My Olympic Life

MY OLYMPIC LIFE

a
memoir

ANITA L. DEFRANTZ

WITH JOSH YOUNG

DORIANNE PERRUCCI, EDITOR

KLIPSPRINGER PRESS
NEW YORK

Copyright © 2017 Anita L. DeFrantz and Josh Young

Photographs from the Personal Collection of Anita L. DeFrantz

Editor: Dorianne Perrucci

Designer: Will Petty

Published in 2017 by Klipspringer Press. All rights reserved. No portion of this book may be reproduced, stored in a retrieval system, or transmitted in any form or by any means, mechanical, electronic, photocopying, recording, or otherwise, without written permission from the publisher.

ISBN: 978-0-692-88567-3
eISBN: 978-0-9992319-0-6

Library of Congress Control Number: 2017943735

Printed and bound in the United States

10 9 8 7 6 5 4 3 2 1

K

Klipspringer Press
http://klipspringerpress.com
New York

Dedication

This book is dedicated to my parents, Anita Page DeFrantz and Robert David DeFrantz, and to my brothers, Robert David DeFrantz, Jr., James Earl DeFrantz and Thomas Faburn DeFrantz. My parents were dedicated to preparing us for our world. They insisted that we learn about, and stand on, the foundation of our ancestors and the many generations that participated in the struggle for freedom in our nation. Thank you for teaching me to ask why — as well as to ask why not.

Chapters

Preface	A Celebration of Human Excellence	I
Chapter 1	My Family: Meet the DeFrantzes	1
Chapter 2	Growing Up in the Land of Milk and Honey	13
Chapter 3	Four Years of Discovery	21
Chapter 4	Messing Around in Boats	27
Chapter 5	Learning the Language of Power and Ethics	35
Chapter 6	Becoming an Olympian	45
Chapter 7	Crossing the Finish Line	55
Chapter 8	An Activist Athlete	63
Chapter 9	Protesting President Carter's Call for an Olympic Boycott	75
Chapter 10	Laying It All on the Line	85
Chapter 11	1980: The Team with No Result	95
Chapter 12	The Los Angeles Olympic Gold Rush	101
Chapter 13	My Dream Job at the LA84 Foundation	115
Chapter 14	Becoming an IOC Member	127
Chapter 15	Opening the Games to All Athletes	135
Chapter 16	A Dark Cloud Forms over the Games	143
Chapter 17	Running As Hard As I Can	153
Chapter 18	The Push for Olympic Equality	161
Chapter 19	The Olympic Movement Is Compromised	171
Chapter 20	Honoring My Ancestors	189
Chapter 21	Women and Sport Should be a Non-Issue	197
Chapter 22	Keeping Politics a Spectator Sport	207
Chapter 23	A Call to Arms on Doping	221
Chapter 24	The Future of the Olympic Movement	231
Addendum	The Olympic Movement's Alphabet of Organizations	237
Acknowledgments		241
Index		249

Author's Note

My mother was a stickler for grammar and the usage of proper names so, to honor her, I adhere strictly to her teachings when it comes to discussing the Olympic Movement. The Olympic Games are the official name of the Games held in the summer, and the Olympic Winter Games are the official name of the Games held in the winter. The word Olympic is an adjective defined as "relating to the ancient city of Olympia or the Olympic Games." Therefore, despite their common usage, neither the Olympic Games nor the Olympic Winter Games can accurately be called the "Olympics."

Preface
A Celebration
of Human Excellence

That first race, on July 18, 1976, at the Olympic Games in Montreal did not turn out as we had hoped. One of our rowers lost her blade (oar), a mistake that almost certainly should have doomed us to defeat and, in our eyes, to lasting disgrace. But the eight of us plus our coxswain, who were racing together for the first time, had worked hard to win a seat in the boat on the first U.S. women's Olympic rowing team. Somehow we pulled together and recovered in the next two races to win the bronze medal. The finish was short of our goal of gold, but we had proved that we were among the best in the world at our sport: We had become Olympic medalists.

The experience also set me off on a new path. Competing at the Olympic Games and living in the Olympic Village radically transformed my view of life. We all knew that there were not enough Olympic medals for everyone in the village, and yet we all were there to do our best and to capture one of the precious few medals available. This reality — that people of every shape and color and both sexes could live and work together peacefully — was no longer just a dream. I began to believe that if these ideals could work for four weeks, then perhaps they could make them work forever!

Since that day in 1976, I have been at the center of the Olympic Movement, experiencing its most triumphant times, and enduring some of its most troubling ones.

I believe that the Olympic Games are a celebration of human excellence based on the principles of mutual respect and fair play. The Olympic motto is "Citius, Altius, Fortius," which is Latin for "Faster, Higher, Stronger," a *hendriatris*, or Greek figure of speech, expressing a single idea in three words.

Certainly, the competition in the 120 years of Olympic Games has lived up to this dictum.

The Olympic Games are a unifying force. The five interlocking rings, colored blue, black, red, yellow, and green, set against a white background, were designed by Pierre de Coubertin, the founder of the modern Olympic Games, to represent the five continents that compete: America, Africa, Asia, Europe, and Oceania (Australia, New Zealand and surrounding nations).

The Olympic Games provide us with some of our greatest memories in sports: Wilma Rudolph becoming the first American woman to win three gold medals in track and field, the U.S. men's hockey team's "Miracle on Ice," the swimmer Mark Spitz winning seven gold medals, and Michael Phelps topping him with eight, swimmer Janet Evans passing the Olympic torch to Muhammad Ali to light the Olympic cauldron. They have given the world moments that transcend sports — Jesse Owens winning four gold medals at the 1936 Olympic Games in the face of Adolf Hitler trying to use the Games as a show of the superiority of the Aryan race.

Because of their lasting ideals, the Olympic Games continue to endure, despite having also produced tragedy that complicates the message of international peace, such as the boycotts by some African nations in 1976, by the U.S. in 1980, and by the former Soviet Union in 1984. No event shattered this message more than the 11 Israeli Olympic team members who were taken hostage and killed by Palestinian terrorists at the 1972 Munich Olympic Games.

As the most watched event worldwide, the Olympic Games have become a multi-billion-dollar enterprise, a showcase like no other for the host country and, yes, even a potent political and economic tool. Putting on the Games in different countries around the world with different values has led to numerous geopolitical challenges. In our era of increasingly precarious world order, every Olympic Games encounters some degree of controversy. But once the athletes begin their competition, these issues fade away as people focus on the beauty of athletic competition.

As an Olympian, I have fought to sustain the integrity of the Olympic Movement. I have served the Olympic Family in the United Sates, as a member of the U.S. Olympic Committee and its Executive Board; around the world, as a member of the International Olympic Committee and its Executive Board and a vice president, as well as vice president of the International Rowing Federation (FISA); and in my adopted hometown, as a member of the 1984 Los Angeles Olympic Organizing Committee, and president of the LA84 Foundation, which has helped millions of youth with sports programs. Currently, I am an advisor for LA 2024, the bid committee for the 2024 Olympic Games.

The roles of these organizations are discussed regularly in many forms: in the media, in high-level government meetings in every nation, at sporting events, and even in bars around the world. Most of these discussions occur in the wake of a controversy putting the Games in a negative light — the Games being hosted in a nation run by a dictator or in a city struggling economically, the awarding of the Games being rigged, the doping of Olympians, and the enormous cost of staging the Games. But what these organizations do and are the people who serve on these organizations is often lost, misrepresented, and misunderstood.

The story of the Olympic Family is vast, complicated, and messy, but it is also an inspiring and enduring story of individuals from all walks of life coming together. At its core, the central tenant of the Olympic Movement is inclusion, and that has made it easy for me to persevere.

Though I did not set out to take this path in life, I have followed its course for over four decades. I have traveled millions of miles the world over, advocated for athlete rights, and taken part in the major decisions related to the Olympic Games. What goes on behind the scenes is often much different than what is reported.

It has been a rewarding journey to date, but by no means an easy one.

Today, I celebrated my 41st year as an Olympian. I embarked on this journey because, in the words of Althea Gibson: "I always wanted to be somebody. If I made it, it's half because I was game enough to take a lot of punishment along the way." The other half is because I really had no other choice.

Anita L. DeFrantz
Santa Monica, California
July 18, 2017

Chapter One
My Family: Meet the DeFrantzes

If you hear the dogs, keep going. If you see the torches in the woods, keep going. If there's shouting after you, keep going. Don't ever stop. Keep going. If you want a taste of freedom, keep going.
— Harriet Tubman

Throughout my childhood, my parents and grandparents were very conscious of making my brothers and me aware of the world in which we lived. They weren't overly preachy, but they didn't sugarcoat anything.

One of the formative events in my childhood occurred when I was just three years old. One day in 1955, my parents bundled my brother and me in the car and drove us to a place just outside of the city of Greenwood, Indiana. When we reached our destination, I distinctly remember getting out of the car and walking through the snow. My father said something like, "We know you kids are really young, but we want you to know that you were here at *this* place in *this* state — in *this* country — that has this sign up." I couldn't read yet, so my father read the sign out loud in a halting tone of voice that I seldom heard him use.

"Don't be here after dark — nigger."

That sign was being forced to come down by a date certain, but my parents took us there while it was still up. They wanted us to realize later in life, when we were fully able to understand, that such a sentiment was held by people in our community and tolerated by our own authorities. At the time, of course, I did not realize the impact, or the emotions that would bubble up to this day when I recall the story. Now I can see that it planted a seed in my personal constitution that ultimately led me to spend the rest of my life speaking up at the first blush of any injustice.

My family comes from a long tradition of fighting for equality and justice. My family's birthright was to stand up to injustice, without considering the personal cost. I learned this at a very young age by watching my parents' actions and listening to the stories they told about their parents and grandparents around the dinner table. The present, I was taught, was not a consolation prize for the future. It was the time to take action to incite necessary change.

This responsibility can be traced all the way back to my great-grandfather, Alonzo David DeFrantz. He was part of the Benjamin "Pap" Singleton Movement in the mid- and late 1800s, named for Singleton, a Tennessee man who escaped slavery to freedom and became an abolitionist. After returning to Tennessee and fighting for equality in society for Negroes, Singleton concluded that the only path to freedom was for them to migrate to neighboring Kansas, which, although not totally free, offered them more rights and bulwarks against exploitation. The migrants were known as "Exodusters."

Alonzo took a lead role in the Exodus of 1879, as it was known. The initial movement arrived in Kansas, but also stretched to Oklahoma and Colorado. It consisted of 40,000 pioneers determined to move families to freedom. The work was physically dangerous, mentally exhausting, and came with no recompense for his own lost opportunities. But it defined him. He reportedly helped over 200 Tennessee migrants relocate to Dunlap Colony, Kansas, and made it possible for families to buy small farms and be put on the road to economic independence.

Alonzo's son (my grandfather), Faburn E. DeFrantz, Sr., attended the University of Kansas and played football at a time when "colored" people or "Negroes," as we were called, were not allowed to compete in contact sports. One day, his leather helmet came off and the opposing team realized that he wasn't a white dude. That was the end of his football career — and the beginning of his activism fighting for opportunities for African Americans.

My grandmother was named Myrtle May Summers, known affectionately throughout my family as "Myrtle the Turtle." She, too, came from an activist family. The Kappa Alpha Nu fraternity chapter was founded at Indiana University in 1911 in her mother's basement. Ten African Americans pushing back against the Jim Crow laws that enforced racial segregation in the South took the historical step of starting a fraternity. Later the chapter changed its name to Kappa Alpha Psi, and more than 100 years later, while still primarily African American, it has opened its doors to men of all color.

My grandmother Myrtle's brother, my great-uncle Frank L. Summers, was also an advocate for the disenfranchised. He, too, had gone to IU and wanted to be a college athlete. His favorite sport was basketball, but he was denied the opportunity to try out for the team because it too was a contact sport. Undeterred, he found that track and field was open field and became the first African American to earn a varsity letter at IU.

Uncle Frank went on to become a well-known attorney in East St. Louis. He financially supported a number of promising African Americans, including the sociologist Harry Edwards and the pathbreaking tennis player Arthur Ashe. As I learned his story, he became yet another example of the life our family led and what was expected of us.

* * * * *

DeFrantz was known as "The Chief" among his colleagues, because of his physical stature and because his mother was a member of the Creek Nation of Tennessee. He moved from Kansas and put down roots in Indiana in 1913. He became involved in the Negro branch of the segregated YMCA at Senate Avenue in Indianapolis. In 1916, having spent many selfless, tireless hours there, he became its executive director. Through his leadership and the work of his dedicated staff, the Senate Avenue Y became what University of Notre Dame historian Richard Pierce called, in the *Indiana Magazine of History*, the "most significant African-American Y in the country."

African-American YMCAs played a crucial role in the lives of black people during that time. They listed their street addresses as their name so that traveling black men could easily locate a Y if they needed a meal or a place to sleep. The YMCA in Washington, D.C. didn't drop its street name until the mid-1970s.

The Senate Avenue Y was an important gathering place for the African-

American community at a time when Indianapolis politics were heavily influenced by the Ku Klux Klan. The Senate Avenue Y hosted a speaker series called "Monster Meetings," so named because they drew such large crowds. Under The Chief's leadership, these meetings became one of the nation's most highly-respected public forums on issues of race.

These meetings brought leaders of the African-American community from across the country, including W.E.B. DuBois, George Washington Carver, Langston Hughes, and Mordecai Johnson, the first black man to be president of Howard University. In an effort to unify the community, white leaders were also invited to speak, notably the *Indianapolis Star*'s publisher Eugene Pulliam and Indiana University Law School Dean Paul McNutt, who was elected governor of Indiana in 1933.

The Chief's philosophy held it was not the passage of time, but individuals, who created progress. "Little progress 'happens,'" my grandfather once said. "Usually it must be wrested from influences that — either belligerently or indifferently — deny it."

The first self-made, African-American female millionaire, Madam C.J. Walker (whose given name was Sarah Breedlove), lived around the corner from "The Chief" and "The Little Chief" (as his wife, Myrtle May, was known), or as we kids called them, "Pappy" and "Nana." Madam Walker began selling hair care products and cosmetics door-to-door to African-American women and eventually grew her company to 20,000 employees. She focused on training African-American women and putting them in decent wage jobs. She was also active in many national and local social causes, including the Senate Avenue Y.

One year, Madam Walker donated $500 — then an enormous sum — but still was not allowed to speak because she was a woman. She took the floor anyway and asked, "Why are you lettin' these other people speak who have given so much less?" No fool, The Chief handed her the microphone.

With the Senate Avenue Y as his bully pulpit, a phrase I don't use lightly, as my grandfather was intimidated by no one, he branched out to fight injustice in the black community on all fronts. He worked diligently trying to break the Indianapolis school board's segregation policies and succeeded in a push to desegregate Crispus Attucks High School. He also lobbied for full membership of black high schools in the Indiana High School Athletic Association, which had a policy preventing black schools from competing against white schools.

In 1947, The Chief seized on Jackie Robinson breaking the color barrier in baseball and used it as a catalyst for change in Big Ten college basketball. He took an active role in pushing Indiana University to allow an African-American student named William Garrett to play on their National Collegiate Athletic Association basketball team. Garrett had led Shelbyville High School to the Indiana high school championship and was named "Mr. Basketball," the state's highest honor. But when Garrett arrived at Indiana University, he was not allowed to play due to a "gentleman's agreement" in the Big Ten athletic conference that black men must ride the bench.

In a face-to-face meeting, The Chief pressured the president of Indiana University, Herman B. Wells, and the basketball coach, Branch McCracken, to understand how important it was to let this talented man have a chance to play, regardless of his skin color. Working together, after an initially unsuccessful attempt, they finally succeeded in getting Garrett off the bench. Garrett proved himself immediately and moved into the starting lineup, making him the first African-American basketball player in the Big Ten to become a starter.

Though Garrett faced open hostility from fans and players on other teams, who didn't welcome his presence on the court, his game thrived. He led the team in scoring and rebounding each year from 1949 to 1951. In the 1950-1951 season, he led the Hoosiers to a 19-3 record and a No. 2 ranking and was voted the team's MVP. After earning All-American honors, he was drafted by the Boston Celtics, making him the third African American selected by an NBA team.

The Chief continued to serve as executive secretary of the Senate Avenue Y until he retired from the position in 1952. During his tenure, he grew its membership from 350 to 5,270. The Monster Meetings and the Y's activist role have been credited by historians such as Dr. Pierce with helping the desegregation of schools, public housing, and recreation centers throughout Indianapolis. He continued his community activism until his death in 1964.

Pappy wrote a memoir for his grandchildren and their children. One passage sums up his activism: "All I have attempted, all I have accomplished with individuals and in movements has been motivated by the theme: I WANT TO BE FREE. With the desire is the knowledge that I cannot be free unless all men are free."

On October 20, 2016, an Indiana state historical marker commemorating The Chief and his work was placed at the location of the Senate Avenue YMCA. Had he been alive to know that his granddaughter snapped a photo of it during the second term of an African-American president of the United States, he would have declared that progress had finally been made.

* * * * *

The Chief's son and my father, Robert David DeFrantz, was born in 1925 in Indianapolis and followed his father's lead. While attending graduate school at Indiana University in 1949, he served as president of the campus chapter of the National Association for the Advancement of Colored People. One of the NAACP's activities was to integrate student housing, which had been segregated since the university was founded. Black women were confined to a place ironically named Lincoln House, while the men lived in a former barrack.

During this period, my parents met at IU. My father was pursuing a master's degree in sociology, and my mother, Anita Page, was an undergraduate. They were in complete sync on their advocacy. At the beginning of her sophomore year, my mom was one of five African-American women who participated in the integration of student housing spearheaded by the NAACP campus chapter. My father told us a story about a time when he went to the movies in college and a white man sitting in front of him raised a newspaper to block his view. My father took out his pocket knife and cut a hole in the paper so that his view wasn't obstructed.

Aside from the influence of his own father, my father's world was informed by his own experiences. During World War II, he served in the Army. He was eligible to become an officer because he had a college degree, but he was faced with a very racist, uphill climb. One question on the officer's exam asked, "What color was Queen Nefertiti?" He answered that she was black. Wrong, the examiner told him. In the mind of the white officer, she wasn't black, she was Egyptian. So my father was denied leadership roles and relegated to menial tasks while he fought for his country during the war.

My father didn't finish his first attempt at a master's degree. He told me that his professor insisted that he take out a section from his master's thesis about the NAACP and its challenges on the IU Campus. When my father refused, the process ended. He later returned to IU to earn a master's degree in social work.

My father spent his life working as a community organizer. I loved going to meetings with him and hearing people exchange ideas and debate issues. Even before I understood what they were discussing and what was at stake for my own future, I was taken by their sense of purpose and their passion.

* * * * *

Mom was still a junior at IU when they moved to Philadelphia and got married. Actually, I believe they went to Philadelphia to elope, but be that as it may, I was born in the City of Brotherly Love in 1952. Their first child, my oldest brother David, had been born there in 1951. For years as a child who paid close attention in church, I wondered why David and my two younger brothers, James (born in 1956) and Thomas (born in 1962), had such Biblical names, but later I found out their names were family names.

My name, Anita Lucette, also comes from family, or what can be loosely described as near family. I was named Anita in honor of my mom, but my middle name came from my father's European girlfriend during World War II, Lucette, whom he met prior to my mother. He saved a picture of his young love even after he married my mom. He held onto some apparently fond memories, too, because he gave me "Lucette" as my middle name.

When I was still very young, I asked my mother who this lady Lucette was and why I was named after her. My mother was a very practical woman who had plenty of challenges growing up in Muncie, Indiana and saw no need to create another one. "Here's the situation," she told me. "She's there and we're here, so it doesn't really matter." And that was that.

My parents moved back to Indianapolis when I was two and a half, so I have few concrete memories of toddling anywhere in Philadelphia, but I remember clearly the day that my brother, James, was born in 1956, because it was two days before my fourth birthday party.

Knowing that my world was about to be rocked with a new baby demanding the family's full attention, my mom had built up my birthday party. She kept telling me how wonderful it would be, and how much fun everyone would have. Cake and ice cream dreams abounded for me, but these were not realized because she went into labor and missed my party. So from that tender age on, I associated birthday parties with my mother's absence and asked to never have another one.

My mother was very driven professionally. Our family life in Bloomington revolved around my mother's final semester of school. I remember living in a tiny trailer, with her and my brother. Dad would visit every weekend, making it even smaller.

After completing her undergraduate degree as a speech therapist and audiologist, she worked as a grade-school speech therapist in the public school system. Later, when I was in fourth grade, my mom went back to Indiana University for her master's degree.

To accommodate her, our family moved to Bloomington, Indiana — which we called "Bloomingulch" — again for one summer and one school semester. My brother and I were the only two African Americans in the entire public school system. This turned out to be much worse for my brother, who was forced into numerous fights. I was in one fight. I was being attacked by a boy, but as he swung at me, I ducked. Both of us fell over on the ice. I fell on my hand and broke my wrist. I went to the nurse's office, but she said nothing could be done and sent me to class. I sat in pain the rest of the afternoon. That day after school, my mom took me to my weekly visit to the allergist. He took action and sent me a doctor who set and cast my wrist. My mother was furious.

After earning her degree, my mom found a job at the IU Medical Center in Indianapolis working with people who had suffered strokes to help them regain their language capabilities. But this was at a time and place in the workforce when African-American women could not get promoted. As a child, I was somewhat aware of her struggles, but it was really later in life that I realized the unfairness.

Undeterred, she pressed on. After I was in law school, she earned a Ph.D at the University of Pittsburgh and was offered a position as a graduate professor of education at the University of San Francisco, necessitating a move to California for my father and youngest brother. It was rare then for a husband to move for the wife's employment, even more so in the African-American community.

Her career also turned out to be fortunate for me in the long run. She made us all — including my father, whom she loved to correct as he spoke frequently in public — very conscious of how we pronounced our words. Due to her linguistic coaching in my childhood, I don't have a Hoosier accent. So Washington is "WASHington," not "WARSHingTUN," and so forth.

* * * * *

Athletics entered my life early. I was four years old when I learned to swim at the Senate Avenue YMCA. By the time I was eight I was swimming competitively, along with my older brother. My dad wanted nothing less than my brother and me to be the first African Americans to make the U.S. Olympic swimming team. He pointed out that we knew one Olympian: Jo Ann Terry (now Grissmon), my physical education teacher at James Whitcomb Riley PS 43, who had competed in the women's hurdles in the 1960 Olympic Games and in the long jump in the 1964 Games.

In retrospect, I believe that he set this goal for us less to turn us into Olympic swimmers, but more because swimming was largely denied to African Americans and he wanted us to think more broadly about opportunity.

We swam on a team at Douglass Park, one of the few in the African-American community. What I remember most is the size of the pool, an oval that was more than 50 meters across the middle — and the darkness in the locker room. The locker room's ceiling and floor had stalactites and stalagmites, downward- and upward-growing columns of mineral deposits that made the place look like a haunted cave. To make matters worse, I was usually the only girl on the team, so I had to change into my suit alone. After practice, I often refused to go back in and wore my wet suit home.

Aside from the locker room at Douglass Park, only two things scared me as a child. Racism was not one of them, because my parents showed me that there was a path to fighting prejudice. The Cuban Missile Crisis and multiple sclerosis frightened me and, oddly enough, both were associated with the corner grocery store.

I would often go to the corner store after school for a piece of candy. When the Cuban Missile Crisis happened over 13 days in October 1962, I remember first hearing about the possible apocalyptic fallout at the corner store. I overheard a group of adults talking about how nuclear war would melt down buildings and wipe out large swaths of the population. I didn't have to ask many questions, because shortly thereafter, preparations ramped up for a possible Soviet attack.

In school, we were shown movies about what happened after the U.S. dropped atomic bombs on Hiroshima and Nagasaki during World War II. My parents told me that if something bad happened and we were not together, that I was to make a beeline for Pappy's and Nana's (my grandfather's and grandmother's house), because they had a basement where I would be safe. Though I was scared, even then I remember thinking that the standoff between the United States and the Soviet Union could be solved through sports. Both countries would gather their best athletes and compete. Whichever country won the most contests would be the winner — and nobody would have to die in the process.

At the corner store, I was also fascinated by the jars on the checkout counter that collected money for different causes. Each jar had a cardboard sign with a rendition of the disease. The one I became most attached to — and frightened of — was multiple sclerosis. The sign cautioned that it was "A Killer of Young Adults" and no cure existed, though one must be found.

Though I didn't know exactly what MS was, from the age of 10 I carried this notion that MS was something I needed to fear only until I became an adult. When I turned 30, I distinctly remember breathing a sigh of relief that I was out of the danger zone.

Our team had swim meets against the Broad Ripple Amateur Athletic Union swim team. Compared to our pool, Ripple was like a five-star resort. We competed well against stiff competition. I was a decent swimmer, compiling a few third-place finishes over the course of my childhood career.

When I was nine years old, my swim coach told me I would be receiving the high-point award for girls at the end of the next meet. I told him I didn't think I could accept the award and needed to talk to my dad first.

I told my dad that I felt awkward accepting the award. He asked me if I had supported my fellow team members. I told him that I had. He asked me if I put in the work. I felt I had. Then he asked why I had reservations. I said I didn't feel right because the rest of the team, including my brother, had worked just as hard as me and weren't getting awards. He suggested that I discuss the situation with my mom.

"Remember, this is going to have to be your decision," he said. "I'm sure you'll make the right one."

What was bothering me?

I was the only girl on the team.

For years, I never felt right about accepting that swimming award. I felt I didn't fully deserve it. This gnawed at me as a kid, and frankly still does. But looking back, I clearly learned something from that experience.

One summer later at the 10-day Flatrock YMCA sleepaway camp, I encountered a related dilemma that forced me to act on principle. I had worked for three summers to achieve the "Mind, Body & Spirit" award, a hallmark of the camp. I had Mind and Body, but I couldn't quite get Spirit, which required excellence in archery.

The third year I tried for the award, I was determined to put enough arrows in the target. As I was shooting, I noticed there were more arrows in my target than I had shot. It was apparent that my counselor had shot the extra arrows in the target to help me. When she told me that I done it, I told her I had not. "I have to do this myself," I said, and eventually I did.

That was surely a lesson that I had learned from watching my father as a community organizer and seeing my mom persevere in her career. The principles my parents lived by held great sway over my feelings and actions as a child, and over time, as I recalled the conversations around our dinner table about some of the most serious issues shaping America, such as the civil rights movement and the fight for women's equality, and I learned about the work of my ancestors, these principles collectively shaped the person I became.

* * * * *

Throughout my youth, my family encouraged me to believe that opportunity had no boundaries, no skin color, and no sex. Around the age of nine, I had one conversation with my mother and my great-grandmother on my mother's side, Laura Ethel Lucas, that has stayed with me all these years.

Grandma and Grandpa Lucas had essentially raised my mother. Her mother, Savelia Ann (later Mansfield) had moved to New York shortly after my mother was born, so that she could become involved in creative pursuits that were not open to minorities in Muncie, Indiana. Although Savelia Ann's mother, Cora Nash, stayed in Muncie, she grew up poor and did not have the ability to support my mother. But Laura Ethel Lucas, her step-grandmother, had worked hard enough to own her own property before she married Grandpa Lucas, and was prepared to take on any challenge that came her way.

I asked my mother why Grandma Lucas (who I called "Grandma Lucas" because I didn't quite understand the "great" part at that age) didn't have a better job. I said, "She works for other people, cleaning houses, washing clothes, but she's so smart. She tells me so many interesting things about the world." My mom looked at me after a moment of reflection and said, "You ask her."

So I did. Grandma Lucas sat me down. "Well, sweetheart, I wanted to be a nurse so I could help people," she said. "But when I was little, colored girls didn't get to go to school for that. My formal education ended with fourth grade. Things have changed now. You can do whatever you want to do. You just have to be very good in school and continue your education. If you promise me you will do that, you can be whatever you want."

"Yes, Ma'am," I said. "I promise."

When she heard me say those words, a tear welled up in her eye, followed by a smile on her lips.

Looking back, the best gift of my family's activism and beliefs was that nobody sat me down and preached a series of bedrock principles that I must follow. Rather, I learned them the best way we can learn such standards: by people who set an example and lived by it. That is how the principles of my fighting DeFrantz family became a part of me.

Chapter Two
Growing Up in the Land of Milk and Honey

My father, Robert David DeFrantz, called Indianapolis "the northernmost Southern city." That was a polite way of saying it was racist. When I grew up in the 1960s, the Ku Klux Klan was a heavy presence in all aspects of society, and most schools and public recreational facilities, were segregated. But there were flashes of hope during my formative years.

The biggest one came in 1966 when I entered Shortridge High School. By the time I reached high school, I was itching for a wider window on the world to open up. I needed a more inclusive and positive experience to show me that possibilities existed, and Shortridge provided that. Despite the deep racial bias that permeated the city, Shortridge was an oasis where black kids actually got along with white kids, and vice versa.

To put a modern cultural twist on it, Shortridge was a combination of the TV series *Glee*, which focuses on the social and racial issues confronting a high school singing club, and the film *Love & Basketball*, a romantic drama about two high school students who fall in love pursuing their basketball dreams. This sounds highly romanticized given the times I lived in, but I truly felt transported at Shortridge.

From its founding in 1864, Shortridge was an innovative high school. The first free high school in the state, Shortridge was also one of the first to hire female teachers. Practically, that was because budgets were low and women would work for less pay. As backwards as that sounds, it actually provided women teachers with an opportunity to work at a time when most schools wouldn't hire them.

From its early days, Shortridge had allowed African Americans to attend. Though the school had a rocky history with black people for years, it persisted with an open door racial policy. In my time, the "white flight" to the suburbs in the 1960s became an issue. As the black population increased, there were efforts to redraw the school district's lines to bring white people back to the school, a movement that was greeted with protests. The U.S. Justice Department sued the Indianapolis school board, charging it with *de jure* (forced by law) segregation.

But there was no doubt that Shortridge was a leader on many fronts. In 1898, the school launched the first daily high school paper in the country. Much later, the great American writer Kurt Vonnegut, Jr., a 1940 graduate, served as editor. The paper continued as a daily during my four years. It was repeatedly named one of the top high schools in the U.S. by *Time* magazine.

Shortridge was highly competitive. The year I entered, students had to apply and be accepted to attend, which was rare for a public high school.

At Shortridge, I fell in love with singing. Music was in my family. My mother was a pianist and a violinist. She was very talented, but there was no room when she grew up for talented black women to do much of anything in Indiana. She infused me with the spirit of music and showed me how it connected people from different cultures. In 1967, my family went to see the Red Army Chorus in Montreal at Expo 67, the World's Fair in Canada. She also knew members of the highly-regarded, all-female *a cappella* group Sweet Honey in the Rock. I, it must be noted, take credit for bringing the excitement of The Pointer Sisters into our home.

Music became my team sport. I joined chorus and the Madrigals, an elite singing group. My Shortridge music teacher, Thomas Preble, was fantastic. He had unlimited faith in our abilities, and his confidence was contagious. He arranged for the chorus to perform at Clowes Memorial Hall, the premiere concert venue in the city located on the campus of Butler University.

Talk about ambitious — Clowes Hall was the home of the Indianapolis Symphony Orchestra. We raised money to be able to perform there. But that proved to be the easy part. We performed Ernest Bloch's "Sacred Service," an incredibly complex piece, accompanied by members of the symphony orchestra and a professional singer.

I was also a member of the marching band and the orchestra. In the orchestra, I played the bassoon for four years — or rather attempted to play it. My problem was that I was playing music solos far beyond my ability and that of most high school band participants. When it came time to compete at the state contest with my bassoon solo, I bombed. I was given a second chance but didn't do much better. I realized that this instrument needed a great deal more of my time. Using that as a wakeup call, I dug in and gave it the time needed.

I was also a member of the honor society and was on the editorial board of the magazine *Quill and Scroll*, the beginning of my interest in the printed word, and the birdwatching club, owing to my love of nature.

My grades were solid A-/B+. My only real academic snag came in chemistry. The teacher told my mother that I was a B student. Telling my mother that her daughter was a B student was a big mistake, even if it was true. She had such great pride and confidence in me. The truth was, I was barely a B student in chemistry. The class was immediately after lunch, and I had the worst time keeping my eyes open while watching movies featuring owl-eyed men pouring steamy concoctions out of beakers.

The only thing that I didn't have in my high school experience was sports. Even though my competitive swimming days were long over, I was interested in sports. Oddly, there were no high school sports teams open to girls. I often sat in the bleachers and watched my brothers play basketball or sports. The closest I got to a sport was taking the football field at halftime as part of the marching band. That did not make any sense to me. Girls were being denied the right to compete solely because they were girls?

I don't recall having any in-depth conversations about why this was the case, but it did bother me because it was unfair and discriminatory. Looking back, that was one of the experiences of injustice that I held onto and used as motivation later in life.

* * * * *

During the spring of my junior year, on April 4, 1968, Martin Luther King, Jr. was shot. Dr. King was a public representation of what generations of DeFrantzes stood for. With white progressives like Robert F. Kennedy, who was seeking the Democratic nomination for president, hope was on the rise for a more unified society.

That day, Kennedy was campaigning in Indiana. He delivered speeches at the University of Notre Dame and Ball State University. As he was boarding his campaign plane bound for an evening rally in Indianapolis, he learned that Dr. King had been murdered.

Kennedy continued to Indianapolis, where he was met at the airport by local authorities who urged him to cancel his rally. They were certain that the largely black audience would incite a riot when they heard the news, as most would be coming directly from work. Riots were already breaking out in other cities. Kennedy refused, and headed to the heart of the city's African-American community, at 17th and Broadway.

Standing on the back of a flatbed truck, Kennedy delivered the news of King's assassination. There were wails and cries from the crowd. Though Kennedy spoke less than five minutes, his speech that day was later hailed as one of the greatest political speeches of the century.

In part, he said: "What we need in the United States is not division; what we need in the United States is not hatred; what we need in the United States is not violence or lawlessness, but love and wisdom, and compassion toward one another, and a feeling of justice toward those who still suffer within our country, whether they be white or whether they be black."

At the end, the shocked and saddened crowd peacefully dispersed.

In our house, there was a sense of lost hope that could not be regained, of helplessness that so much progress had been stopped by a single bullet, a feeling that our leader who had been slain could not be replaced. Beyond being sad, I remember being confused about what black people should do next. My father, who had turned his life over to seeking civil rights, was crushed. He fought on in the ensuing years, but I'm not sure he ever fully recovered.

* * * * *

In high school I was hungry to learn about how others before my parents had fought for civil rights. I was captivated when I first learned Harriet Tubman's story in grade school, and I learned more about her life in high school. In 1849, Tubman was enslaved but decided that she would be free. That was not something that women, or even men, had the courage to do.

She asked her husband and others to come along, but no one joined her because it was too dangerous. Alone, she made her way to freedom. But when she arrived, she realized that it wasn't just her freedom she was seeking — it was everyone's. Rather than remaining in the safety of Canada and the North, Tubman decided to return and attempt to rescue her family and others in her community who were living in slavery.

Tubman's life's mission began. She became a "conductor" on a network of safe houses known as the Underground Railroad that transported enslaved people to freedom. Historical treatises record that she helped free more than 300 people, always at great personal risk. Her ingenuity and cunning fascinated me. She once donned a bonnet and carried two live chickens to make it appear that she was a slave out shopping for her master.

During the Civil War, Tubman became a scout and a spy for the Union Army. She was probably the first woman to carry a weapon in the Union Army. Eventually, the Union leaders told her what she was doing was too dangerous. What could be more dangerous than what she had already accomplished? She then became a nurse for the Union Army. After the Civil War was over and in her later years, she cared for her parents and other needy relatives, and turned her house into the Home for Indigent and Aged Negroes, which opened in 1908.

What resonated most with me — and still does to this day — was that she was always giving of herself. She lived the most unselfish life possible. I call this amazing woman my "shero." I jumped with joy when the decision was made to honor her by putting her face on the $20 bill, relegating President Andrew Jackson, a slaveholder, to the back.

So while my mother was my first and most important role model, and my great-grandmother the woman I admired most for living against the grain and motivating my mother and me, the historical woman I admire most is Harriet Tubman.

Alongside her stands Sojourner Truth. The African-American abolitionist born Isabella Baumfree, Truth was the first black woman to win a court case against a white man to free her son from slavery in 1828. Throughout the mid-1800s, Truth delivered some of the most moving and meaningful speeches on women's rights, notably what became known as her "Ain't

I a Woman?" speech to the Ohio Women's Rights Convention in 1851. Though she never learned to read or write, she spoke powerfully from the heart with wit and insight. In an effort to bring about sweeping reform, she linked abolishing slavery to women's rights and universal suffrage.

As a consequence and a motivator, my company, The Tubman-Truth Project, bears their names. The project is in its infancy and will be a big part of the next chapter of my life. Its goal will be to help end human slavery and trafficking, which persists to this day, even in the U.S.

* * * * *

Compared with what might have been if I had been forced to attend an exclusively black high school, the overall Shortridge experience was nothing short of life- and confidence-affirming. As the school song goes:

> *"In the land of milk and honey*
> *In the central west*
> *Stands a school of many virtues. Ranked among the best*
> *Glorious Shortridge is her title*
> *Loved by old and young*
> *Let her name be duly honored*
> *Let her praise be sung."*

Indeed.

The time came in my senior year to apply to college. My older brother, David, had followed the family tradition to Indiana University. I was certain of only one thing: I did not want to go to IU. I wanted to find a liberal arts college where I could expand on my Shortridge experience. I leaned toward being a music major, but my parents encouraged me to consider studying law and becoming a judge someday. The teenager in me processed that and thought, I think I'm pretty judgmental already, and besides I really love music.

I applied to Radcliffe College (then the female version of Harvard), Yale University and Connecticut College. Guess where I went?

I really wanted to go to Radcliffe (as much as I still hate to admit it), but I was turned down. I was also turned down at Yale. One extremely smart guy from my class, Bartram Brown, was admitted to Harvard and matriculated there. He went on to law school and now teaches at the University of Chicago. A'Lelia Bundles, the great-granddaughter of Madam C.J. Walker, who had attended Sunday school with me, was accepted to Radcliffe.

But for me, it would be Connecticut College. I like to say they chose me. I was awarded a partial scholarship and funded the rest with student loans and work study. My parents weren't in a position to stake me the tuition.

Connecticut College was a place for what I'll politely call dilettantes. Many people were outstanding in a number of areas, but none was a star in any one area. On paper, the school appeared to be a good fit for me. An older brother of a friend of mine who was in the first class that included men assured me that I would love its liberal nature. Many of my friends from Shortridge were heading to the East Coast for college. After living in Indianapolis, I was sure that the more broad-based and inclusive the experience, the better the college would suit me.

Chapter Three
Four Years of Discovery

Connecticut College was founded in 1911 as Connecticut College for Women after Wesleyan College converted to an all-male institution in 1909. The story goes that Wesleyan decided to exclude women because they were dominating in academics, making up a disproportionate number of *cum laude* students and regularly becoming valedictorian. In response, Wesleyan alumnae formed an all-female college 40 miles up the road from Middletown in the seaport city of New London, Connecticut.

My entry year was only the second that men were admitted as freshmen. The name had been changed to Connecticut College in 1969 when the school became co-ed. As empowering as the college's history was, I would not have attended had it remained an all-female institution — I was a principled 17-year-old, but also a social one.

By the time I arrived, Connecticut College had long since patched up its relationship with Wesleyan. Students at both schools could take classes and participate in extracurricular activities on the other's campus. For a semester, I played bassoon in a group at Wesleyan. There were even ride-sharing programs. Connecticut College had a similar arrangement with Yale on class exchange and clubs.

Connecticut College turned out to be the perfect fit for me. Being on the East Coast was a considerable improvement in my quality of life. I had felt geographically confined and philosophically trapped in Indianapolis. Now, I was easily able to travel north to Boston and Providence and south to New York, Philadelphia, and Washington, D.C. to experience more diverse and vibrant American cultures.

Though Connecticut College was liberal-leaning, it wasn't particularly diverse. The student body numbered 1,400 my freshman year, and only around 50 were African Americans. The students were pushing a movement to increase the number of African Americans, dubbed "74 by '74." The goal was not exactly a huge number, but it did show a willingness on the part of the administration to expand its minority population, one that was shared by many Northeastern liberal arts colleges.

I still felt comfortable there. My freshman residential hall, Brandford, was next to the aptly named Blackstone Hall, which was where most African Americans lived. (Where did they get these Dickensian-like dorm names?) I met students from different backgrounds, ranging from wealthy New Yorkers to those who grew up in rural areas. I remember being shocked the first time I met someone whose family had more than one house.

* * * * *

My family name followed me to New London. While I thought that I was figuratively leaving my family behind by striking out to Connecticut, instead of following tradition and attending Indiana University, that notion did not last long.

During the third week of my first semester, I was walking down the corridor of the administration building. The Dean of College, Dr. Jewel Plumber Cobb, walked out of a door in front of me. Dean Cobb, who was African American, stopped me.

"I wanted to introduce myself," she said. "I'm the dean of the college."

I managed a nervous smile. "Yes, Dr. Cobb, I know," I said.

"You're a DeFrantz, aren't you?" she asked me.

"Yes, ma'am," I replied, unsure where the exchange was headed.

"Any relation to Faburn or Bobby DeFrantz?"

"Yes, I think you are referring to my uncle and my father." (Like my grandfather, my uncle was also named Faburn.)

DeFrantz is such a distinct last name that it was obvious that I was somehow related. I had never given much thought at that time to my name being a dead giveaway about my relatives. Dean Cobb turned out to be a strong influence on me in my college years.

* * * * *

With her support, and my own appetite to be involved, I carved out a place at Connecticut College. As a music major, I continued my extracurricular interest in music, joining the *a capella* singing group The Concords and the chapel choir, but I also took a particular interest in public policy on campus.

At the time I entered college, students across the country were focused on securing individual rights, and Connecticut College students were no different. I entered college in the fall of 1970 after the Kent State University shootings. The previous May, during a student protest of the U.S. invasion of Cambodia, the Ohio National Guard had killed four students at Kent State. There was tension on many college campuses across the country, as students bucked authority and administrators pushed back.

Getting involved in student government felt like something I needed to do. My sophomore year, I was elected class president. My junior year, I was elected chairman of the student judiciary committee, a student committee that heard cases involving violations of the college's honor code. I ran for student body president that year, but lost.

One of the richest traditions at Connecticut College that appealed to me was its honor code. Prior to 1970, the school held a special ceremony for incoming freshmen, who signed the pledge and agreed to live under the honor code. The honor code dictated the tenor of life on campus. One of my first acts as chair was to bring back that tradition.

The campus atmosphere was a civil society of students who were responsible for themselves. There were no adults living in the dorms. Each dorm had what was known as a house fellow, a senior who supervised the residents.

We had self-scheduled exams that weren't monitored by teachers. Students were expected to report others, as well as themselves, for any violation of the honor code. In fact, the code was so strong that it was not unusual for a student to turn himself or herself in for an infraction. The student-run Judiciary Committee adjudicated the cases.

Individual rights greatly interested me, and I felt compelled to participate in ensuring that all students had rights. When I joined the judiciary committee, I realized that despite the strong commitment to integrity fostered by the honor code, the school did not have a student bill of rights.

Leading the work with support from the faculty, I authored a student bill of rights. The treatise laid out what rights students had and what responsibilities they needed to undertake to earn and maintain those rights. This ensured that the administration's primary function was oversight, provided that the principles of self-government by the students were faithfully upheld.

There was one tradition, however, that none of us wanted to revive: parietals. This was the process whereby students were required to check in at their dorms each evening by a time certain. I didn't have to do that at home in high school, so why would I do it in college? Due to predictable student opposition, this tradition was not reinstated.

I was also involved in supporting community life. I spent senior year as a house fellow, a position that made me responsible for the life and well-being of a dormitory.

Being a house fellow had its perks. My room had a sitting area with a fireplace, an *en suite* bathroom, and a convenient window to climb out if I needed to escape. But the position was also a serious undertaking.

I had two near suicides on my watch. One day I returned to the dorm and found a picture of a sinking boat drawn on my door's bulletin board with a grease pencil. Though it wasn't signed, I had a pretty good idea who drew it by the way the individual, a freshman, had been acting. I went straight to her room. We talked for a while. She was so distraught that I insisted she call her parents.

The second time was a closer call. I arrived at the dorm on a Sunday evening after being away for the weekend. A student informed me that one of her fellow students hadn't been out and about all weekend. We went to her room and found her on the verge of suicide, after taking several pills. I called 911. Luckily, she was fine. She ended up taking a semester off and returning the following year to graduate.

* * * * *

Academically, I did well all four years, earning mostly B's and a few B+'s. One C found its way onto my transcript, which annoyed me to no end and kept me from graduating *cum laude*. Overall, given all of my extracurricular activities, it was a good result.

Initially, with such a heavy writing load, I struggled finding my voice. I had never written a paper longer than three pages in high school, and the second week of my freshman year, I was expected to deliver 10-page dissertations. As the professor commented on that paper: "You tend to ramble and digress but reach sound conclusions." That was because I only needed three pages to make my point, but was forced to expand it to 10.

During the last semester of my junior year, the college decided to initiate "Student Designed Inter-Disciplinary Majors," which allowed students to create their own majors based on their interests.

Up until that point, I had been a declared music major, although I also loved philosophy and government. By the end of my junior year, I had enough credits, except for one in each discipline, to be a major in each one. But based on some principle I had adopted, I refused to take the missing class in each. I was able to persuade the faculty that I was qualified to spend my senior year working in the inter-disciplinary area of the field that I named "political philosophy."

I drew up a curriculum and petitioned the faculty selection committee to sanction my major. I convinced the powers that be that even my music credits, given the concentration on the history and philosophy of music, were ideal for this inter-disciplinary study. I recruited a faculty adviser to oversee my solo program and ended up being the first — and likely the last — Connecticut College graduate with a B.A. in Political Philosophy.

I also wrote an honors thesis. My paper focused on my belief that there is not just one truth in the world, and that the more perspectives one knows and understands, the closer we get to a universal truth. In some ways, the seed for this was planted in me as a child when I attended community meetings with my father. Everyone in those meetings who spoke about issues had slightly different points of view and bent the facts to support them. I watched as my father listened to a dozen people speak and then synthesized the points of view in his own speech to build a consensus.

My thesis was entitled "The Philosophical Value in the Plurality of Ideas." In the introduction, I wrote: "We find that in daily life, the problem of differing accounts is treated as a question of determining who is right and who is wrong. That habit of choosing one view over another tends to preclude the possibility of recognizing the merit to be found in different perspectives. In short, I believe that there must be great value in learning to understand the various perspectives that may be brought to describe any particular situation."

Although I had no idea at that time, this would become a useful tool in my life many years further on. Discovering this idea in college laid the foundation for how I approached my work on the International Olympic Committee, which is composed of disparate points of views informed by differing life experiences. The hope was — and still is — that a better understanding of multiple points of view leads to better decision-making.

Chapter Four
Messing Around in Boats

Sport is a great, unexplored part of what we are and how we live in this world. We humans enjoy playing sport, talking about sport, watching sport. We are the only species on the planet that sets up hurdles and then races across them to see who can get to the finish line first. I've seen ants use twigs to cross a puddle, but I've never seen them line them up to race to the other side.

We speak of being "in the zone" in sport, especially where there is an extraordinary performance by athletes. How do we get there? If we understood it in sport, could we get there in other parts of our daily lives? Then, of course, there are the other parts of sport — the ethical questions that arise. Is sport based on situational ethics? Are there certain ground rules of ethics required for sport to exist? We have to agree to abide by a set of rules or sports won't work. Why are we willing to do so to play a game? Does that mean we should be able to do that to "play life?" There is so much to the world of sport, and we do so little with it outside of competitive events.

For me, sport is the mind directing the body through the dimension of time and space. In no athletic pursuit is this truer than rowing. As David Halberstam wrote about rowers in *The Amateurs: The Story of Four Young Men and Their Quest for an Olympic Gold Medal*:

> *"During their college years the oarsmen put in terribly long hours often showing up at the boathouse at 6:00 a.m. for pre-class practices. Both physically and psychologically, they were separated from their classmates. In many ways they were like combat veterans coming back from a small, bitter, and distant war, able to talk only to other veterans."*

Though my relationship with rowing has shaped my life, I entered the sport entirely by chance.

* * * * *

One of the most exciting things about being at Connecticut College was that women could play competitive sports. Although this was two years before the passage of Title IX, the legislation that sought to end discrimination against women and women professors in particular, colleges were beginning to field more women's sports teams. Little did I know how this would permanently alter the course of my life, nor did I ever think that I would be in competition in sport after college.

I took the first athletic opportunity I saw my freshman year. I tried out for the basketball team. My only previous experience was shooting hoops on the playground with my brothers and watching their games from the bleachers, as my high school had no team sports for girls. I had never been taught anything formally about the sport. I knew a few of the basics; if you bumped into somebody, that was a foul. However, I didn't want to admit I was a complete novice because I was trying out for a college team.

On the first day of tryouts, the coach told me to take the high post. I had no idea where that was. I looked around. I figured it couldn't be too far away from where I was standing. I shuffled a few feet and stood in place, awaiting further instructions or a rebuke. Apparently I was close to the high post, because the coach never scolded me — and I made the team.

Because I was tall, I played center and learned how to take the high post. We competed against the Ivy League schools, all of which had larger pools of women. I don't think we beat anyone that first year.

The most important thing that happened to me during my time playing basketball was that I learned about moments of excellence. At the time, I didn't know what to call the feeling, but I knew it was special. My first one occurred during a game. I grabbed a rebound and threw a blind outlet pass to a teammate running up the court. She caught it and glided in for a lay-up. The experience was sublime, both for me and for those who saw it.

We often call such moments "being in the zone." Yes, I could play basketball, but not like that all the time. On that particular play — for one moment — I had a sixth sense of exactly where my teammate would be and how to get her the ball, despite being swarmed by our opponents. These moments where something happens that is extraordinary and flawless, and everyone knows it is superior, should be studied so that they are better understood. I'm sure they happen in all fields.

Though opportunities for women athletes in college existed, there was no formal system of recognition during my college years. It wasn't until some 20 years after graduating from college that I was invited to receive a silver award from the National Collegiate Athletic Association. It took me several weeks to understand that I had retroactively been considered NCAA Division III athlete who had excelled in academics. At that time, there was also no next level for women college athletes, unless they aspired to be Olympians.

* * * * *

With my spot on the basketball team secure and my commitment to two singing groups, I wasn't looking for any more activities. That changed one afternoon in the fall of 1971. I was walking across the campus admiring the fall foliage when I passed in front of the Crozier Williams Building, the hub of student life. A man was standing next to a recruiting display for the rowing team. Out of curiosity, I stopped to admire the long boat and the oars and asked what it was there for.

The man eyed me. I was 5 feet 11, with legs a little too long for my frame, and fit. "It's for rowing, and you'd be perfect for it," he said.

I thought that was quite a line because I had never been perfect for anything. I was happy to be on the basketball team, but I wasn't exactly the smoothest player on the court. I said, "I know how to swim, so tell me what to do so I don't need to use my swimming."

The man was crew coach Bart Gullong. We struck up a conversation about rowing, an outlier of a sport if ever there was one. Coach Gullong spoke passionately about the dedication of rowers, saying that there was nothing more elegant in sports than watching the visual symmetry of eight athletes dropping their blades in the water and pulling at precisely the same moment to glide a boat across the water.

I decided to give it a try.

* * * * *

Rowing was actually the initial intercollegiate athletic event. The first regatta took place in 1852 when Harvard rowed against Yale. That regatta happened on Lake Winnipesaukee in New Hampshire. In the ensuing years, it has moved around several times and is currently contested on the Thames River near Connecticut College.

At the collegiate level in the U.S., men and women both rowed in an eight-oared shell, called an 8+, a boat of eight rowers plus a coxswain who directs the boat. There was also a 4+, which is four rowers plus coxswain; a 4 without coxswain, called a straight 4; and a 2 without coxswain, called a straight pair.

There are two types of boats, sweep boats and sculling boats. In a sweep, each person has one oar (always referred to as a blade) and uses two hands on it. The rowers sit in a single line and are paired so that there is an equal number of oars on each side of the boat. In sculling, each person has two blades, one in the left hand and one in the right. In all the boats, each rower sits on a seat on wheels that go back and forth on runners, which helps propel the boat.

In my era, the sculling boats and the "blind" boats (those without a coxswain, the person whose responsibility it is to steer the boat, manage the race, and convey the coach's strategy) — called the straight pair and the straight 4 — weren't contested at the collegiate level.

I took to rowing immediately. I may not have been perfect for rowing, but it was perfect for me. I loved the outdoors, and rowing for me was about being outdoors and in nature. In addition to being part of a team, I liked the fact that the sport didn't cause any harm to its competitors or to the environment. Over time, I also found that while I was rowing, the rhythm of the motion allowed me to meditate and solve all sorts of problems at the same time I was becoming better at rowing.

The basketball and rowing seasons barely overlapped, so I was able to do both, despite the fact that Coach Gullong frowned on the arrangement. Basketball was a late fall and winter sport, while rowing competitions took place in the spring. Fall rowing practices took place early in the morning, while basketball practice and games were scheduled in the afternoon and evening.

The team rowed on a nearby lake at a boathouse called Blood Street Sculls until my senior year. The boathouse was owned by a wealthy man from Wisconsin named Fred Emerson whose family had made their money in the shoe business.

Emerson was the patron saint for women's rowing. He was devoted to creating and funding women's rowing programs at liberal arts colleges across the Northeast, including ours at Connecticut College. He was also supporting all small college teams in Connecticut for both men and women.

In 1972, my junior year, women's rowing was voted onto the Olympic Games program for the 1976 Montreal Olympic Games. I rowed varsity that year, but I didn't give this development much thought until my senior year.

If I were to try to make the Olympic team, I would need to devote the two years after graduation to training. This came with huge obstacles, namely financing. There were no subsidized programs for rowers' training for the Olympic Games. The only way would be to find a training program and pay my own way.

There were only two viable options, the Long Beach Rowing Association in Southern California and the Vesper Boat Club in Philadelphia. I was applying to a Coro Fellowship program in Los Angeles that helped college graduates prepare for careers in public service and then placed them in government jobs. I had never been to Los Angeles, but exploring the West Coast sounded enticing. If I did go west, I had the possibility of training at the Long Beach Rowing Association.

At the encouragement of Dean Cobb, I was also applying to law school. I applied to the University of Pennsylvania law school, which had a joint doctorate program in law and peace studies. I reasoned that I had been born in Philadelphia, so I had some kinship with the city. There was also a possibility that I could train at the Vesper Boat Club, a world-class rowing team.

A member of our Connecticut College team had spent the previous summer rowing at Vesper. Perhaps, I started to think, I could row at Vesper while attending law school at Penn to keep the Olympic possibility open while also not losing time advancing my education. So I began corresponding with Vesper, in the event I went to Penn.

As I was thinking about this, however peripherally, I was thrown a curve ball my senior year. I failed to make the varsity 8, and I was demoted to junior varsity. Or rather Coach Gullong came to me and asked me to row in the JV 4 boat. My pride, as a senior, was dented.

That night, I thought about the situation. I asked myself, what is he really saying to me? He was saying that the team needed me to row in the JV 4 boat, and, unless I did, there would be no JV boat because you can't row a 4 with three rowers. Without me, the coxswain and those three rowers who had blistered their hands every morning at practice, teammates of mine, would not be able to compete. And clearly, if I didn't row in the JV boat, I would not be rowing at all on the team; for all practical purposes, my rowing career would be over.

I did the only thing I could: I got in the JV boat and rowed with vigor.

Though any hope of rowing in the Olympic Games had all but become an illusion, Coach Gullong told me that he believed I could make the Olympic team if I trained hard for the next two years. My first thought was, how in the world does he think I can make the Olympic team if I can't even make varsity at a small liberal arts college? My second thought was, I certainly won't make it if I don't try.

A plan started to come together. I was accepted for the Coro Fellowship in Los Angeles. I looked again at the rowing program in Long Beach. What I didn't initially realize was how far apart Los Angeles and Long Beach were from each other. The commute to and from the fellowship to practice in terms of distance and cost would be unworkable.

Fortunately, just after I was accepted to the Coro program, I was also accepted at the University of Pennsylvania Law School. This was lucky, because for some reason Penn was the only law school I applied to — not a great strategy unless it works. Actually, Dean Cobb had wanted me to apply to Harvard, but there was no way I was giving Harvard another cent of my money after they had rejected me as an undergraduate.

I chose Penn over the Coro Fellowship. I had very little money, but my parents had made it in Philadelphia and so I reasoned I could, too. I decided to enter law school and then re-apply to the peace studies program later. This would also free up some time for me to row at Vesper and see if I had what it took to make the U.S. women's Olympic rowing team.

Chapter Five
Learning the Language of Power and Ethics

The political environment in the U.S. in 1974 when I graduated from Connecticut College was toxic. The country was mired in the Nixon years. The Watergate scandal had played out in newspapers and on the nightly news during my last two years in college. I was personally distressed by the revelations being reported about the abuse of power by President Nixon and his top advisers, and particularly their efforts to illegally and immorally cover their tracks. One thing stood out to me: Those in power on both sides of Watergate had legal backgrounds. That's when I decided I needed to learn the law, because there was no question that those who spoke the language of law spoke the language of power and were the arbiters of what was going on in government.

Since early childhood, I was very sensitive to any injustice. Law would offer an avenue for me remedy that. In the macro scheme of things, I had studied and lived through the civil rights movement, and on a smaller scale, I had seen what my mom had endured trying to overcome racial bias and get a deserved promotion at the university hospital where she worked. Besides, my parents always said that I was very judgmental and suggested that I should take advantage of rendering opinions by becoming a lawyer or a judge.

At the same time, I loved music, but I knew I didn't have the chops to make it as a singer, and contemplating life as a bassoonist was unappealing. So, in the fall of 1974, I returned to my birth city and entered the law school at the University of Pennsylvania.

I first moved into a room in the house owned by the head of women's rowing at Vesper. The place was a hovel, with cracked plaster walls, a barely-functioning toilet, and enough mold to knock out a small town. My parents, who drove me from Connecticut, weren't happy when they saw the conditions. They called old friends of theirs who lived in the city, and I moved into their friends' place while starting a search for new housing.

* * * * *

Their friends welcomed me with open arms. They lived in a row house near the university that had a spare room. Before I even began looking for a new place to live, they offered me their spare room for the summer. I gratefully accepted.

My next step was to find a job to pay for rent, food, and rowing dues. Vesper had agreed to let me start rowing for a reduced fee, but my parents weren't in any position to carry me financially. In my job search, I reasoned finding food and money in the same place would be beneficial, which led to waiting tables. That way, I could make money and eat my main meal of the day for free at the restaurant. But after the third customer asked me if I was doing this so I could afford my education, I decided I was not cut out to be a waitress. A month into the job, I let them know I would not be coming back.

I paid for law school with a combination of loans and work-study. The summer before law school, I somehow scraped together enough money to fly to San Francisco to compete with the Vesper team in the national championships. It wasn't an auspicious debut.

I rowed what was generously called the "single." The boat was a gig so antiquated that it is no longer produced. It was 24 feet long and weighed in at 40 pounds, compared to a normal single, which weighed 22 pounds. Mine had the added handicap of not having a fin, so if I didn't row with precision, the boat veered off to one side. The upside was that if I hit anything it was unlikely to damage the boat. It took me a long time to make my way down the course, but I managed. I ended up second of four boats.

I jokingly call it "the gig that I got," but it was an important race for me. A flickering of light — not as bright as the Olympic flame, mind you — had begun to shine through. I hoped it wasn't a will-o'-the-wisp. I was also beginning to believe that I belonged in rowing, despite the fact that the entire sport was inhabited by white people. I felt that I was proving myself both to Vesper and to the rowing world.

Learning the Language of Power and Ethics

* * * * *

I lived in an apartment in West Philadelphia. It was a rough area of town at that time. Gang issues and crimes against individuals were common. Very close to the law school was a soup kitchen called Mother Divine's where low-income and down-and-out people could grab a meal for $2. That place saved me. I ate there more than I should have. I was actually ashamed of going there, because I knew at some point that I would be earning a decent living as a lawyer. I felt obligated to give back once that occurred.

In the fall of 1975, after leaving behind food service, I had found a job working nights at the police headquarters in Philadelphia called the Roundhouse, where defendants were taken and held before their bail hearings. Roundhouse was aptly named: There were two round structures connected by a straight one. If you looked at it from above, the building was in the shape of a pair of handcuffs.

I worked in a city pilot program called "Release on Your Own Recognizance," or ROR for short. ROR's central premise was to decide whether or not criminal suspects should be released without bail based on their promise to appear for all court hearings. ROR catered to those who couldn't afford a lawyer. We interviewed those who had committed crimes ranging from larceny and drug possession all the way up to killing another person for one reason or another.

My job was to interview the charged individuals, prepare them for their bail hearings, and then recommend to the judge whether or not to release them on their own recognizance. The accused would then appear before the judge, who would make the final determination. In nearly all cases, if they did not make ROR, they were incarcerated pending trial, as most did not have the resources to make bail.

The job was interesting and challenging, to say the least. I interviewed people we called "pilots," drunk drivers who were the worst type to interview, because of the smell of alcohol on their breath and their difficulty in coming up with coherent answers. I also interviewed people who had murdered, or were about to be charged with murder.

There were moments of frustrating levity. I frequently interviewed people from the MOVE group, a black liberation organization with Rastafarian tendencies that engaged in demonstrations against police brutality, making them regulars in the ROR program. They were impossible to talk with. I would ask, "What's your mother's name?" "Moon," the person would reply. What's your father's name? "Sun." How old are you? "Eternal." It would go downhill from there.

I wasn't necessarily scared of my clients, although I did often wonder what would happen if I ran into someone on the street who had not received an ROR recommendation from me. In the three years I worked at Roundhouse, there were also plenty of recidivists. It was difficult to recommend ROR for them because of the likelihood that they would end up across the table from me again in a few months.

The experience taught me a lot. It taught me about my willingness to work hard for something I believed in. I would arrive at police headquarters at 10 p.m. and conduct my interviews through the night. I would finish my shift and maybe have time to go to my house for a quick nap, but more often than not, I was due at the boathouse by 5:30 a.m. for rowing practice.

It was great to have Cathy Menges (now Zagunis), another Connecticut College grad who was attending Penn, rowing at Vesper with me.

Practice for me was always a great release. My energy spiked every time I saw the boathouse. After practice finished around 7 or 7:30 a.m., I would shower, change my clothes, and head to class.

In the middle of the day, because I had a Penn law student ID, I'd head to the gymnasium to do my weight workout. Often, Cathy would join me. We had some memorable workouts with the coach of the football team, who could not believe the amount of weight we moved. In the wintertime I would run stairs, or "stadiums" as they are known, in one of the high-rise dormitories, and then change and go to class. After class, I returned to the boathouse for our evening workout. And I biked everywhere.

Afterwards, I'd go home. If I was scheduled to work that night, I'd show up at the Roundhouse. On nights I didn't work, I alternated between sleeping and studying.

With not much variation, that was my schedule for my first two years of law school.

Rowing at Vesper was intense — and intensely rewarding. We rowed on the Schuylkill River in an area known as Boathouse Row, just north of downtown Philadelphia. Comprised of 15 boathouses, Boathouse Row is located on the east bank of the river. Each house is lined with clear lights that frame their edges at night.

Founded in 1865 and rechristened Vesper in 1870, Vesper is located at #10 Boathouse Row. Its mission is to "produce Olympic and world champions." When I entered the club in 1974, Vesper had a long list of male gold medal winners, many of them with multiple medals. The 1964 8+ team had won the gold medal in Tokyo. Three men had been members of the 1972 team. The Olympic team and Harvard coach Harry Parker, an Olympian who had rowed at Penn, were among the club's most prominent members. In 1970, Vesper had broken a barrier by organizing a women's rowing team, the first all-male club to do so.

Every morning, the rowers arrived before sunrise to have the boats in the water at first light. In the winter, the predawn sky was black, and when the sun rose, it turned dishwater gray. But in the spring, the sun would bounce off the Schuylkill and onto the city's buildings. Whatever the season, seeing the sun meant only one thing: now came the pain.

Rowing was a test of will, which appealed to me. We were constantly battling against the elements, while doing nothing to harm nature. At one practice, the guys had returned from rowing on the choppy Schuylkill River in near-freezing, foggy conditions just as the women were going out. It was so bad that their boat's runners had iced over. (The seat is on wheels that go up and down the runners, which is how you propel the boat, so if the runners ice over, mobility is severely restricted.)

Hearing this, the women's team assumed we weren't going out, but our coach, John Hooten, had other ideas. It would be practice as usual, Hooten (as we all called him) informed us. Since we were lighter than the men, the boat would not have the same problem of water coming in.

Within a few minutes, my hair froze. Not long after, a huge wave came across the boat and completely engulfed our coach. The water was bone-chilling. I lost sight of Hooten in the fog.

I yelled out, "Hooten, are you there?"

A few seconds went by. "Yeah, I'm here," came his voice after a crackle of ice. "But I'm thinking we turn back at the next bridge."

Another appealing aspect was that rowing was uniformly a team sport. In rowing, those moments of excellence that occur in sport needed to involve everyone in the boat, not just one or two people. One such moment that stuck with me at Vesper came in a race against Yale, at a time when private clubs rowed against colleges.

The race took place on our home water, the Schuylkill River, so we knew the course well. We got off to a decent start, but for some reason, our coxswain, Carlye Byron, was holding us back. We could all feel this, but we continued to row at her direction. As we reached the halfway point of the race, the Yale boat walked through us, crew talk for, "they passed us." Carlye told us to hang in there, meaning she was not yet ready to call for the sprint.

"Hang in there. We aren't ready…we are going to sprint when I tell you…okay…SPRINT!"

Like a rock shot out of a slingshot, we blew past the Yale boat as if they were anchored in place, and won the race. Carlye had focused all eight of us and controlled our energy until just the right moment — a collective moment of excellence.

Vesper was tight as a team, but our unity was challenged in 1975, my second year there. USRowing, the sport's governing body, decided for the first time that the boats going to the world championships would be boats made up of the best rowers from different clubs. The organization announced that there would be a camp held in Boston to select the eight rowers who would represent the U.S. women's team at the worlds. In the past, there had always been a time trial, and the club's boat that won was designated the national team boat. USRowing changed that in preparation for fielding a team in the Olympic Games.

The selection camp would create a hardship for us even beyond the likelihood of our boat being split up. All the women on the Vesper team worked; none of us had the financial means to take time off to attend the camp in Boston.

Vesper filed for arbitration with the American Arbitration Association against USRowing, requesting that the Vesper 8 have the right to compete as a team if we won the national title.

Because I was in law school, my teammates looked to me as a leader in this legal process and asked me to speak on behalf of Vesper at the arbitration.

To prepare for the hearing, I read the constitution of the USOC. It was my first exposure to the minutiae of the rules of elite sport and to fighting for athletes' rights. The arbitration ended in Vesper's favor. The experience also became a personal test for me: If Vesper won the national championship in the 8, then we would have the right to go as a boat to the world championships. If not, then the 8 would be determined at the camp.

Heading into the national championships, the pressure mounted. Vesper had several boats competing, and not everyone fully understood what the outcome would mean for team selection for the world championships. The coming Olympic Games — the first for women's rowing — were also in the back of everyone's mind, because results would dictate who was invited to the Olympic tryouts.

At the nationals, the University of Wisconsin beat Vesper in the 8, and Vesper won the 4. These results meant that the 8 for the worlds would be selected at the camp, while Vesper would represent the U.S. in the 4. Then things became tricky.

The assistant coach of the national team approached Pam Behrens, who was the stroke (the closest to the stern) in our 4+ boat, and me, the three seat (two seats from the coxswain, who is at the rear of the boat). He couldn't promise, he said, but there was a high probability that we would both make the 8 going to the worlds if we came to the camp on weekends.

For starters, I wasn't sure an offer like that would hold up until the coaches saw us row at the camp. Further, Pam and I would still have to pay our way to Boston each weekend, which raised an ethical dilemma: If Pam and I decided to accept the offer (and the offer stuck), it would break up the Vesper 4, which had won the right to go to the world championships. If the two of us bailed on the Vesper 4, then it would be impossible for the two other women in the 4, as well as the coxswain and the coach, to have that opportunity. They would need to find other rowers.

Pam's decision was basically made for her. She was not able to leave town for the camp because she worked as a critical care nurse. I had to make a choice.

It didn't take me long to decide. Even though this was my first chance to be on the national team, a probable gateway to making the 1976 Olympic team, it was my first year rowing for Vesper at the national level. The club had accepted me into their program, and allowed me to finance my dues. Consequently, I felt my allegiance had to be with them. Ethically, I did not see how I could accept the offer to be in the 8 and abandon my teammates, so I made the decision to stay with the Vesper 4+.

The U.S. national team won a silver medal in the 8 that summer at the worlds in Nottingham, England. The Vesper 4+ finished fifth. Colleagues in the rowing world still believe I was in the winning 8. They can't imagine me dropping the opportunity, but I felt very loyal to my team. Ultimately, that silver medal would have taken its place next to my "high-point" award for swimming in grade school that I didn't deserve.

In my first international regatta, I learned that rowing is the noblest of sports. Rowers have a deep respect for one another. At the end of the regatta, the teams have a tradition of exchanging and negotiating for shirts or parts of uniforms with their opponents, what we in the sport call "betting shirts." At the collegiate level, the winner takes the shirts. At the international level, you negotiate and make deals with one another for different items of team gear.

From my first regatta, Thomas Keller, the longtime president of the International Rowing Federation, was eager to hear from the athletes about how we all felt. Thomi, as he was known in rowing circles, welcomed feedback to improve the regattas and better the sport.

I assumed that this level of open communication was *de rigueur* for all international sports federations. Unfortunately, this proved not to be the case. To this day, I take great pride in how devoted the rowing community is to its athletes and its sport.

* * * * *

I became somewhat disillusioned by the University of Pennsylvania.

Inarguably one of the elite academic institutions, Penn had a closed-mindedness that surprised me, particularly for my expectation of an Ivy League school. Interestingly, a year later, my brother, James, experienced far worse as an undergraduate at Dartmouth College.

My Penn law school class was the second smallest of the Ivy League schools, at about 175. There were only 13 minorities in my class, including three African-American women. Across the university, there was an inexplicable stigma against the minorities. Despite the fact that Penn was highly selective, many undergraduates verbally attacked and belittled the few law school minorities, saying that we were charity acceptance cases admitted on reduced standards and therefore unfit to take up space in the prestigious law school. The school newspaper published stories echoing these unfounded comments. Even more surprising, the law school staff did not do anything to correct that notion in our defense.

The entire situation left me with a nagging, uncomfortable feeling.

I also realized that most of my classmates just wanted to learn what they needed to in order to graduate and make a lot of money at blue chip law firms. That was anathema to the kind of educational experience I had had at Connecticut College, which was an open and honest forum for learning, self-improvement, and the betterment of society.

In my second semester, I took a course from a wonderful professor by the name of Ed Sparer. In a voice tinged with incredulity, he said: "Look around you. The first year after you graduate, every one of you will be making $50,000 or more." In 1977, our graduation year, the median U.S. household income hovered around $9,500 annually, which made Sparer's prediction an enormous sum.

Of course, Professor Sparer's point was that it was outrageous that someone would be paid this kind of money merely for making it through law school. "I won't be earning that kind of money, because I'll be in public interest law," I thought. My starting salary in my first job at the Juvenile Law Center of Philadelphia was $14,000.

I became close friends with three classmates, Gerald Early, James "Jimmy" Johnson and Reese Couch, one who changed careers, one who earned big money, and one who headed off in an altruistic direction.

Gerald ended up leaving law school to pursue his doctorate at Cornell University and become a writer. He now teaches at Washington University in St. Louis and is often seen in documentaries about baseball and jazz. Jimmy went on to become in-house counsel for Boeing. Reese, with whom I shared a house, eventually changed his name to Gurujodha Singh Khalsa. He is now a Deputy County Counsel in Bakersfield, California, and runs "spiritual warrior" workshops in yoga and martial arts.

For me, the most challenging part of law school was finding enough money to pay tuition and living expenses and also fund my rowing training. Even in the 1970s, the cost of law school was high (though I'm sure today's law students would laugh at the amount we were paying then). Because I intended to be on the national rowing team, I would be required to spend my own money for the privilege of representing the United States. We had to contribute to our airfare and even our uniforms, and I needed to save for that. My other law school colleagues landed high-paying summer jobs at law firms to finance their next year in law school, but I felt that trying to make the Olympic team was a once-in-a-lifetime opportunity, regardless of the challenges faced.

Chapter Six
Becoming an Olympian

The 1976 Olympic Games were the first to feature women's rowing. Men's rowing had been a part of the Games since the beginning — with an asterisk. Rowing was on the program at the first Olympic Games in 1896, but it was never contested because a storm blew the regatta off the bay.

The popularity of rowing increased in the early part of the 1900s. In the 1920s and 1930s, collegiate crews received the same level of press coverage as baseball. Regattas regularly drew 100,000 spectators. Special train cars were available for people to ride in alongside the river and take in the race from a mobile perspective. Betting on the sport was prevalent, especially in the singles races.

The popularity of rowing peaked in 1936, the year the American Olympic team won gold over the Germans, which is well-chronicled in the best-selling book *The Boys in the Boat*, by Daniel James Brown. The advent of World War II triggered a falloff of rowing audiences, and the sport never fully recovered. After the war, other more heavily-promoted sports, notably baseball and then basketball, crowded rowing out.

But the sport persisted, in large part because of its collegiate history and presence in the Olympic Games. By the early 1970s when I took up rowing, there was an increase of women's programs in the U.S. Still, it was an uphill struggle to get the sport on the program at the Olympic Games. Thomi Keller, the president of the International Rowing Federation, and Nelly Gambon de Vos of the Netherlands, patron saint of women's rowing, worked tirelessly for years before finally succeeding. And Monique Berlioux, the longtime Secretary General of the IOC, was a big help, as she declared that all six women's rowing events were accepted.

The inaugural rowing competition at the Olympic Games for women, it was decided, would have three sweep boats and three sculls, an 8 with coxswain, a 4 with coxswain, and a straight pair. The sculling boats were the single (1x), double (2x), and quadruple (4x) with coxswain. However, the women would row 1,000 meters, while the men rowed 2,000, which we all found insulting. Nevertheless, the fact that six boats would race in the debut of women's rowing was exciting, as most people had expected only three.

Camp for the U.S. women's sweep tryouts began the second week of June, just four weeks prior to the start of the Games. The camp for the sweep boats (I rowed in the 8+, 4+, and 1) was held in Boston, while the scullers went to Long Beach, California.

The beginning of the Boston camp was delayed until the annual Harvard-Yale regatta was finished, because Harvard men's coach Harry Parker was the women's coach, too. Parker was a demi-god to his male rowers, and a legend in the sport. In his first year as coach, Harvard snapped a losing streak to Yale, beating their arch rival 18 consecutive times.

Perhaps because we were older, we were less reverent than the legions of men who had been coached by Parker. Much to their chagrin, we called him "Harry" rather than "Coach Parker," and often sprayed him with the hose, a transgression that would have resulted in a timed mile run for the men under his tutelage. One of his Olympic assistants was Vesper coach John Hooten. The two others were Nat Case of Yale and Jay Mimier of Wisconsin.

Approximately 100 women rowers attended the camp. We lived in a massive dormitory at Boston University known for good reason as "The Zoo." We each received a weekly stipend of $50 for food, but in a somewhat cruel move, coxswains, who were told to keep their weight below 98 pounds, received only $25.

Selection lasted for four weeks. As it became clear that a rower wasn't going to be selected, she packed up and went home. There were many mind games, because rowing is a mental sport as well as a physical sport. During the seat racing, we would all wonder who was going to be the next one switched. However, there was nothing close to trash talking. In rowing, once the boat goes in the water only the coxswain speaks until everyone is out of the boat.

The mental toughness required in camp would, however, be beneficial.

When you're sitting on the starting line of a regatta, you must be totally there, in mind and body. By the time you reach the competition, there's nothing more to do for your body. It's all up there in your mind, which is why rowing is a sport better suited to older, more mature people, older meaning in their upper 20s.

Early each morning, we would make our way from the dorm down to the boathouse on the Charles River. We would receive our boat assignments and then move out on the river. Because a rower could only compete in one boat in the Olympic Games, everyone's primary goal was to make the 8, the most prestigious boat for the USA.

The team was chosen through a grueling process called seat racing. Seat racing determined which rowers did the best job of moving the boat. In seat racing, two boats would row against one another for, say, three minutes. The boats would then pull up side by side, and the coach would select two rowers to switch boats. The rowers would climb from one boat to the other. The boats would start from the same place and sprint for the same amount of time. Whichever boat was in the lead determined which rower won that seat race.

We did this for four weeks, over and over and over again. In addition to the physical aspect, it was psychologically draining. At one point, my best friend and roommate, Cathy Menges (Zagunis), was pitted against me because we rowed on the same side. We had gone to college together, were both in graduate school at Penn, and both rowed at Vesper. Now, we were competing against each other for a seat in the Olympic 8. For such a noble team sport, this seemed downright primitive.

I was worried about Cathy and what would happen if I were the one who knocked her out of the Olympic 8. The first race started, but the result was discarded because the coxswains made a mistake. Just before the second race, I thought, I need to start worrying about myself and row the best race I can. I did, and I ended up winning the next two races. This didn't mean I would be in the 8 for sure, although it was a big step. But it likely meant that Cathy would not be selected for the 8.

* * * * *

In addition to the rowing itself, the trials were a stressful time for me. I was an African American in a sport where there was no one else with my color of skin. I also did not feel particularly comfortable in Boston. Schools were desegregated, but there were parts of the city where my teammates went where I did not feel comfortable.

The day before the team selection was announced, I was talking to Hooten, my Vesper coach and the team's assistant coach, about my anxiety over making the team. I told him that I was worried. He asked why.

"I've done all I possibly could, but I'm just not sure they are ready to put an African American on the first women's Olympic rowing team," I said.

That was my feeling. I was in Boston at a time when racial tensions were running high. Even in the bubble of the camp, I felt like an outsider, as I was the only African American.

Hooten was rattled. "I'm shocked you would say that," he said.

"I'm shocked, too," I said. But that was how I felt.

As much as I was an anomaly in the rowing world, I never felt any racism from the other women competitors. We all wanted to make the team and win a gold medal: That was the basis on which we were all operating.

But there were racist comments, and they lingered not with me but with others. Many years later, a male rower who had rowed at Vesper approached me at the San Diego Crew Classic. He told me that he wanted to apologize for something he had once said to me at Vesper. "I should not have said that, and to this day I am ashamed of myself," he said. With little hesitation, I accepted his apology, because I knew his words at that time were more about his place in life than mine.

Though I didn't clearly recollect his exact words, I remember that he had essentially told me that I didn't belong at Vesper, that I should not be a part of rowing and, in particular, his club, and that I should leave before I was forced out. I did my best not to dwell on racist comments, from him or anyone else. I'm not saying they didn't happen; they most certainly did. But my folks had taught my brothers and me to resist being thrown off course by listening or responding to any bigoted statements — and so at the time I must have let his remark pass me by. As I grew older, I learned how to address such comments directly. But at that time, the defense I had learned was to ignore them.

A rowing tradition is that the lineup is written on a sheet of paper by the coach and nailed to the boathouse door. The morning after I told Hooten that I didn't think I would make the team, I walked down to the boathouse with the other rowers to see who had been chosen. The list was handwritten: Lynn Silliman (coxswain), Jackie Zock (stroke), Anita DeFrantz (seven seat), Carie Graves (six seat), Marion Greig (five seat), Anne Warner (four seat), Peggy McCarthy (three seat), Carol Brown (two seat), and Gail Ricketson (bow).

The list was not written by Harry Parker, though; as tough as he was with the men, he couldn't bring himself to say no to any of us, and so he had John Hooten and the assistant coaches write out the list.

The bottom line was, I had made the United States Olympic team. My feelings were somewhere between ecstasy and exhaustion. I remember calling my parents and telling them that I was an Olympian. But when I hung up, I realized that I wouldn't have any proof for another 10 days, when the team would travel by bus to Plattsburgh, New York, and then on to Montreal. We would not be receiving our Olympic gear and clothing with the five interlocking rings signifying that we were Olympic team members until then; the gear was not for sale anywhere.

After the camp, there were trials in the pair (the boat with two rowers and no coxswain) and then seven days at Dartmouth rowing together as a unit for the first time. The scullers, whose camp and trials had been in Long Beach, joined us. Compared to the Long Beach scullers, we sweep rowers who had gone through the trials in Boston looked a bit scraggly. They had cute shorts that showed off their tan legs, while we walked around in mismatched clothes. Our policy was to wear whatever we had that was not walking on its own due to a lack of laundering where we roomed.

Finally, we were ready, and boarded a bus to Plattsburgh *en route* to Montreal.

Because our camp had started so close to the Games, we were the last team to arrive for processing, just four days before the Opening Ceremonies. By this time, they were almost out of uniforms. For whatever reason, the USOC had failed to order, or Adidas had failed to supply, enough uniforms for the women's rowing team, but the men's team was fully outfitted. We had our racing uniforms from USRowing, but few of our team members received all they were due. I was crushed by the slight.

By this point, I had been elected team captain and made it my duty — not only as captain but also as someone who had earned the uniform, too — to make sure we received the gear we were entitled to. While that may seem trivial, I felt this was a major issue for us as the first U.S. women's rowing team: The sweats, jackets, shorts, and shirts with the five rings would be our lasting proof that we were Olympians. We all needed to receive what we had earned.

During the Games, I found the USOC office in the Olympic Village. Every day after our arrival in Montreal, I visited the USOC office to ask if they had received our uniforms. The officials working there all came to know me. Though I didn't realize it at the time, I was making relationships and building in-roads with people that I would be working with for the rest of my life. I didn't hound them, but I was there every day. Some became irritated, but Col. Don Miller, the USOC executive director, was impressed with my persistence.

Finally, I got to talk with someone who had answers. He told me that Adidas had not made enough gear and were not going to make any more before the Games. "They're too busy with other things and other teams, and they just don't care about the U.S. team," he said. A lot has changed since then, but at that time, the United States team wasn't important to a German apparel company.

Stunned as I was by that information, it didn't change anything. Respectfully, I said, "I am going to keep coming to the office and keep asking — even after the closing ceremonies — because my job as team captain is to ensure we receive our gear."

In the end, I accomplished the task. It took me an entire year, but I did not stop until everyone had every piece of their Olympic gear, including rain suits, warm-ups, and anything else given to team members emblazoned with the words "United States Olympic Team."

* * * * *

I wasn't prepared for the political overtones of the Olympic Games. The bus ride into Montreal was my first indication that the Games had another dimension to them beyond athletic competition. The scene was surreal. Because of the terrorist attacks at the 1972 Munich Olympic Games, the freeway was closed to traffic. We were protected to the extent that authorities even shut down bridge crossings over the freeway. I remember seeing a helicopter almost land on the hood of a car to prevent it from driving over a bridge as our van passed under it.

Two days before the Opening Ceremonies, I learned firsthand how the Olympic Games can become mired in international politics. My teammates and I were waiting at the gate to the village where the credentials were issued when I noticed a delegation from an African nation sitting off to the side.

I went over and greeted them. "Are you guys excited about the Games?" One of them who spoke English replied that they weren't.

"Why not?" I asked.

"We're going home," he said, motioning to a fairly large group of athletes.

"Why?"

"Our nation is boycotting because New Zealand played a rugby game in South Africa," he said. "We don't know much about it, but now we're being forced to go home."

It turned out that because New Zealand had played a rugby match in South Africa, which had been expelled from the Olympic Movement over apartheid in 1964, twenty-eight African nations were pulling their teams out of the Games.

I couldn't believe what I heard. I knew plenty about apartheid, growing up in a family devoted to fighting for civil rights. But I didn't understand the connection: What did a rugby match — contested in a sport that wasn't even on the Olympic program — have to do with these African athletes competing in Montreal?

"I am so sad for you," I said.

"So are we," the man said. "It's just terrible. We've been here for a week and now we have to leave."

"I'm going to learn more about this," I told him. "I know that doesn't help you now, but I will commit to learning all I can. I want to help to make sure this will never happen again."

He looked me in the eyes and said, "Thank you, Sister."

That was my first direct experience with an Olympic boycott, and it showed me that being an Olympian was more than earning sore muscles from training, spending grueling hours on the river for the past several years, and more than the mental grind of the camp. It was being part of a global community.

From the moment I entered the Olympic Village, my life changed. There was a palpable feeling of respect among the nations. The village encouraged socializing. There was a movie theater and a discotheque, which stayed open until midnight. Back then, the average age of the Olympians was around 25, much younger than in today's Games. There were several married couples on many of the teams.

Those of us on the U.S. rowing team were very close in more ways than one. Fourteen of us were crammed into one apartment in the Olympic village. The unit had two bedrooms and a small kitchen/living room, leaving four of us in the larger bedroom, three in the smaller one, and the rest in the living room. We joked about our rule to keep things moving: no fewer than three people in the bathroom at any one time.

Joking aside, we had heard rumors that Olympic officials would make us strip to prove that we were female, but those proved to be unfounded. That had actually happened at the 1966 Track & Field World Championships in Europe and had been instituted because the Eastern Bloc countries were presenting men to compete in the women's competitions. Among the theories we heard were that some of these men may have been women by birth, but due to the high levels of testosterone they had been forced to take, it was probable that their gender had changed. In fact, that year, it was determined that the world champion women's downhill skier Erika Schinegger was actually a man.

For us, as disturbing as the gender test was, it was far less of a breach of privacy than a strip search. On our second day, the day before Opening Ceremonies, we all met in a classroom building across the street from our dorm. We were told to wait in the hallway until called. One by one, an official called us into the room. A doctor took a quick mouth swab that was whisked to the lab, and we were done.

And with that, we entered a unique and vaunted community. Yes, everyone was at the pinnacle of their sport. But more importantly, it was a community where everyone was successful. They had been selected to represent their countries. We were all sharing a rare experience, and everyone was speaking the language of the Olympic Movement.

* * * * *

The Opening Ceremonies were held on July 17, 1976. Queen Elizabeth II opened the Games to a stadium packed with 73,000 people and an estimated half billion people watching on TV around the globe.

That afternoon, while preparing for the Opening Ceremonies, the U.S. women athletes ran into a wardrobe issue. We had all received Halston dresses for the Opening Ceremonies, the same ones all the U.S. women had received, but as we put on the dresses, it became clear that the designer felt the less seen of athletic women, the better — the long blue dresses covered us from neck to ankle and from wrist to wrist.

The USOC women's team administrator took one look and changed the dress code. She instructed us to wear blue pants and white jackets, which we dubbed "marshmallow jackets." We later learned that the Canadians were upset because they had wanted to be the first women's team to wear slacks. It wasn't our intention to upstage our host team; we just didn't want to wear those ugly, shapeless dresses.

Other women's teams wore tracksuits. The German team had wonderful tracksuits, made by Adidas, with white tops and bottoms accented with the country's colors. I made a trade for one of those suits.

The other funny moment occurred when American broadcasters completely missed our team marching in. Montreal was in the French-speaking part of Canada, so they used the French alphabet, which placed "United States" not at the end of the list, but as "Etats-Unis d'Amerique." The U.S. broadcaster, ABC, had gone to commercial break before we marched in. They were probably thinking, "A-B-C-D-E, okay, nothing for the U.S. audience there."

A more serious concern was the first rowing race, which was scheduled for the following day. The most important part of the body for rowing is the legs, and also the part of the body that would be the most fatigued from participating in the Opening Ceremonies. Yet our coach, Harry Parker, never said a word. Others coaches warned us that we would be too tired to row if we took part, but Harry knew how much this once-in-a-lifetime experience meant to all of us.

That afternoon, we walked down the path from the Olympic Village. At first, there were a few people on either side of the path, but as we approached the venue, there were solid lines of people on both sides. People were standing three and four deep, applauding and cheering us on. Finally, we turned a corner, and there before us was a hillside packed with people cheering for us — cheering for all of us. It did not matter that we represented the United States; what mattered was that we were Olympians.

We proceeded into the stadium tunnel and out onto the field. The roar was deafening. I remember smiling so hard that my face hurt. I don't know if my legs were exhausted, but I clearly remember feeling that I had been lifted up by the joy expressed throughout the stadium that evening.

Chapter Seven
Crossing the Finish Line

The rowing course for the 1976 Olympic Games was built on Notre Dame Island, a man-made island in the middle of a wide swath of the St. Lawrence River, which runs alongside downtown Montreal. The island was created for Expo 67, the world's fair held to celebrate Canada's centennial, which my family had attended. Nearly all of the other pavilions had been moved or demolished while building the rowing course, but I recognized the Buckminster geodesic dome, which was still standing, immediately. The course, the largest of its kind in North America, was essentially a long rectangle, with the St. Lawrence River on both sides. An isthmus on the east side of the course was so thin that steamboats passing parallel to the course were easily visible.

The first time the women's U.S. Olympic 8+ raced as a boat was in the first race in the Olympic regatta. This was also true for the 4+. In fact, we had only rowed together a dozen times in our practice week at Dartmouth before traveling to Montreal. Our coxswain, Lynn Silliman, had the race planned out, although she wasn't exactly sure what we were capable of.

We came out fast and were leading at the 500-meter mark, ahead of even the powerful East Germans, or "Easties," as we called them. The plan was to start the sprint with 250 meters to go. When we reached that point, the Easties had pulled slightly ahead of us. Lynn called for the sprint. It was as if we hit a brick wall. It felt like everybody froze.

With the boat barely moving, two strokes later, Lynn again called for the sprint. I thought, I am going to pull this boat across the finish myself if I have to. Apparently, everyone had the same thought. We started sprinting, cutting through the water faster than we ever had in practice.

A few seconds later, out of the corner of my eye, off to my left, I noticed a blade abandoned in the water. It was definitely ours. Someone lost an oar!

We crossed the finish line second of the six boats, despite losing an oar, which is well within the rules. Under the rules, only the boat and its coxswain must cross the finish line.

Gail Ricketson, who was rowing bow, had caught what's called a "boat-stopping crab," so named to suggest that an underwater critter has grabbed the oar. "Catching a crab" happens when the blade doesn't slice smoothly into the water, and, as a result, the pressure of the water locks on the oar and drags it down. Because we were moving forward with everything we had, the pressure of the oar hitting the water was so fierce that it popped out of the oarlock. Gail had no choice but to let it go.

I was surprised that Gail was even able to walk. The pressure of the oar popping out and hitting her mid-section must have been horribly painful. At that speed, it could have created substantial abdominal injury, or thrown her out of the boat into moving blades.

We still managed to finish second to the Easties, which kept our medal hopes alive. In rowing, *repechage* (second chance) allows the highest finishers that fail to win the first heat to race for spots in the finals and advance directly into the finals.

The team never discussed what had happened. One of the coaches may have talked to Gail privately, but the rowers simply moved on. "Catching a crab" is a rookie error virtually unheard of at the Olympic level, but there was no point in belaboring a race that was over. We had another race to focus on in two days, and it was a must win for us to make the finals.

We won the *repechage* and secured our spot in the finals.

Years later, I saw a picture of Gail in that first race as the boat crossed the finish line, head buried in her hands. I'm not sure if it was from frustration, pain, or shame. To this day, we have never discussed it.

* * * * *

The day of the finals was incredibly windy. The wind was whipping across the man-made Notre Dame Island from west to east. The grandstand, located on the west side, created a barrier that made the water over the last 200 meters in front of the grandstand like glass, while the water further away, in the higher numbered lanes, was incredibly choppy. The outermost lane was also closest to the St. Lawrence River and the steamers passing by.

Every U.S. boat in the finals, with the exception of the single scull, drew Lane 6, the one furthest from the grandstand. There was such disparity: Lane 1 had completely calm water, while Lane 6 was so rough it was nearly unrowable. The conditions were so different that the officials moved everyone over one lane, which meant that no one rowed in Lane 1 and boats would row in Lanes 2-7. But now the issue was, newly-created Lane 7 was so close to a rock buildup that the water hitting the rocks created a backwash.

Well, we have a couple of relevant sayings in rowing. The first one is: "It's an outdoor sport," meaning there's no point complaining about the weather. The second one is: "Someday you'll get Lane 1" — or in this case, Lane 2 — because the lane closest to the stands always has the most shelter from the elements. Unfortunately, that didn't happen for the U.S. team. We drew Lane 7 for the finals.

The eight of us and our coxswain who had only rowed together twice — and lost an oar in one of those races — took our places in the boat and rowed up the course toward the starting line. Although you are taught not to look out of the boat, I have always had a bad habit of doing just that. What did I see? On the St. Lawrence River, running parallel to the race course, a steamboat with a giant smokestack was chugging along. Painted on the smokestack was a red hammer and sickle, the symbol of the Soviet Union. My only thought was, how could they time that so perfectly?

Whether or not that was meant to psyche us out, we had more pressing problems. We were rowing in white caps. There is a picture in the Olympic yearbook that captures us perfectly: a tight shot of the stern four glaring at the water, trying to will it to calm down.

With the boats positioned at the starting line, the announcer took to the PA system with the lineup. Counting out from Lane 2, it was Canada, the German Democratic Republic (East Germany), the Federal Republic of Germany (West Germany), Romania, the USSR, and the United States. The commands were all in French: "Etes vous prêts, partez!"

The starter's flag dropped. Years of preparation came down to the next three-and-a-half minutes.

The water was so rough that we looked like a cement mixer coming down the course, but we were rowing like there was no tomorrow — and as I would learn, when it comes to the Olympic Games, there may not be. We took it out well for the first 400 meters, but then someone's blade hit the water wrong, throwing off our rhythm. The boat wobbled just enough for us to lose speed. The Easties moved through us. We were still in contact with the USSR (what else could they be then but "the Soviets"), who had taken the early lead, but the Canadians were coming up fast at the 800-meter mark.

I don't remember a thing that happened in the last 200 meters.

All I remember is the boat slowing down and coach Harry Parker jumping off a small platform. "Anita, did we do it!?," he yelled.

"Yes, we did," I yelled back, more as a feeling than a fact.

The results came up on the board. We had won the bronze medal, though not by much. The Canadians, due partly to the fact they were rowing a different course in the calm waters of Lane 2, nearly ran us down. We crossed the finish line just over a second ahead of them. The Easties won easily, with the Soviets taking the silver medal, finishing 2.5 seconds ahead of us.

We went directly to the medal stand, and turned the boat around. There was no opportunity to row down and calm the lactic acid rushing through our bodies.

Next, I heard my nephew, who always called me by my middle name, saying, "Lucy, get out of the boat." He paused. "Put some shoes on!" (We all rowed in socks or barefoot.)

I knew that my family was planning to attend, but I hadn't seen or talked to them since the Games began because it was difficult to communicate outside the village. There they all were — my parents, my three brothers, one nephew, and my paternal grandmother, Myrtle May.

We all got out of the boat. One of the team, Marion Greig, turned green. I thought she was going to pass out, which actually helped the rest of us stay upright because we were tending to her. The ceremony lasted a few minutes. At the time, I remember being disappointed because we had come to Montreal to win the gold medal. Yes, we had medaled, and represented our country to the best of our abilities. But there was something missing: a gold medal.

An interesting *coda* to our boat was that we were not friends, rather we were athletes united in our goal. We were teammates with the same vision who had survived a grueling process of elimination. We all shared the triumphant moment, but then moved on. The next time we were all together, except for Marion Greig, who didn't attend, was 40 years later, when we rowed together in Sarasota, Florida, for a special event during the trials for the 2016 Olympic Games.

* * * * *

After the rowing competition ended, we had the opportunity to stay in the Olympic Village, attend other competitions, and participate in the closing ceremonies. The only catch was, by staying the USOC gave us a $100 expense stipend, as opposed to giving us $200 if we had left. Naturally, I chose to stay and absorb more of the Olympic Games.

I watched sports that I had never heard of, like team handball. I went to the track and field competition to watch high jumper Dwight Stones. The day I saw him, the track was very slippery and he was being very careful about his run up. I also saw part of the decatholon with Bruce Jenner.

The lack of a gold medal notwithstanding, I was leaving Montreal with wonderful memories. One of them was meeting Queen Elizabeth.

The chance occurrence happened when one of my teammates and I came back from practice and found the elevators in our dorm were locked. We decided to hoof it up the eight flights of stairs. More than half-way up, we got word that the reason the elevators were closed was that the Queen was there with Prince Phillip visiting their daughter, an equestrian who had been injured.

When we reached the sixth floor, we exited the stairwell. Queen Elizabeth was standing in the hallway. I went up to her and asked if I could give her one of my Olympic pins. The pin had the Olympic torch and rings and the year 76 on it, but nothing distinguished it as American.

The queen extended her gloved hand and received the pin. "Oh, this is lovely," she said. "Where are you from?"

"The United States," I replied. Then, alluding to the 76 on the pin, I couldn't help but add: "We are celebrating our Bicentennial."

"Thank you, darling," she said politely.

I was nothing if not a patriot.

* * * * *

The day after the closing ceremonies, I hitched a ride with a teammate's brother back to Philadelphia. We departed in a VW long past its warranty with a bench for a front seat, a car of dubious roadworthiness. Though the car held up, we were detained at the U.S. border.

I was wearing the top to my Olympic tracksuit. I gave my name to the border guard. For some reason, he insisted that I was Haitian. I told him that I was American, so much so that I had just competed for the U.S. in the Olympic Games. But he refused to let us back into the country until I dug out my passport.

After arriving in Philadelphia without further incident, I flew to visit my parents in Indianapolis. They had planned a celebratory reception for me.

My parents were extremely proud of my medal. My dad, of course, had wanted me to be the first African-American women's Olympic swimmer. Instead, I became the first African-American women's Olympic rower. He was so pleased that his daughter, who had grown up in a city where girls had few opportunities to take part in organized sports, had managed to win an Olympic medal.

Truth be told, they were most proud that I became an Olympian while remaining in law school and staying on the path to graduate in 1977. Education was the prime motivating force in my family, viewed as a building block to help create a productive life. I had also made a promise to my Grandma Lucas that I would see my education through to bring me those opportunities that she was not afforded.

The summer and the Olympic Games over, I returned to Philadelphia to begin my final year of law school. My first day back I visited the Vesper boathouse, my second home for the past two years. John Hooten, the women's coach, was there, and we got to talking about the experience at the Games.

The conversation was very positive. People in the rowing world were applauding the U.S. women's 8 for winning bronze in our first regatta together. But as a competitor, I remained unsatisfied.

"Hooten," I said. "This is not a gold medal I won. I am willing to continue to train until 1980, but only if you think that I truly have a chance to make the team and win a gold medal. You know my skills. You saw what was on display. Do I really have a shot at doing better than a bronze medal?"

He mulled it over and took a while to answer. "Yep, you do," he finally said. "You are going to have to work hard, but if you do that, you can win a gold medal."

I was 23 years old, two months from my 24th birthday, meaning I would be 27 by the 1980 Olympic Games. There was no guarantee that I would even make the 1980 Olympic team, much less win gold. But I felt I had to go for it. I decided then and there that I would devote myself to rowing for the next four years, with the sole goal of winning a gold medal. After the 1980 Games, no matter what happened, my rowing career would be over.

After the 1976 Olympic Games, my plan had been to finish law school at Penn, become an attorney, and then someday become a member of the Supremes — and I'm not talking about the singing group. Lofty as it was, that was my goal, but the road would fork and take me in another direction.

Chapter Eight
An Activist Athlete

People talk about the three pillars of the Olympic Movement: the National Olympic Committees, the International Olympic Committee, and the International Federations representing each sport. To me, this is grossly incomplete, because it doesn't include the athletes. Without athletes, you can't have the Olympic Games. So instead of the three pillars, I prefer to call the Olympic Movement the Olympic "Pyramid," because a pyramid has four sides. Being an Olympian clarified this for me.

Throughout my childhood, I had been imbued with the spirit of standing up for individual rights, no matter how big or small the issue. I'm sure, in part, that was why I took up the quest to secure the official uniforms for the women rowers at the 1976 Games, which didn't end at the Closing Ceremonies. After the Games finished, I continued to pursue the matter. It wasn't until the summer of 1977 that the women's rowing team received all of their Olympic gear.

I had started to realize that athletes were often treated like children in an elementary school, and constantly told what to do by the teachers (coaches in this case) and the principal (the USOC). The athletes themselves were expected to compete, to be content — and to be quiet.

The 1976 Olympic Games exposed me to other issues affecting athletes that I wanted to learn more about, such as performance-enhancing drugs. The boycott by the African nations over an unrelated rugby match was another issue that concerned me. The Olympic Village also inexplicably separated men and women — even husbands and wives — which I felt was not in the inclusive spirt of the Games. And worst of all, only one in five athletes at the Games was female.

All of these issues collectively illustrated the complex administrative and political issues of the Olympic Games, areas which I felt did not have enough input from the athletes themselves. I wasn't sure exactly how I could help correct this, but it was clear that something needed to be done.

* * * * *

My future was taking shape, and it was becoming clear that it would focus on advocacy for individual rights. Following the Montreal Games, in the fall of 1976, I had what turned out to be a rewarding and ultimately fortuitous experience. I applied and was accepted into an internship for third-year law students at The Center for Law and Social Policy in Washington, D.C. It was an important experience, because I began to understand the process of public interest law and made contacts in that field.

When I graduated from law school the following spring, I was offered a full-time job as a staff attorney at the Juvenile Law Center of Philadelphia. I had seen a listing for the position on a bulletin board and bicycled to their offices wearing my running shoes. I thought nothing of it — I didn't have any other shoes to wear. Evidently, they were quite taken with the fact that I appeared at the interview in running shoes. I guess I was a good enough fit, because I was hired on the spot and began working that summer.

The organization was only in its second year of existence when I joined. Working on behalf of children is something that I wanted to do. I have always believed that the way we treat children is a reflection of how we treat ourselves as society. And, too often, the picture is not pretty.

In late 1976, my work on behalf of athletes had also begun to take up much of my time. As a result of the people I had met at the United States Olympic Committee, the International Olympic Committee, and other National Olympic Committees during the uniform chase, and due in part to my pursuit of a law degree, I was one of the athletes elected to the recently expanded USOC Athletes Advisory Council. The AAC was the only body representing athletes from all the Olympic sports.

Then, in January 1977, I became one of two athletes elected to the USOC administrative committee (later renamed the Executive Board), along with track star Willie Davenport. To this day I don't know how that happened.

Because I was participating in the Olympic Movement, I saw it as my continued responsibility to be an advocate for athletes. At that point, I had no intention of making it my life's pursuit. I intended to finish my time on the AAC, which had a two-term limit that would last until 1984 if I were re-elected in 1980, and then I would focus on my pursuit of a legal career in public policy. At least that was the plan in the back of my mind.

* * * * *

At that time, there was a battle going on over the hearts, minds, and bodies of amateur athletes. The AAC was working with Senators Ted Stevens, Richard Stone, and John Culver to enact the recommendations of the President's Commission on Olympic Sports. President Gerald Ford had created the commission on Olympic Sports to deal with problems that had come up during the 1972 Olympic Games. The PCOS had encouraged athletes from one sport to study a different sport at both the trials and the Games and report their findings to the commission. Rafer Johnson, the gold medalist in the decathlon in 1960, chose to immerse himself in rowing, and we struck up a valuable, lifelong friendship.

In its report, the commission described how the U.S. amateur athletic world was being marred by power struggles between competing athletic organizations. It detailed horror story after horror story of athletes who were denied the right to compete by one organization or another, notably the National Collegiate Athletic Association and Amateur Athletic Union. The report deplored "the actions of governments, which deny an athlete the right to take part in international competition." Legislation would be necessary to remedy the situation.

The main issue was an ongoing turf war in several sports between the NCAA and AAU. Though the USOC technically chose the Olympic team, many of the trials were run by the AAU. The AAU, however, did not allow its athletes to compete in certain NCAA events and vice versa, leaving amateur athletes caught in the middle with nowhere to turn. The PCOS report also recommended that the USOC restructure itself vertically, meaning that it would incorporate each and every amateur sport.

In October 1977, the U.S. Senate Commerce Committee called a hearing on the matter of amateur athletes' rights. AAC chairman Ed Williams asked me and three other Olympians to testify before the committee. The others were skater/cyclist Sheila Young, water polo player Carl Thomas, and marathoner Kenny Moore, who had become a writer for *Sports Illustrated*.

Part of the reason Ed wanted me to testify was that I was a lawyer. I had been admitted to the Pennsylvania State Bar in 1977 and gone to work as a staff attorney for the Juvenile Law Center of Philadelphia. I was well-versed in athletes' rights, after serving on the board of directors of the Vesper Boat Club, the USRowing Association, and the USOC as an athletes' representative. I had also become a trustee of Connecticut College.

My workload was something of a joke around Vesper. I remember going to Coach Hooten one afternoon in October of 1977, asking to be excused from practice.

"Anita, you can't continue to do all of this and still row for me," he said.

"I know," I told him, "but this one is kind of important. I have to testify before the United States Senate."

The Senate hearing took place on October 18 in Room 5110 of the Dirksen Senate Office Building. None of the athletes had ever testified before Congress. We were seated behind a long conference table with name cards in front of us facing the senators. The senators, who were seated on an elevated platform with their staff behind them, very much had the home field advantage. Looking out at a row of U.S. Senators seated behind a table of microphones was a bit intimidating. However, we held our own, and everyone contributed.

The three of us drew straws to determine the speaking order. Kenny went first. He addressed how runners had been made "pawns in a turf war" between the NCAA and the AAU, and said that athletic directors should be "consultants, not dictators." He closed by saying that an athlete's unilateral ability to compete should be recognized by federal law.

When Kenny finished, Senator Culver leaned in to his microphone. His words barreled out and filled every corner of the hearing room.

"You are saying they (meaning the coaches and athletes) ought to talk it over, but the athlete ought to be the one to ultimately decide," he rumbled. "Be free to go. No coach, college, or parent should stand in the way."

He paused, landing on a question. "What if one parent wants him to go and the other parent doesn't want him to go and the young athlete wants to go? How would you resolve it legally?"

Kenny hesitated and looked at a loss for a response (which he later confessed he was). As the Senator's words hung in thick air, I stepped in.

"I can answer that question," I said. "Because athletes are decision makers. When they compete, they make hundreds, even thousands of decisions during their competitions. That's what athletes are, they are decision makers. Of course they should have rights. All of us are not children. There are a few who are very young who compete at the Games, but more and more athletes are adults who have made the decision to compete. Therefore, we must have rights."

Years later, Kenny wrote of my performance in *Sports Illustrated*: "It was clear that Olympic athletes had found a forceful new advocate."

I was flattered, and I didn't feel that at the time. I certainly had no idea where things were headed. But I did feel a responsibility to advocate especially to the U.S. Senate, which had the power to grant that athletes be free to compete where they chose.

* * * * *

As a result of the hearing and the work of the three supportive Senators, the U.S. Senate inserted athletes' rights into the resulting legislation, the Amateur Sports Act of 1978, which restructured Olympic sports governance in the U.S. The Act, which was signed into law by President Jimmy Carter, removed the AAU from the equation and provided national governing bodies for each Olympic sport. The Act also gave athletes the right to decide on their competitions, the right to lodge complaints against the USOC if they felt they were not being treated fairly, and the right to compete in the Olympic Games.

During this period, I met other women on the frontline. One of the leaders was Donna de Varona, an Olympic medalist in swimming who had a career as a sports commentator at a time when few women were behind the microphone. She was also a member of the PCOS. We have now worked together for four decades on various issues, as she is devoted to making certain that especially girls and women, as well as men and boys, have equal opportunity to compete in sports.

The NCAA pushed back. Its basic argument was, how could students who were subservient to the NCAA have rights? That would completely undo what the NCAA had put together over the years, namely the right to control college athletes. The NCAA threatened to scuttle the legislation entirely, leaving it up to the USOC to safeguard athletes.

Tension came to a head in April 1978 at the USOC House of Delegates meeting in Orlando. During the meeting, AAC Chairman Ed Williams became so emotional that he left the room and could not be found. Someone had to speak to put forth a compromise, so I was designated.

I went off to the ladies' room to write the speech. I sat down on a small couch and wrote out what I believed was a solution to make the NCAA back off of its threats, while still providing athletes some control over their own destiny. I showed the speech to several AAC members for feedback. After a few modifications, it was show time.

The compromise I presented was straightforward. The athletes' rights would exist in the USOC constitution, but would not be detailed in the Amateur Sports Act, thereby placating the NCAA. The USOC accepted, followed by the NCAA. It wasn't perfect, but it was a step in the right direction.

* * * * *

Things were moving fast for me in the Olympic arena. The Los Angeles Olympic Organizing Committee had been created in 1978 to organize and operate the 1984 Olympic Games. The USOC had a certain number of members to represent them on the LA board. I became one of the board nominees proposed by the USOC, and I was elected. As a member of the Los Angeles Olympic Organizing Committee, I would represent the USOC and look after the needs of the athletes as the 1984 Olympic Games were being organized.

* * * * *

But there was also the matter of training for the 1980 Games. From the fall of 1977 until the fall of 1979, I spent my mornings and evenings rowing at Vesper and the rest of my day working at the Juvenile Law Center.

The Juvenile Law Center is a wonderful institution that accomplishes remarkable work. One of my proudest moments there came when I enabled a 16-year-old girl to become emancipated from her abusive parents. Her case file had been transferred to me from one of the other attorneys. The girl, who was white, had managed to escape her parents. She had found a place to live and a job and was paying her own rent. She wanted to complete high school, but parental permission was required for her to enroll. I filed a case in federal court, represented her before the federal bench, and succeeded in convincing the judge to grant her emancipation.

The law center was very forgiving of my rowing life, allowing me to take off three weeks for the World Rowing Championships each year.

In 1977, the worlds were held in Amsterdam. I rowed the pair, which is truly my favorite boat. It is the purest form of rowing — no coxswain, just two rowers sitting front to back. I rowed with Anne Warner, and though not blazing fast, we were a formidable duo. Unfortunately, I contracted bronchitis just before the worlds.

I pushed through the first two races, and we managed to make the finals. By then, I was very sick and could hardly breathe. Ann was upset, but there was nothing we could do about it except row. In the finals, we went off at some ridiculously fast pace. It was my job to call out the commands. I could barely get the words out. It's hard enough to breathe when you have bronchitis, let alone trying to breathe as you are putting your body through extreme torture. We wound up finishing sixth, and just as my body had let me down, I felt that I had let Ann down, too.

As much as I liked the pair, I wanted to win a gold medal in 1980. That meant focusing on the 8. In 1978, the world championships were held in New Zealand. I rowed both the 4+ and the 8+, taking a silver in the 4+, and just missing a bronze in the 8+. These results made me feel like I was on a path to make the Olympic team.

* * * * *

By the fall of 1979, it was time to make the final push for the 1980 Olympic team. I decided to take a leave of absence from the Juvenile Law Center and train at Princeton University with the coach of the women's Olympic rowing team. Though focused on the 8, to log extra time on the water I agreed to row in the pair with Connie (Coz) Crawford, who had been in our 4 the previous year. She was continuing her master's in engineering at Princeton. Because the head coach of the U.S. rowing team was head coach at Princeton, it made sense for me to leave Philadelphia and move to Princeton to train.

The coach was Kris Korzeniowski, who had an interesting story. Born in Poland, he had rowed in his native country for 10 years. In Poland, as was the case in most Soviet countries, coaches required a great deal of education and skills. To further his coaching opportunities, Kris defected from Poland and landed in Canada, where he coached the Canadian women's team to medals in the pair and the 8 at the 1977 world championships. His goal was always to come to the U.S. where there are more rowers and a larger talent pool, so he left Canada to take the position of head women's coach at Princeton. In 1979, he was selected as one of four coaches of the U.S. national women's team.

Princeton University was very generous to me. They gave me a job as an assistant housemaster and a pre-law adviser. There was a small salary — so small that I didn't have to file a tax return — but the job provided me with a place to live in a dorm and meals in the dormitory when school was in session.

Princeton has an amazing rowing facility on Lake Carnegie, so named because of its benefactor Andrew Carnegie. The man-made lake was built with a donation from Carnegie, a Princeton alum, who wanted to endow a sport other than football or track. He decided to give enough money to purchase a large tract of land on which a dam from the Millstone River was built to create a private reservoir for rowing. A state-of-the-art boathouse was also constructed. The facility became a home of the U.S. Olympic rowing team, and remains so to this day.

Through the fall of 1979 into the winter of 1980, I rowed two practices a day, called "doubles." I was up before dawn every morning for the first workout. I returned to the dorm to handle my duties. Midday, it was weight training and then back to the boathouse in the evening for a two-hour workout. I would also hold office hours for my pre-law students in the afternoon.

All of the rowers who had moved to Princeton had low-paying, full-time jobs, as there was no training money available to the team. Those of us who had the time adhered slavishly to the doubles, which were actually triples. The truth is that we were overtrained by the time it came to the team selection, while those who weren't were much better off because the doubles were physically a killer.

* * * * *

On January 20, 1980, an unexpected plot twist in my Olympic training occurred. I was celebrating a friend's birthday party in a bar in downtown Princeton. A breaking news flash, rare in those days, came across the television saying that President Jimmy Carter was breaking in to regularly scheduled programming to make an announcement. Out of natural curiosity, I moved closer to the TV to listen.

President Carter appeared on the screen. He talked about the Soviet Union's invasion of Afghanistan, which had taken place on December 27, 1979. Hundreds of thousands of Afghan citizens had since fled their homeland. The country's ruler had been deposed and killed, and a Soviet-sponsored government had been installed. It was an illegal international act intended to spread Communism, President Carter said, and it could not be tolerated. If the Soviet Union didn't withdraw its troops from Afghanistan within one month, he declared, then the U.S. would not send out spectators and athletes to the 1980 Olympic Games in Moscow.

At first, I wasn't sure if I had heard him correctly. My mind started racing. "What does the Olympic Games have to do with the Soviets invading Afghanistan? Doesn't he know that we are hosting the Olympic Winter Games in Lake Placid, New York, beginning February 9? Will the Soviet Union boycott the Olympic Winter Games with the cloud of a U.S. boycott hanging over the Moscow Olympic Games? And what does all this mean for the Olympians?"

The more I thought about what he had said, the more I realized that there was a lack of understanding on President Carter's part about how the Olympic Movement worked in our country. Athletes funded their own training without any federal money. Spectators paid their own way to the

Games. It wasn't the President's decision to send the team or make them stay home. That power rested with the USOC.

Three days later, on January 23, 1980, the president delivered his State of the Union address. In the speech to both houses of Congress, he drew a line in the sand. He said that he would not support sending American athletes to Moscow as long as Soviet military forces remained in Afghanistan.

This declaration resulted in Congress taking action in the following days. On January 24, the House of Representatives passed, by a vote of 386-12, a resolution opposing participation by United States athletes in the Moscow Olympic Games unless Soviet troops were withdrawn from Afghanistan by February 20.

On January 28, the Senate Foreign Relations Committee held a hearing to consider the House resolution before sending it to the full Senate for a vote. To provide the Olympians' perspective, I was called to testify before the committee, along with Olympic gold medalist Al Oerter. Others who testified included Deputy Secretary of State Warren Christopher, USOC Executive Director Don Miller, and Senators Bill Bradley and Ted Stevens. I held nothing back.

"My experience as a black woman in this country has taught me that there are many things that defy rational explanation," I said in my prepared opening remarks. "These last few days I have tried to understand why it is that the Olympic Games should be used to punish Russia. If the President, the House, and I submit, this committee and the American people, truly believe that the Games are so important to the Russians that the U.S.A. could effectuate a withdrawal of Russian troops from Afghanistan by refusing to participate in those Games, then why weren't the Games used to prevent the invasion of that country and prevent subjugation of the people?"

I implored the committee to recognize the courage that the athletes were demonstrating in continuing to train for a Games they may not compete in. "Please," I concluded, "if you must use us and use our Olympic Games, don't destroy us in the process. There are future generations of Americans who need the U.S. Olympic Committee. Support us; stand with us, as we have stood for and with the people of this country."

It was to no avail. The Senate Foreign Relations Committee recommended the House resolution to the full Senate, which passed it the following day by a vote of 88-4. However, I believe that my testimony and that of the others planted the seed for the team to be selected.

What was clear was that the battle over the hearts, minds, and bodies of Olympic athletes that had just played out with the AAU, NCAA, USOC, and the U.S. Senate was about to escalate into an entirely different arena. All of this troubled me deeply. The more the situation sank in, the more I realized how personal this was for so many athletes — and for me. Everything we had worked for hung in the balance.

I vowed to stand up for the athletes. I set up what could very loosely be described as a "war room" in the living room in my dormitory apartment. I collected every USOC document I could get my hands on to search for a way to stop the president and the Congress from taking action against the Olympic team.

I also phoned Joe Onek, a senior adviser to President Carter working in the West Wing. I had met Joe while working for the Center for Law and Social Policy in Washington during my third year of law school. Joe took my call. I explained why I felt the president was wrong, and I told him that I planned to fight any attempt to keep us from going to Moscow. He made no reassurances, but I knew that, at the very least, we were being heard at the highest level.

The day after the State of the Union, reporter Jane Gross of *The New York Times* came to Princeton to do a story on me and the rowing team. In her feature story, which appeared on the front page of the Sports section on January 27, 1980, she detailed how hard we were working for the Games and how much we had all sacrificed.

In very personal terms, I alluded to my upbringing and said I was surprised that many people were simply saying we should do whatever the president says. "They seem to think the president must be right," I said. "I'm black, so my experience isn't America first, last, and always. I don't think there's any other country I'd like to live in, but I don't think this country is always right. America didn't help me a lot, but I'm proud America taught me do it myself. If you're going to make it here, you make it on your own. I don't like being told what I must give up."

I also said that I felt the Olympic Games was being wrongly used as a geopolitical negotiating tool. "I just don't see that [a boycott] will have any effect on anybody but the athletes, and I don't believe the world is with us on this," I said. "What does it say about our foreign policy that our only weapon is the Olympic team? That is just plain shocking."

Chapter Nine
Protesting President Carter's Call for an Olympic Boycott

It was March 21, 1980, the day my future came into view. The U.S. Olympic team was invited by President Jimmy Carter to the White House — actually, summoned might be a more appropriate verb — where he would address my Olympic dream and the dreams of all the other athletes.

The U.S. Olympic Movement was stronger than ever. The 1980 Olympic Winter Games had taken place in Lake Placid, New York in February, although under cloud of a potential U.S. boycott of the summer Games. In what was dubbed the "Miracle on Ice," the U.S. men's hockey team had upset the heavily-favored Soviet Union, winner of the past four Olympic golds, to win the gold medal. Speed skater Eric Heiden had won five gold medals and broken four Olympic records in the process. And Los Angeles was busy preparing to host the 1984 Olympic Games.

But that was all background noise. I, and others, had been challenging President Carter's authority to withhold the U.S. team's participation from the Moscow Games very publicly and rather vociferously. My pushback to his call for a boycott was widely circulated.

The athletes gathered in the East Room. Chairs were set up in a horseshoe pattern facing a podium with the presidential seal. It certainly wasn't a setting conducive to a two-way conversation. It looked more like we had been invited to the White House to hear why the president was giving the team what amounted to a death sentence.

National Security Adviser Zbigniew Brzezinski took the podium. Using a pointer and a map, Brzezinski gave us a tutorial on the situation in Afghanistan. He told us that that Soviet Union had invaded Afghanistan, killed its ruler, and installed its own Communist leaders to run the country.

At present, Brzezinski said, an estimated 100,000 Soviet troops were in Afghanistan. He also talked about how the Soviets were trying to cut off U.S. oil supplies with their actions. The result of these actions, he said, was spreading Communism and devaluing freedom. We needed to stop them.

I was certainly sympathetic to the Afghans' plight, but I couldn't see what the situation had to do with the Olympic Games. Nonetheless, the threat of Communism was the hot button issue of the day, and the administration was sounding the alarm bells that boycotting the Olympic Games was a way to curtail evil from spreading across Eastern Europe.

Senior adviser Joe Onek spoke next. He talked about the sacrifices that were necessary in these extraordinary times. He told us that the president would address all the issues shortly. At the end of Joe's speech, I rose to ask a question. I wanted to ask why the Olympians would not be able to speak to the president and give him our perspective.

Joe called on me to speak. Just as I started, President Carter entered the room. Everyone stood but, as we later learned, for the first time in Carter's presidency, no one applauded.

For 20 minutes, President Carter spoke in a somber tone. He had asked us to come to the White House to discuss "a serious and very vital matter, one that does directly involve human life," he said.

He talked about the thousands of lives that had been lost in Afghanistan as a result of the Soviet invasion, the villages wiped out, and the hundreds of thousands of lives that could be lost unless our nation was strong and willing to sacrifice. By that, he meant the Olympians.

"The highest commitment that I have in my official capacity as president is to preserve the security of the United States of America and to keep the peace," he said. "Every decision that I make, every action that I take, has to be compatible with that commitment."

President Carter compared the current situation to the 1936 Berlin Olympic Games, in which Hitler promoted Nazism and barred Jews from competing. The president said that history would have been different had those Games not been held. He also likened the sacrifice he was asking the Olympians to make to the Iowa farmers who had suffered from the grain export embargo he had imposed on the Soviet Union – despite the fact that his administration had already relaxed the embargo.

"I can't say at this moment what other nations will not go to the summer Olympics in Moscow. Ours will not go," he declared. "I say that not with any equivocation; the decision has been made. The American people are convinced that we should not go to the summer Olympics. The Congress has voted overwhelmingly, almost unanimously, which is a very rare thing, that we will not go. And I can tell you that many of our major allies, particularly those democratic countries who believe in freedom, will not go."

The president told us that he felt the decision was in the best interest of the Olympic Movement. "In my judgment, what we are doing is preserving the principles and the quality of the Olympics, not destroying it," he said.

At one point, he tried to strike an empathetic tone. "This is obviously a difficult decision for me to make. It's much more difficult on you. I'm not saying it's worse for me."

He closed by saying that he hoped we would support him, but added, "This is a free country, and your voice is yours, and what you do and say is a decision for you to make. But whatever you decide, as far as your attitude is concerned, I will respect it."

Indeed, it is a free country, I thought, except when our president is restricting our freedom.

Like so many other athletes, the 1980 Olympic Games would be my last chance at reaching the pinnacle of my sport. I had put my life on hold to train. There was no tomorrow, no next competition, no turning pro. I decided that I could not sit back and let anyone — not even the President of the United States — strip me and my teammates of the right to compete.

Following his speech, the president took no questions and then hastily departed. It was hardly a "meeting" with the Olympians, as he called it. That night on the ABC News, Sam Donaldson called the event "a grim moment for President Carter."

Following the president's speech, 45 of us opposed to the boycott gathered for a press conference across Lafayette Park at the Hay-Adams hotel. Six of the most vocal, including me, stood at the microphone.

One reporter asked me, "Why didn't you clap when the president appeared?"

I knew this was an important moment. I had to be respectful, but also respect the position of the athlete. I took a deep breath and replied, "Because we are athletes, so we are not impressed that someone can walk across a room."

There was a laugh, which broke the tension.

I said that I felt that the Olympic Games had survived two World Wars, but now President Carter was using the Games as a political bargaining tool in the Cold War. I refused to accept this. I explained that the president did not understand how the Olympic Games worked.

"The president is not the one who sends athletes, the athletes go of their own volition," I said. "The president is the honorary president of the U.S. Olympic Committee, and he has no jurisdiction over the athletes." In fact, he needed the USOC to vote for the boycott.

It all came down to the individual rights of the athletes. The Amateur Sports Act, which I had testified in support of before the U.S. Senate Commerce Committee in 1977, gave athletes the right of due process and barred anyone from denying an athlete's right to compete. Ironically, it was President Carter who had signed the act into law.

I wasn't about to give in.

* * * * *

The day after President Carter's White House address to the Olympians, France, Spain, and Italy declared that their teams would compete in Moscow. Great Britain reaffirmed its previous commitment to attend, and ended up competing under the Olympic flag rather than their own national flag (as did many European nations) to prevent angering the U.S. Puerto Rico, a U.S. territory no less, also voted to participate. Nevertheless, in days following his speech, President Carter shored up his position.

White House Counsel Lloyd Cutler drafted an executive order that would give the president the power to prevent the USOC from sending a team to the Olympic Games and would also ban U.S. media outlets from sending reporters. The Department of Justice pushed back on this directive, which was controversial at best, unconstitutional at worst, as even during wartime the president did not have the power to control the movements of the media.

President Carter also sent the Secretary of Commerce a memorandum that prohibited international transactions related to the Moscow Olympic Games under the Export Administration Act.

But he still had to convince the USOC not to send the team.

An emergency meeting of the 13-member USOC Administrative Committee (later renamed the Executive Board) was called in New York to discuss the impending boycott. The meeting was organized by Bill Simon, the former Treasury Secretary under President Nixon who served as the USOC treasurer (and would become its president in the next quadrennial).

As if things were not tough enough for me as an Olympian whose dream was being stripped away, the meeting was held at the New York Athletic Club. I knew that the NYAC had a history of not being open to people of color or women, and it upset me that we were meeting there. It was the place where, in 1936, the USOC had held its debate over whether to go the Berlin Games.

When I arrived at the meeting, I let my feelings be known. I didn't care if there was a feeling, "Anita is complaining about everything." I told the panel that it was wrong to ask me to come to a building, where save for the fact that this organization was meeting here, I would not be allowed to enter. It just was not right for the USOC to meet in such a venue.

In the meeting, I again voiced my opposition to the president's call for a boycott, saying that neither the president nor the USOC should be taking away an athlete's right to compete. "Nowhere does it say the USOC should keep athletes home, except when there is a clear threat of danger, and there is no threat of danger to the team," I explained.

It was decided that the USOC would gather all of its delegates at its headquarters in Colorado Springs and take a vote.

* * * * *

As the Carter Administration's drumbeat for a boycott grew stronger, I was invited to attend a briefing at the U.S. State Department on the issue. General David Jones, the Chairman of the Joint Chiefs of Staff, was there. During the event, I decided I had to ask him a question that had been troubling me.

I asked him straight out: "Can you tell me if one life will be spared if we stay home from Moscow?"

"No, I cannot," he said.

White House Counsel Lloyd Cutler was also at the briefing. I met Cutler through my friend Joe Onek, who worked in the West Wing with him. Cutler was in the process of drafting legislation that would give the president legal authority to unilaterally prevent the U.S. Olympic Committee from participating in the Games and to ban all U.S. media organizations from sending reporters to Moscow.

Cutler asked me if I could meet with him at the White House. Though I had a plane to catch that afternoon, I told him that I would be happy to. He suggested we ride there together in his car. So we did, in silence.

The car pulled up to the rear of the White House, where the president comes and goes. We walked through the Map Room and then through a corridor. We passed an entire wall filled with pictures from the Olympic Winter Games in Lake Placid. I couldn't believe that a White House so enamored with pride in our winter athletes was so consumed with restricting the summer athletes from participating.

We reached Cutler's office, and I waited outside while he took a phone call. Joe dropped by to say hello to me. Cutler called me in to his office, and we had a polite but tense conversation.

When it became clear we were not making any progress, Cutler moved from behind his desk and sat next to me. "At some point you have to feel in your gut that something is just plain wrong, and you have to do something about it," he said.

"You are so correct, Mr. Cutler," I replied. "I do feel that right now. It is absolutely wrong to keep the athletes home from the Olympic Games when they have dedicated their lives to pursuing this goal. And the fact that it will make no difference and not save one life, as General Jones admitted, says to me that all of this is just plain wrong."

Cutler leaned back in his chair. "I take it I have not convinced you how important this is to the administration," he said.

"No sir, you have not," I said. "It may be important to the administration, but it is more important to this group of citizens who have invested and made life decisions in order to compete at these Games. And there is nothing you can do that will come close to filling the hole that will be created by the administration's actions to prevent us from competing."

Cutler thanked me and offered to have his driver take me to the airport.

I walked back past the wall of Olympic images and out to his chauffeured car. The driver greeted me warmly. I got into the back seat. I noticed a telephone console in the middle of the seats. I had never seen a car with a telephone. I asked if I could make a call. He smiled and told me it was fine. I called three people. None of them answered their phones, as if to underscore the fact I was having trouble getting through to anyone.

* * * * *

On April 10, President Carter upped the ante. In a speech, he declared, "If legal actions are necessary to enforce my decision not to send a team to Moscow, then I will take those legal actions." Among the legal measures the president was apparently contemplating was invoking the sanctions of the International Emergency Economic Powers Act, a recently-passed federal law that authorize the president to regulate commerce after he declared a national emergency in response to a threat against the United States. Applying this to Olympians, I felt, would grossly overstep his authority and was a ploy to influence the USOC House of Delegates vote scheduled two days later.

On April 11, the USOC Administrative Committee met in Colorado Springs in advance of the full House of Delegates meeting to discuss the president's actions and the boycott. We took a vote on a resolution to support the boycott and keep the team from Moscow. I voted no, so the final tally was 9-1. I was the lone dissenter.

The USOC's special meeting of all delegates to vote on the boycott was held on April 12. Each sport was allotted five delegates, one of whom had to be an athlete, with the exception of Swimming and Track & Field, which had 10 delegates each because of their outsized influence. It was the largest USOC meeting ever held, so big that it had be held in a hotel ballroom.

The White House marshalled its resources. Vice President Walter Mondale arrived to carry the boycott message to the athletes. It was clear from our New York meeting that former Treasury Secretary Bill Simon, the

USOC treasurer, was a supporter of the administration's position.

At a news conference the day before the vote, I told reporters that if the USOC or the Carter Administration barred the athletes from the Games, then we would file a lawsuit. "Possible defendants of the lawsuit are all members who may vote against the law and in favor of President Carter's boycott," I said.

The story was widely covered in the national media. In a front page story in the *Chicago Tribune* on the day of the vote, Vice President Mondale was quoted as saying: "The House of Delegates is now on the eve of a decision critical to the future of our whole nation. A great deal is at stake in this vote, not only for our athletes, who have been asked to make an enormous sacrifice, but also for all Americans and all civilized people everywhere."

The meeting was held in the Antlers Hotel ballroom. After introductions were made, Vice President Mondale spoke. He delivered the same party line that the president had given us, asserting that the boycott was crucial to national security. "History holds its breath," he said, calling on the USOC to support the boycott.

Bill Simon spoke next. He delivered a passionate plea in support of the boycott. "I am somewhat incredulous that a group of mature and what I consider to be among the most patriotic of Americans — our Olympians — can seriously discuss defying the president of the United States on a national security issue," he said. "We aren't defying a man. We are defying the office, the highest-elected office in our land."

Simon's speech received a standing ovation.

Then it was my turn. I implored the Olympic Family that surely they must sense what was right. "The boycott trivializes the Olympic Games by bringing them down to the level of trade embargoes," I said. I rebutted Simon with a quotation from Benjamin Franklin: "Those who would give up essential liberty to purchase a little temporary safety deserve neither liberty nor safety." In closing, I said: "We define our liberty by testing it. This is such a test."

The 300 delegates cheered my speech, but I was outmatched. Simon's speech won the day. The vote was 2-1 in favor of the boycott. A year later, Simon was elected president of the USOC.

But there was another avenue available: asking the courts to intervene. I had chosen to attend law school because I wanted to speak the language of power and use my legal background to stand up for people's rights. Long before I expected, I was about to put this to the test.

Chapter Ten
Laying It All on the Line

Time was critical in overturning the boycott. Under the rules of the International Olympic Committee, the U.S. Olympic Committee needed to formally accept the invitation to attend the Moscow Games by May 24th. Rowing tryouts were not being held until June, so it was now or never. Feeling that I had no other choice, I decided on now.

I would file a lawsuit against the USOC seeking to stop the boycott and defying the directive of the President of the United States, which both houses of Congress supported.

The legal path was complicated by my lack of funds. Luckily, a benefactor named Robert Zagoria appeared out of nowhere. Robert, a former collegiate athlete, was a solo practitioner based in Princeton. After he saw me quoted in the press about the boycott, he called to volunteer his legal services.

Robert took the lead in the process. I needed co-plaintiffs, he said, including a coach and a board member, as well as other athletes, to demonstrate that all parts of the Olympic Family were affected by the boycott. He was instrumental in recruiting the American Civil Liberties Union *pro bono*. Their board agreed by a mere one-vote margin to join the case, which seemed to underscore how sensitive the issue had become. Robert also brought aboard the heavyweight national law firm of Covington & Burling *pro bono*.

On May 16, 1980, I filed suit against the USOC. The unprecedented class action was joined by 25 other athletes and one member of the USOC Executive Board, Col. Don Hull, and, most importantly, the ACLU.

DeFrantz et al. v. United States Olympic Committee moved for an injunction barring the USOC from carrying out its resolution. The suit argued that in preventing American athletes from competing in the Moscow Olympic Games, the USOC had exceeded its statutory powers, and had violated the Amateur Sports Act of 1978 by abridging the constitutional rights of those athletes who wanted to compete.

The media reaction was mixed, at best. *The New York Times* had published an op-ed prior to the vote entitled "Olympian Hubris" arguing that the will of the public should be considered in any decision to send U.S. athletes to the Moscow Games. Shirley Povich of *The Washington Post*, the unofficial dean of sportswriters, accused us of playing "petty, whining law games" and called those who voted against the boycott and brought the suit "self-interested."

I believed with all my heart that I was on the right side. While my larger point was that that the Olympic Games belonged to the world and not just to one city, the suit also had another goal: to ensure there was a 1980 U.S. Olympic team. But I needed the support of Congress, which had already voted for the boycott, for there to be an official Olympic team. I was determined that even if the boycott held, a team would be both selected and officially outfitted. (I had presented the case for team selection during my January testimony before the Senate Judiciary Committee.)

Under the Amateur Sports Act, the U.S. Congress had jurisdiction over the USOC. Although the legislation doesn't specifically state their powers in the relationship, many believed Congress could stop the process of selecting a team. I felt that they might just do that, because we were past the Rubicon and had crossed the point of no return. No law said that the president could order us to stay home.

* * * * *

I understood that I was possibly putting my future in jeopardy. I had planned to pursue a career in public interest law, a career that I had started with my work at the Center for Law and Social Policy in Washington and the Juvenile Law Center in Philadelphia. But if things turned out badly and I ended up with the U.S. government as my enemy, my goal of forging a career in public policy law could be very difficult.

I was receiving hate mail and even death threats, and I had a few visits from people I'm positive were FBI agents wanting to "sympathize" with me. I received a call from members of a group called the Stalin Society, who were offering to fly U.S. athletes to Moscow to watch the Games, making me feel even more like a pawn in a political game.

The Princeton University staff was very supportive. When the threats started coming in, Dean Joan Girgus called me into to her office. I was sure she was going to ask me to leave for the safety of the students. Instead she told me that mail intended for me had ended up in her box.

She held up the letters. "These are some rather troubling messages."

I apologized for bringing undo attention to the university and volunteered to leave.

"Absolutely not," she said. "I just wanted to be sure you were safe."

The truth is, I had never considered the personal cost to me, but I had to consider the potential impact on others, including my family. Being named DeFrantz is not quite the same as being named Smith. The surname is so unique that there were would be no confusion that my family members were related to the rower pushing back against the president and Congress.

Shortly after President Carter made his first declaration of a boycott, I told my family that I was going to fight it. My parents accepted my position. They told me that I needed to stand up for what I believed in, even if I was standing against the president.

My father had suffered a massive heart attack in 1979. He was the CEO of the advocacy organization Community Action Against Poverty. He went on disability while he was recovering. During this time, he was falsely charged with embezzlement. I feared that it would be harder for him as he worked to prove his innocence with the DeFrantz name in the media fighting for something that many opposed.

While there is no way to know the impact, the allegations against my father were wrongly and, doggedly, pursued for some time. In the end, the truth came out and the charges against him were dropped. It turned out that the treasurer was skimming money to pay for his wife's cancer treatment. The situation took so long to unravel because the treasurer also contracted cancer. Even though my father was exonerated, to this day I feel responsible for his ordeal because of the decision I made.

Throughout the boycott, my parents kept telling me to do what I thought was right. My actions were based on the life I was working to lead — one of inclusion, one free of discrimination and oppression, and one that shined a light on individual rights. I felt that I had to ask myself, what are the principles that make up a life? What had so many who had come before me fought for, if I didn't fight now?

My family is a mix of European, Native American, and African — known as "Indian" and "black" in those days. Generations of my ancestors had been involved in an ongoing struggle for freedom at all levels, but at its core, theirs was a struggle simply for what was just. So while the Olympic boycott had nothing to do with race, I felt that it had everything to do with what was just.

* * * * *

Justice was not delivered in the courtroom, however. William H. Allen and Edward R. Mackiewicz of Covington & Burlington appeared on my behalf, because I was busy training, and argued the case. However, on June 8, 23 days after it was filed, my suit against the USOC was dismissed by U.S. District Judge John H. Pratt. In his decision, he did not agree with our assertion that the government preventing athletes from going to the Olympic Games constituted a "state action" that violated our constitutional rights.

I felt that Judge Pratt, who had served our nation and lost an arm fighting in Korea, had skirted the merits of our case out of his openly "America First" stance. He seemed to be swayed by the argument that the boycott would help pressure the Soviet Union to bring an end to the conflict in Afghanistan. In the final paragraph of his decision, he wrote that the "responsibilities of citizenship fall more heavily on some than on others," and likened the sacrifice to military service.

We immediately filed an expedited appeal to the U.S. Court of Appeals, but the appeal was dismissed the following day. We also thought about appealing to the U.S. Supreme Court on an expedited basis. Justice Byron White would have to recuse himself, however, because his daughter was a member of the Olympic field hockey team. That meant that we had no chance of getting enough votes — and that meant that the 1980 U.S. Olympic team would not compete in the Games of the XXII Olympiad.

Several legal scholars disagreed with the courts. In 1981, legal scholar Jeffrey M. Marks reviewed Judge Pratt's decision in the *New York University*

Journal of International Law and Politics. He argued the President's order contravened the Amateur Sports Act of 1978, which had chartered the USOC as a private organization designed to be immune from government action. Marks concluded: "The court lost sight of this overriding principle. It should have invalidated the USOC decision not to send a team, thereby compelling the Carter Administration to devise other methods to implement its foreign policy."

* * * * *

In the spring of 1980, as the fight over the boycott was intensifying, I began having trouble hearing in my right ear. I was preparing to race in the pair with Coz Crawford and joked to my friends that losing my hearing was a defense mechanism against all the mean things being said about me. It grew worse and worse until finally I lost all hearing in my right ear.

My mom, who was an audiologist, insisted that I get checked out. I went to an audiologist, but the doctor wasn't able to figure out why I had a greatly diminished ability to hear in my right ear over my left. He suggested it could be the result of a fever or a cold. I rarely got sick, so that seemed unlikely.

Though my hearing slowly returned, the ailment had consequences. My rowing partner's mother advised Coz that she shouldn't row in the pair with me. She felt that the stress of rowing in the pair, combined with the boycott fight, had caused my hearing to go out, and she didn't want Coz to be responsible. Consequently, Coz refused to row with me.

I was disappointed, because I had originally moved to Princeton to row with her. But I was so caught up in fighting the boycott, I brushed the issue aside. I needed to stay focused. I still had to make the team.

The Olympic rowing camp was held in early June, just after the court decision was handed down. After the third day, I noticed that my left leg was going numb. I was pretty sure I was exerting the same amount of power as usual, but it was hard to tell with a numb leg. I pushed on for another day and then decided to see the trainer.

I didn't want the coach to know, because that might diminish my chances to make the team. Unfortunately, when I was in the trainer's room another team member came in to be attended to as well. She was a port (meaning she rowed on the left side) so I knew she wouldn't go after my seat, but as an athlete competing for a spot on an elite team, you don't want anybody to know that you have a weakness.

The trainer's best guess was that I had a pinched nerve in my rear. He suggested putting a pad on the seat to provide some cushion. I tried the pad, but it didn't help. In fact, my other leg started getting numb.

My performance suffered. I pushed my hardest when I was on the water. I had to make sure that by the time I got back to the dock, my leg was functioning well enough so that I could climb out of the boat without any visible handicap. There is no room for injuries in Olympic sports.

Camp was a grueling process. The coaches again used seat racing to determine the best rowers for the 8. In the end, I made the team, but I was a shadow of my best self. I was assigned to row in the 4, which dinged my pride. I had faith that I could fight my way back to the 8 that summer at the summer tune up for the Games.

The day that the names of the team were announced, Coz informed me that she was leaving the camp. She had made the team, so I was shocked. I clearly hadn't been paying attention to her. She said she was disappointed with the impending boycott and felt there was no reason to go through all the pain and work if we wouldn't have the chance to compete.

Her decision troubled me. I took it very personally. I felt that I was letting down my teammates and all Olympians by not winning the fight against President Carter. I honestly believed that if anyone could get the U.S. rowers in the Olympic Games, I could.

The only positive news was that Congress had given their de facto support to a team being selected by not standing in the way. They apparently reasoned that it was a positive thing to have an Olympic team even if it didn't compete. However remote, for me, having a team meant that the possibility of competing still existed.

* * * * *

In June, the Olympic rowing teams traveled to Germany for international regattas leading up to the Games. The plan was for the team to train and race there to determine the final spots in the boats. Even though the U.S.

Olympic team was not going to Moscow, we needed to select a team and continue competing to hold our standing in the rowing world.

I resigned myself to the fact that I could not save the entire U.S. Olympic team's participation, but there was one last chance for the rowers to be entered. During the entire process, I stayed in touch with rowers around the world, and their support kept me going through the discouraging times. My teammates had been asking me if there was something in the Olympic Charter that might allow rowers to enter. We combed through the document and discovered a section stating if athletes disagreed with their National Olympic Committee, then their International Federation could enter them into the Games. In our case, this would be the International Rowing Federation, or Fédération Internationale des Sociétés d'Aviron. My plan was to ask FISA to enter the U.S. rowing team directly in the Moscow Games, thereby circumventing the U.S. boycott in our sport.

I wrote to FISA president Thomas Keller. Thomi knew that I was fighting the boycott and was willing to help. As head of FISA, Thomi said that he would enter the U.S. team in the Olympic Games, despite the fact that USOC, at the behest of the President of the United States, was preventing the U.S. team from competing in Moscow. All he needed was the official list of the U.S. team members from USRowing, our national federation.

I quickly got in touch with USRowing and asked for a letter listing the names of the U.S. team to send to FISA. The team had just been selected at trials, but officials refused on the grounds that since the U.S. was not participating in Moscow, there was no "official" 1980 U.S. Olympic team.

My public response was curt and immature. I said that it was a miracle that those officials could walk given that they had no spine.

We were out of options. This was my lowest point. I was emotionally spent and physically exhausted. I had failed.

Then a small, beautiful thing happened. A team meeting was called. We were in Ratzeburg, Germany, one of the Valhallas of our sport. I had no idea what it was about. I was just going through the motions, brushing my teeth in the morning, eating at meal time, and rowing toward nothing. Athletes always have goals; I now had none.

One of the rowers, Holly Hatton, stood up. Holly was a graphic artist.

She singled me out by name. She held up a certificate that she had designed. "We want to thank you for all that you have done for us and for our Olympic cause," she said. "We all signed this."

She then held up a box. "We also bought you a pair of lederhosen," she added.

There were peals of laughter. I had made it well known that I wasn't leaving Germany without a proper pair of lederhosen. I looked out over the room of these women who, like me, had given years of their lives over to a dream. They had pushed the "pause" button on their careers, their families, and their relationships for a chance to compete in the Olympic Games. Yes, we had lost that dream, but I had won the respect of my teammates, a reward I cherish to this day.

An African proverb came to mind. "You can go fast alone, but you can go far together." For the first time, I felt that we were together.

That summer in Moscow during the IOC Session prior to the Olympic Games, the International Olympic Committee recognized me for my courage in fighting on behalf of the Olympic Movement, and bestowed on me the Bronze Medal of the Olympic Order, despite the fact that I was not physically there. I was the only American awarded a medal in Moscow.

As appreciative and inspired as I was by the honor, I would rather have had the chance for my teammates and me to compete for a gold medal.

* * * * *

With no Olympic Games to attend, two of my teammates, Jan Palchikoff and Coz Crawford, and I headed for Greece. We visited Athens and the Olympic Stadium there. We then went to Ancient Olympia on the Peloponnese Peninsula, the site of the first Olympic Games. The modern-day Olympic torch is lit there using a reflection of sunlight in a parabolic mirror. The torch is then transported to the site of the Games, where the Olympic flame is lit.

We traveled around Greece with just our backpacks. What we had gone through stayed with us for the entire trip. We talked on and off about the Olympic Games, but we didn't grouse. Despite the fact that we wouldn't see the 1980 Olympic flame lit, this pilgrimage made us feel a part of the tradition.

We also visited West Berlin, where Coz's brother lived. One morning, we ventured into East Berlin. We talked to several people about the Olympic Games in East Berlin, where information was parceled out and altered by the Soviet Union. One couple told me they heard that the U.S. team was not going to Moscow because it was afraid of losing on Soviet soil. I assured them that was not the case, but I don't think they believed me.

We were home by the time the Olympic Games started, but there was nothing to watch on TV. NBC owned the rights to air the 1980 Olympic Games, and had paid the highest price to date, $80 million. The network had filmed the events, but most affiliates did not air any of what had been recorded.

Chapter Eleven
1980: The Team With No Result

Our nation does not know us as Olympians. Our sublime moments of exertion and triumph do not exist. We have no memories, and fans have no memories of us. We forever are the team with no result. We are the 1980 United States Olympic Team.

Over 35 years later, I have come to understand my unrelenting feeling of loss. There were some 500 athletes on the 1980 U.S. Olympic Team. For 219 members of that team, the 1980 Olympic Games was their one chance to compete in the Olympic Games. But they were denied. Those 219 athletes never marched in an Opening Ceremony parade. They never experienced the boundless pride in representing our nation. And they never lived in an Olympic Village, where men and women representing every size, shape, and shade of humanity lived in peaceful and respectful harmony for four weeks.

I had the opportunity to experience all of this in 1976, so I know what these 219 athletes missed. We had all done the work, paid the price, made the life decisions that would bring us to the Olympic Games, yet we were denied access to the elixir.

Our team was composed of private citizens who had found a way to finance their dreams. Those dreams were one step from reality. Not one penny of public money — federal, state, or local — supported us as we trained and prepared for our final athletic examination at the Olympic Games. Before corporate sponsorships or financial backing existed, each of us had to make our own way.

To this day, my friends ask why I can't accept what happened. Why it is so hard for me to let go? I have since had the privilege of working at all levels of the Olympic Movement, and achieved so much that I am proud of. But the feeling of loss over 1980 remains palpable. Only athletes who have been forced to stay home can truly understand and share my sense of loss.

Finally, at the inaugural USOC Olympic Assembly in April 2005, I understood why I continue to feel the loss.

The program began with a video presentation of scenes from the 2004 Athens Olympic Games. The athletes' smiles and the wondrous show of mutual respect and fair play that is the basis of the Olympic Games delighted the audience.

Later in the program, another video was shown, of the 1980 Olympic Winter Games. As always, I experienced an overwhelming rush of emotion and pride, watching the highlights of the hockey team win the "Miracle on Ice." I had chills as I watched the vignettes of stories that I know so well. These were my contemporaries. After all, my teammates and I, who had prepared for the 1980 Moscow Olympic Games to be held that summer, were to be their "twins." Our stories would be told just six months later.

Then a flash of understanding hit me. There were no videos, no pictures, no medal ceremonies of us. Nothing could be shown to the Olympic Family or to our nation recounting the efforts of the 1980 U.S. Olympic team. The members of that team will always be members of an Olympic team but never Olympians, *because they did not compete*. Those memories are missing for both the participants and for everyone who has ever been moved by an Olympic moment.

* * * * *

In late July 1980, while the Olympic Games were being held in Moscow, our reward for being Olympians was an invitation to Washington, D.C., for a parade and a chance to shake hands with the man who had denied us our chance to compete. All sports except swimming participated. For some bizarre reason, the U.S. national governing body for swimming staged a mock competition to compare their times against those in Moscow. Their virtual competition seemed to me to skirt the whole point of competing in the Olympic Games — to compete against other nations in the same venue.

On a sweltering summer day in Washington, the U.S. Olympic team gathered to be recognized. Levi Strauss provided us with the full complement of Olympic gear, and the rowing team added to that. We had shirts made.

On the front, they said "U.S. Rowing Team." On the back: "Threat to National Security." Hey, at least we hadn't lost our sense of humor.

We also had stickers made. Holly Hatton, our resident graphic artist, designed them. "We're here to make sure this never happens again," they read. We put those on our cowboy hats and passed them out to other athletes who wanted them. My teammate Carol Brown made certain there were plenty of stickers to go around.

We got all dressed up in our Olympic gear and had our picture taken on the steps of the U.S. Capitol and then rode in open-air buses down Pennsylvania Avenue — for two short blocks. There was no parade announcement. Then we made a U-turn, and returned to the Capitol Building. People were looking at us, wondering exactly what was going on. When they began to figure out that we were the Olympians with no Games, they started applauding.

Back at the Capitol, we boarded a bus for the White House. A reception for the athletes was being held on the East Lawn, and charged back to the USOC. There was a speech by President Carter, which I didn't listen to, and a receiving line to meet the president, which I didn't stand in. I told the media that I wouldn't shake President Carter's hand. I was criticized by many people, mostly the news media, for attending the White House reception at all and called a hypocrite. I felt that it was my right, and even my duty, to speak out against power whenever I felt oppressed. That, however, did not make me an enemy of the president; it showed that I was a citizen.

Parents were also invited to the event. I wasn't going to deny mine the opportunity to be at the White House and meet other parents. They more than deserved that opportunity. In fact, they ended up becoming friends with the parents of Carl Lewis and Edwin Moses.

Some athletes put their best face on the situation. I remember one athlete saying, "This is the best of both worlds. I can say I would've won a gold medal if I could've competed." Truthfully, it was unlikely that he would have won a medal. And besides, that wasn't the way I viewed it.

* * * * *

Years later, in 1995, I had the chance to meet President Carter and discuss the boycott. An organizer of the 1996 Atlanta Olympic Games, a friend of mine, had been President Carter's driver when he was campaigning for the governorship of Georgia. I told my friend that I regretted never having had an in-person conversation with the president. If we had gone to those Games, I would have told him, we could have actually made a much more powerful statement to the world by being there and winning events and showing the strength that we have. Not going meant that we had nothing to say, and achieved nothing.

The meeting was held in President Carter's office at the Jimmy Carter Presidential Library in Atlanta. My friend was there, along with the former president's Secret Service detail.

First President Carter spoke. He had earned the right, after all, as a past president. He was somewhat defensive, telling me that most Americans had been in favor of the boycott. He said that dramatic action was the only way to deal with Soviet aggression. That clearly didn't work in this case, because the Soviet Union had stayed in Afghanistan for a decade after the boycott.

Because I was taught to be polite, I didn't press him or contradict him. I felt that it was his office, and I didn't see the need to reiterate the events in front of others. But I did want him to hear my side, even after all these years.

I told him that I was sorry we did not have a chance to talk at the time. Had we met, I said, I would have told him what it was like to live in the Olympic Village with people from other nations and exchange ideas. I felt that there were ways we could have gone to Moscow without embarrassing the administration or the U.S. by competing under the Olympic flag, like so many European nations had. "All of the athletes were working hard and supporting ourselves," I told him. "We all could have found our own way there, and for that to be taken from us was devastating."

President Carter listened intently, but he didn't address my remarks. Instead, he changed the subject to the Atlanta Games. The meeting ended politely, but unresolved in my mind.

Later, during the 1996 Atlanta Games, I was invited to a luncheon. The organizer told me that President Carter, and Vice President Al Gore, would be there. When I arrived, I found my table. I looked at the place cards, and, to my right, near the end of the table, was none other than President

Carter's seat.

During the meal, we were both very polite and spoke in general niceties. He actually spent most of the time talking to the person on his right. But during dessert, he turned to me and addressed the elephant in the room, just loud enough to be heard by me.

"Anita," he said, "when are you going to stop beating me up over 1980?"

I was taken aback. I felt like my eyebrows arched to the ceiling. "Excuse me, Mr. President?" I managed to say.

He repeated what he had said.

"Well, sir, if you mean speaking out about the boycott, probably never," I said.

He gave me his famous toothy smile. "You know, Congress was unanimous about us not going," he said.

"No sir, they weren't," I corrected him. "There were at least four senators against the boycott, as were a number of members of the House."

"Well, the USOC was unanimous."

"No sir, they were not," I said in a very measured tone of voice. "The Executive Board was definitely not, because I was a member and I voted against it. Then when the House of Delegates voted, at least a third thought it was the wrong way to go."

"In the end, it was Congress and not me who pushed it through."

"No sir, you had everything to do with it," I said.

He paused. I was hoping he would say he was sorry that it happened, but he didn't.

The conversation ended without either of us raising our voices or even speaking harshly. Clearly, he had his point of view, but it was one that did not square with what had actually happened.

Soon after, the meal broke up. Everyone stood. I turned to President Carter.

"President Carter, I want you to know that I voted for you anyway," I said. "I thought you were a great president except for this one thing, which was horrible for the Olympians and will stay that way."

President Carter hugged me, and we parted. There's nothing like telling a politician that you voted for them.

⁕ ⁕ ⁕ ⁕ ⁕

That afternoon, I wound up at the Olympic diving event — after hitching a ride in Vice President Gore's motorcade. Waiting for the competition to begin, I noticed that directly across from me in the same row as me was President Carter, sitting alone. I thought to myself, this is not a good visual for the Atlanta Olympic Games. As an IOC and USOC member, I felt I had a responsibility to do something.

I walked to the other side and sat down next to him. He greeted me warmly. As we watched the diving competition, we chatted about the athleticism of Olympians, and marveled at how the divers sprung, then flipped and contorted, and came within inches of the board. We sat together for an hour but didn't speak of the 1980 Olympics, as we had already aired our views.

That visual, Anita DeFrantz and President Jimmy Carter watching diving together, provided me a decent amount of grief from people with ties to the 1980 Olympic Games who saw it and couldn't believe I appeared to be enjoying a casual afternoon with the enemy. Of course, they weren't aware of the terse conversation that had occurred at the luncheon.

My hope is that the 1980 Olympic team will stand as a barrier against the manipulation of athletes outside sports venues. We know that the only effect is to leave us without results, athletic or otherwise.

It is impossible to change the past, but the disappointment for all of us involved in the 1980 Olympic Games will never leave me.

Though I didn't know it at the time, the entire experience turned out to be prologue for the rest of my life. In 1980, my love of Olympic competition shifted me out of the boat — and into the larger arena of the Olympic Movement.

Chapter Twelve
The Los Angeles Olympic Gold Rush

The 1984 Los Angeles Olympic Games were positioned to become one of the most successful ever — provided everything came together. Although there were not any outward signs that the Soviets would stay home from the Games, the shadow of the 1980 boycott hung over preparations.

Then there were the logistics. The City of Los Angeles was excited, but concerned, about hosting the Olympic Games. On one hand, there is great pride in showing off your city to the world; on the other, the Olympic Games threatened to disrupt daily life in the LA basin.

As a member of the Executive Board of the United States Olympic Committee, I also had a seat on the board of the Los Angeles Olympic Organizing Committee, a private committee responsible for organizing and staging the Games. (For simplicity's sake, I will refer to the Los Angeles Olympic Organizing Committee, also called the LAOOC, as the LA Organizing Committee.) That allowed me to closely follow the preparations. The USOC had six members on the 60-member LA Organizing Committee board because the USOC was financially responsible for the LA Olympic Games.

The USOC had become the guarantor of the LA Games when the city refused, which made the 1984 Games the first not backed by a government entity. Large losses from previous Olympic Games, mostly due to overbuilding facilities that were often not re-used, had been a factor in Denver backing out of hosting the 1976 Olympic Winter Games after voters refused to approve public funding. Still, the USOC financially guaranteeing the LA Games was something of a joke, because we had roughly only five million dollars to our name — counting everything — including our townhouse on

Fifth Avenue in New York. And we were staking this small portfolio against hundreds of millions of dollars in costs.

In retrospect, the situation turned out to be one of the greatest decisions ever for the USOC and for the Olympic Games. When the City of Los Angeles refused to financially back the Games, it allowed them to be put together and run in the private sector without government involvement. This is not to say the city was not supportive; Mayor Tom Bradley was a driving force in making the Games a success and ensuring the city's support in many areas. Los Angeles simply could not take on the financial risk.

Because the residents of Los Angeles refused to be exposed to taxes for construction and the other financial expenditures involved with the Games, another solution was necessary. The first — and only — tripartite agreement in the history of the Olympic Games was signed among the IOC, the USOC, and the LA Organizing Committee. The Organizing Committee had also signed a separate agreement with the USOC in 1978 stating that any surplus from the LA Games would be divided, with 40 percent staying in Los Angeles to fund youth sports programs in Southern California, 40 percent going to the USOC, and 20 percent distributed equally among the U.S. national governing bodies of the sports.

The deal was made at a time when the Olympic Games were not profit centers and were portrayed as losing money, meaning there was no promise of a surplus of any size. The 1976 Montreal Olympic Games ended more than $1 billion in the red. The Games themselves generated a small profit from ticket sales and TV revenue, but when the capital construction cost of several sports venues and a massive upgrade to the city's transportation system were factored in, Canada was stuck with a loss so large that it necessitated the passage of a tobacco tax to fill the hole. In truth, Montreal received several major infrastructure improvements for its investment, including upgrading its metro system and many sports venues that have been used since the Games.

So the bottom line was, the USOC was guaranteeing a potential $1 billion loss with its $5 million balance sheet. We were rooting for Peter Ueberroth and his team to deliver big time.

* * * * *

I met Peter shortly after he had been elected president of the LA Organizing Committee in 1979, two years after I was elected to the USOC Executive Committee. Peter had a successful travel business, but no experience with athletes and sporting events. He was interested in meeting and talking to Olympians. I found him open to ideas and genuinely excited by what could be done with the Olympic Games.

In 1979, I wrote him a letter. The Olympic youth program backed by the LA Organizing Committee was missing an important element, I said. LA hosted several competitions to find out which youngster excelled in each sport, but the program would better serve these youngsters if they treated them like athletes training for the Olympic Games. The way to do this, I proposed, was to help them set goals and then assess achievement toward those goals as they pursued them. Rather than just having a contest to see who was "best," the program would measure the kids' improvement over the years.

It wasn't until late 1980, after the boycott had faded into the mist of the past, that I heard back from Peter. Harry Usher, an entertainment lawyer who served as Peter's No. 2, approached me at a USOC board meeting. By then, everyone knew all too well who I was from my work fighting the 1980 boycott. He said that he and Peter were impressed with my ideas and my commitment to the Olympic Movement and would like me to come to work for them.

I assumed they were just being nice to me because I was an athlete who had been harmed by the boycott. I didn't consider it to be a serious offer.

At the time, I was working in Washington, D.C. for the Corporation for Enterprise Development. A friend I had met during my third year of law school came up with an idea to help people on welfare create economic value and obtain jobs. The project was called Transfer Payment Reinvestment, or TPR. The idea was to help people on welfare realize their business ideas. TPR was trying to show that if you allow welfare recipients to invest some portion of their payment in a business, then within a year or so many of them could be on their feet financially and off of welfare.

In the spring of 1981, my rowing friend and mentor Larry Hough revisited the idea of my going to work for LA Organizing Committee. He assured me that there was a job there for me. Larry, who had rowed in the 1968 and 1972 Olympic Games, was strongly considering joining the committee, which would mean a move to Los Angeles.

I had met Larry in Montreal in 1976, when he was one of the six athletes on the Athletes' Advisory Committee. Though Larry and I may disagree on many things relating to politics and social issues, as he is a staunch Republican and I am the opposite, we fully agree on the Olympic Movement. At the time, Larry even loaned me his straight pair that had been built for him and his rowing partner for the 1972 Games.

Larry offered to set up a meeting with Harry Usher for me to pursue the opportunity. I accepted.

I traveled to Los Angeles with Larry before the board meeting. After spending an hour driving around the City of Angels, I knew it was the place for me. I could feel the energy. I could tell that it was a place where creativity and freedom of expression were a way of life.

I met with Harry at his house, while Larry went to look for a place for his family to live. Harry told me that he and Peter wanted me to come aboard full-time. He asked me what I wanted to do. I told him I was interested in working with the international world, and specifically the National Olympic Committees, because of my firsthand experience with some African nations boycotting the Games in 1976, or set up and run the Olympic Village, which I felt was the most important part of Games for the athletes. He offered me a job on the spot, to start that summer.

I wasn't fully prepared. There were practical concerns, beginning with how I would get my stuff to Los Angeles. He said that he would have it moved for me. Then he paused.

"Do you have a lot?"

"No, mostly just sweats," I said. "But I do have a boat."

He arched his eyebrows. "A boat?"

"Yes, it's 27 feet long — but it only weighs 25 pounds." It was the single scull that I had managed to purchase for training.

Harry seemed relieved to hear it wasn't a fishing boat. He agreed to have the boat, as well as my car and my closetful of sweats, moved for me.

By the time Larry returned from house hunting, I had agreed to move to

Los Angeles in August 1981, and to do my part to ensure the success of the 1984 Games.

I had gained some perspective on the disappointment of 1980. I had come to realize that I never really had a chance. But I had decided to continue to work for athletes' rights. In addition to continuing to serve on the USOC Executive Committee, I had been re-elected to the AAC and elected vice chairman for the 1980-84 term. Now I was going to take a bigger step. I disclosed this move to the USOC president and asked to be removed from the LA Organizing board. I also asked the president if I needed to resign from the USOC position, but the president's decision was that it was not necessary.

I decided to leave the East Coast and detour from the path of my legal career for the unknown and for what I thought to be a temporary job, because once the Games ended I would be unemployed. The one thing that 1980 had convinced me of was that I wanted to do whatever I could to make sure the Olympic Movement prospered. Working on the 1984 Games was a chance to give back to the Olympic Movement in a positive way, and as part of a team with the singular goal: to put on the best Olympic Games ever.

* * * * *

Peter and Harry had organized the LA Organizing Committee like a business. They worked with the group that had won the Games to create a board of directors composed of community leaders in business and finance. The LA Olympic Games were being financed by large corporate sponsorships and television deals, as well as ticket sales and some licensed products, all very new to the Olympic Games at that time.

The backbone of the revenue would come from an unprecedented TV deal. The LA Olympic Games would have wall-to-wall television coverage. The committee, aided by TV producer David Wolper, sold the broadcast rights to ABC for $300 million — provided that the Games delivered a certain level of ratings.

To prevent runaway costs, they took a very budget-conscious approach. Rather than building venues, they realized they could adapt and upgrade the existing ones. New venues were built in very smart ways. The aquatic center, for example, was sponsored by McDonald's and built in partnership with the University of Southern California on the university's campus for future use by USC students and its swim team.

For the 28 months leading up to the Games, I designed and implemented the operational plan for the Olympic Villages with my team. In order to accommodate all the nations, there would be three villages, one at USC, one at UCLA, and a smaller one for rowers and canoe/kayakers at UC Santa Barbara. I focused on USC, while Frank Smith oversaw UCLA, and Claude Ruibal handled his *alma mater*, UCSB. There were endless logistical issues, but I was proud to ensure that each athlete had full access to all three villages.

One condition I was determined to end was the practice of segregating living accommodations by sex. In Montreal, I had been surprised when husbands weren't allowed to stay with their wives. My idea was simple: Allocate each National Olympic Committee the number of beds they needed and then let them decide who slept where. Not only was this practical, but also, it was logistically necessary: We didn't have enough housing to create separate facilities for the men and the women.

I made my case to Harry and Peter that segregating the sexes was backwards and pointless. I wanted the LA Games to take the lead and make this more modern approach permanent at future Olympic Games. Harry and Peter were all for it. "But you get to present it to the IOC," Peter added.

What an introduction. In 1982, I became the first woman to make a presentation to the Executive Board of the International Olympic Committee. I laid out my plan. It would be better if men and women in all sports from a National Olympic Committee stayed together. From a practical aspect, in some sports, such as equestrianism and shooting, they competed together. There were, I concluded, many good reasons for integrating men and women and no good reasons not to. When I finished, one member exclaimed, "Revolutionary!"

The board passed the measure and immediately put it into effect for the 1984 Olympic Winter Games in Sarajevo, as well as for the LA Games and all Games thereafter.

The LA Organizing Committee worked particularly hard to make sure the Soviet Union felt welcome and did everything we could to ensure that their team was coming to the Games. Peter had worked with the Soviet government in his previous position in the travel industry, and he understood that they might need extra convincing. In the spring leading up to the Games, all evidence indicated that they would compete. Soviet team officials flew to Los Angeles several times to look at housing and practice facilities.

We figured that if the Soviets were going to boycott in retribution for 1980, they would do so on May Day, the first day of the torch relay, for maximum press impact. On May 1, the grandson of Jim Thorpe, the first Native American to win a gold medal, and the granddaughter of Jesse Owens, who won four gold medals at the controversial 1936 Berlin Olympic Games, started the Olympic torch relay in New York City. The day came and went without any word from Moscow, leaving us all relieved.

On May 8, however, the hammer and sickle came down. The Soviet Union announced that it would boycott the LA Games. The official word was security concerns and anti-Soviet hysteria being whipped up in the U.S., but we suspected, and our sources later confirmed, that their action was political payback for the U.S. not going to Moscow in 1980. Soviet President Yuri Andropov, a protégé of Leonid Brezhnev, wanted to get even with the U.S. even though his mentor was dead.

Their withdrawal and declaration that no other Communist or Eastern Bloc nations would attend threw planning into a tailspin.

At the time, invitations were sent from the organizing committee, not the IOC. (That changed after 1984.)

The next morning, Peter called a meeting and laid out his plan for keeping the Games on track. He said that we were going to reach out to every National Olympic Committee and make sure they knew they were welcome. We were to ask if there was anything else they needed from us, in order to secure their commitments.

Then he turned to me. "Anita will be in charge of making sure all of the African NOCs come to our Games."

I was a little intimidated, but nonetheless very honored. I had never forgotten talking to the African athletes days before the Opening Ceremonies in Montreal. Athletes from 28 African nations were being sent home unfairly in a protest over a rugby match between New Zealand and South Africa, which had nothing to do with the Olympic Games. I learned the role in sport in combating apartheid, but I disagreed with that use. I had always wanted to do something to help them, and now I had my chance. With my marching orders in hand, I went right to work.

I called Olympic athletes I knew and asked them to reach out to the NOCs. Then I called every African NOC and lobbied them to attend. In the end, only Ethiopia, Upper Volta (now Burundi), and Libya did not compete. The Libyan team traveled to Los Angeles, but withdrew when three of their journalists were not allowed to enter the U.S. National security officials believed that the journalists planned to make news by protesting rather than reporting it. As a result, Libya withdrew its team at the last minute.

The committee was also successful in persuading some of the Communist nations to attend. Romania had its primary source of funding from the Soviets cut off. Ultimately, the LA Organizing Committee agreed to pay Romania for their athletes to attend and promised that they would be well taken care of. To their credit, the Romanians defied the Soviets and attended.

Because we had initially planned to have all nations, we were forced to amend our plan in several ways. Volunteers assigned to certain countries were left with no country, so they were reassigned to other duties. The schedule for the practice facilities had to be reworked. The housing plan, which was my area, also had to be reconfigured.

Even the Opening Ceremonies, with its parade of flags, had to be altered. The great flourish came when everyone in the audience reached under their seat and held up a piece of cardboard creating flags of the nations. The overhead display, showing the flags of all the nations, was dazzling. Without several countries participating, however, the entire production had to be redesigned, like a jigsaw puzzle with some pieces missing.

In the end, only 14 Eastern Bloc nations wound up not coming, a real tribute to the hard work put in by the staff of the LA Organizing Committee.

Through it all, however, I couldn't help but think that if the fight to overturn the 1980 boycott had succeeded, the 1984 Olympic Games would not be in this position.

* * * * *

There is nothing quite like the Olympic Games Opening Ceremonies. In 1976, we had walked from the village and then stood in line to enter the stadium, so I hadn't seen all the other teams. This time around, I helped the teams at the USC village board the busses. Seeing the nations in their Olympic gear is an amazing moment. Seeing that again in 1984, after having missed out in 1980, was a special moment for me, a sight of international unity and an example of the unifying power of sport. I was filled with pride knowing the athletes were going to the Opening Ceremonies at the Coliseum where the traditions of Opening Ceremonies would play out — the administering of the oath of fair play, the singing of the Olympic anthem, and the lighting of the torch, followed by the release of the doves.

Peter and Harry provided a ticket for each of my management staff to the Opening Ceremonies, and I took the last ticket for myself. I went to the L.A. Coliseum, the site of the 1932 Opening Ceremonies, and took in the spectacle.

Earlier that day, Peter had given me the immense honor of running the torch into the stadium, and handing the torch to Gena Hemphill, who then handed it to Rafer Johnson. This was an honor I shared with the small crowds milling around the coliseum hours before the Opening Ceremonies. Then it was back to the village to make sure everything was ready when the athletes returned, all at the same time, and mighty hungry.

During the Games, I lived in the USC Village to make sure everything ran smoothly. My goal was to make the athletes' experience as memorable as mine had been.

There were many firsts. We installed computers with printers that allowed the athletes to pull up schedules and results. The computers also had electronic mail programs designed by AT&T that allowed the athletes to correspond with each other. This was long before the days of laptops and universal email. Each athlete's credential had a number that functioned as that person's password. The athletes quickly learned how to use the system. Much of the correspondence became a bit steamy, as the days went on.

I also made sure that all athletes had the same access to all three villages. No matter where they lived — USC, UCLA or UCSB — they could have a meal and go to the movies or visit the disco at the other villages. On a first-come, first-served basis, the athletes could also go to any competition using their credential as a ticket.

Naturally, there were a few snags, rare as they were. To ensure the athletes' safety and restrict access, the villages had both SWAT teams and uniformed security guards, called the "Blue Berets." Security guards did not carry weapons and were minimally trained. Most of them were college students working summer jobs.

The LA Olympic Committee did not want the village to look like an armed camp. In Montreal, the first summer Games after Munich, the village had to be an armed camp. I told the committee that security didn't bother the athletes as much as they might think. When housing became short at USC, we needed to tell the SWAT team to move out of the dormitories and into trailers.

Moving the SWAT teams was a duty I delegated to my second in command, Steve Kettell. I told him that he would be much better than me at telling people with guns to pack up and move to less comfortable quarters. Ever the team player, Steve took care of it.

One NOC did not like the bunk beds, so they were sleeping in the common room in the dorm. I diplomatically explained to them that we had done our best and treated them the same as every other team, including the U.S. team. I suggested that everyone would be more comfortable if they slept in their rooms, but I didn't press it, adding that they could stay camped out in the common room if they preferred. Eventually, they concluded the beds were more comfortable than the floor.

One morning I received a particularly early call. Typically, I was in my office at 6 a.m., but this call came in from the security office at 5 a.m., just as the sun was rising. There was an urgent matter: One nation's track team was having their early morning training run on the freeway.

At a meeting the day before with the *Chef de Missions* from each nation, I explained that their runners should be careful not to cross the street when the stoplight was red, because it would be dangerous for them and mess up traffic. (In Los Angeles, pedestrians have the right of way.) I told them we would find places for them to run where they didn't have to deal with the traffic lights, but something must have gotten lost in translation. Instead of asking us for a venue, they had found a place where they could run without stoplights — the 10 Freeway.

So I calmly told security to have the team get off the freeway at the next exit, and explain to them that it is not safe to run on the freeways in Los Angeles. I hung up the phone and broke out laughing.

Above all, I strived to have the three villages be havens for the athletes. We were required to allow certain outsiders be admitted, but I made it difficult for them. Except for the athletes, cameras were not permitted. At USC, we had granted 1,000 faculty access to the village because their offices were within the secure boundaries. However, I made them wear red, license-plate-sized signs around their necks for entry. I did the same for the media, but featured yellow passes for them.

I also had the privilege of issuing credentials to members of the USOC Athletes Advisory Council, members of the IOC Athletes' Commission, and a list of non-competing Olympic athletes provided by the IOC. Thomas Bach, the future IOC president, was one of the Olympians on that list, along with his wife. I made sure that all of the Olympians had the best possible access, nearly equal to that of the IOC members. Anyone supporting athletes' rights deserved as much.

* * * * *

The LA Olympic Games became a global event. As part of the television deal, ABC built an international broadcasting center that made it easy for rights holders around the world to broadcast the Games in their territories. This resulted in the LA Games being seen by the largest worldwide audience in Olympic history.

The Games were filled with Olympic memories. My friend, Rafer Johnson, gold medalist in the decathlon in the 1960 Games, became the first African American to light the Olympic cauldron. Track and field great Carl Lewis won four gold medals, equaling Jesse Owens's historic record in 1936. Eight years after taking gold in Montreal, Edwin Moses hurdled his way to another gold medal, and gymnast Mary Lou Retton won gold in the all-around gymnastics, the first non-Eastern European to win the competition. Evelyn Ashford won the gold medal in the 100-meter dash. The men's basketball team, still restricted to college players, won the gold medal behind the play of Michael Jordan, Patrick Ewing, and Chris Mullin.

Naturally, there was also some controversy. In the finals of the women's 3,000-meter run, South African Zola Budd, given British citizenship in order to compete, took on American rival Mary Decker. Budd bumped Decker during the race, causing Decker to fall, an occurrence later deemed an accident by both women. Neither of them won the race.

The television ratings delivered, and ABC paid out the contract. The fees from U.S. television rights totaled $300 million, with ABC paying $75 million for the host broadcast center and $225 million for U.S. territorial rights to the LA Organizing Committee.

The 1984 TV contract was the last one to be negotiated by an organizing committee. Contracts, which since have become increasingly larger, are now controlled by the IOC. It was also the first time that an organizing committee paid the IOC so much in advance of the Games. The first payment that went to the IOC was $20 million in October of 1980, well in advance of the Games.

For some reason, the IOC did not cash the check for 30 days. Because interest rates were hovering around 19 percent, the delay provided the LA Organizing Committee with enough money in interest to cover its operating costs for an entire year.

The success of the LA Olympic Games also created corporate sponsorships for the USOC. In the wake of the 1980 boycott, the USOC had lost some $10 million in corporate sponsorships. The 1984 Games opened the USOC to recognizing the increasing value of the U.S. team.

For his leadership, Peter Ueberroth was named *Time* magazine's "Man of the Year." Immediately after the Games he became the commissioner of Major League Baseball.

The City of Los Angeles was also a big winner. The traffic nightmares and logistical snags predicted never materialized. Television coverage showed Los Angeles in its best light, as a connection of communities diverse in terrain and population. Financially, the entire LA basin was a winner.

The total surplus from the LA Games was $232.5 million. Under the agreement with the USOC, 40 percent of the revenue stayed in Los Angeles. A foundation created to benefit Southern California youth sports programs was endowed with roughly $93 million.

The 1984 LA Olympic Games became a model for cities in the future to use a combination of public and private resources to stage a successful Olympic Games. Many other cities have done well with the Games, but none have been as financially successful as LA84.

As lucrative and civically uplifting as this was for Los Angeles, it also was personally rewarding for me. Working for Peter Ueberroth, who was exactly the right person at the right time for that job and masterfully guided our team to success, remains one of the privileges of my life. He was a remarkable leader and visionary. Under his leadership many lasting contributions to the Games were created. Working on the Games reinforced my love of, and devotion to, the Olympic Movement and helped remove some of the disappointment I still felt from 1980. It also provided me with my next career opportunity.

Chapter Thirteen
My Dream Job at the LA84 Foundation

After the 1984 LA Olympic Games were over, Harry Usher asked a few of us, including Steve Montiel, Terri Jones, Dean Cruz and me, to figure out what was most needed for youth sports in Southern California. This would become the focus of what became the LA84 Foundation.

We discovered that Southern California's rich history of sports opportunities for youth through its parks and recreation departments had suffered in recent years due to budget cuts. We spread out across Southern California for our due diligence. Over the course of two months, we put together a detailed report on where resources could be best directed. There were an abundance of facilities, we learned, but what was missing was equipment and coaching. We recommended putting the focus there.

Stan Wheeler, who was on faculty of the Yale Law School, came aboard as the president of the Amateur Athletic Foundation of Los Angeles, the name of the organization created with the surplus left over from the LA Olympic Games. Stan had grown up in Los Angeles and spent his formative years playing jazz on Central Avenue. He had come back to LA to re-live his younger days, as he still played occasional trumpet gigs, and to help put together the foundation.

In June of 1985, Stan asked me to give him my thoughts on a youth sports festival the foundation was planning. The festival would feature a contest that would bring the winners together for a major competitive event. I suggested other approaches would be more meaningful. I was concerned that the focus was more on winning than skill development, which is far more important over the long run.

Stan apparently agreed because he offered me a job. Going to work at the foundation seemed like a natural step for me. I was passionate about the development and treatment of children, something I had carried with me from my days working at the Juvenile Law Center in Philadelphia.

I started work as a senior associate on the day the foundation opened its new offices, in a museum that housed the Helm's Hall of Fame Collection, a treasure trove of Olympic and sport memorabilia. This collection began its life as a part of the Southern California Committee for the Olympic Games. Its assembly began in the late 1930s after the 1932 Games in Los Angeles by Paul Helms, a former coxswain, and a member of the noblest of sports, who owned the famed Helm's Bakery. He kept his memorabilia at his bakery on Venice Boulevard. After the bakery closed, the Helms Collection moved around until Peter Ueberroth and his wife, Ginny, bought the collection and a house to showcase it. The foundation moved into the former museum house and later built a library and meeting center in that location.

In the summer of 1987, Stan returned to Yale, and I was elected president of the AAF. (The AAF would eventually be renamed the LA84 Foundation in 2006. For simplicity's sake, I will refer to it as the LA84 Foundation.) For the next 30 years, the foundation became the central focus of my professional life.

* * * * *

The LA84 Foundation is a wonderful place. If I could have created my ideal job, it would have been working there. It is both a showcase for sport and a laboratory to create a new and lasting understanding of sport, a place for undertaking research, commissioning studies, and, most importantly, developing ways to deliver sports to our youth.

My team was first rate. Conrad Freund was already on board as vice president of finance. He had been Treasurer of the LA Organizing Committee from the beginning and he stayed at the Foundation until 2012. Steve Montiel, who had also been in the press department at the LA Organizing Committee, was vice president for communications at the foundation. He left a year later, but we have remained lifelong friends. Judith Pinero Kieffer was vice president for grants and programs and stayed at the foundation through our tenth anniversary. She is currently president of another foundation.

My first hire was Wanda L. Dowding. We had worked together at the LA Organizing Committee, and she was willing to join me at the foundation as my executive assistant. Her assistance for me was well beyond executive. Her title should have been "Supreme Assistant." Next was Wayne Wilson, who had been consulting with the foundation on our library. I asked him to become full time, and he remains there as vice president for education. The library and education services is his masterpiece. My next hire was Patrick Escobar. He had also worked at the LA Organizing Committee in the communications department. He replaced Steve Montiel and went on to manage our growing communication needs, and also joined the grants and programs work, taking over after Judith departed.

There were other staff members who worked at the foundation under my presidency, and many still do, having passed the 20-year mark. I am grateful for all of their work in keeping the mission clear and our services to the community first rate. This team was never deterred by a challenge — and we had many — and their loyalty and dedication helped the foundation realize its enormous potential. Through it all, we also had a very supportive board of directors. Without them, I could not have been successful in doing my work at the foundation, and also spent time doing my volunteer work on behalf of the Olympic Movement.

I felt the foundation was an ideal way to demonstrate that organized sports could unite areas of the city torn apart by crime and poverty, as well as to provide solid alternatives to keep young people out of street gangs. Sports, I believed, could be a central force in unifying communities. I also believed that sports could provide educational avenues for kids. The kid who loves baseball and keeps statistics, for instance, could end up becoming an expert in physics.

When we started, there were areas where children were using broom handles for baseball bats and a bundle of rags for a soccer ball. There were kids wearing secondhand shoes three sizes too big for them. These were issues that the foundation could remedy if we executed properly.

The initial board was composed of heavy hitters, including Mayor Tom Bradley, Los Angeles Dodgers' owner Peter O'Malley, TV producer David

Wolper, movie mogul Lew Wasserman, and Southern California Edison Co. CEO Howard Allen, people who had the ability to expand our influence.

While the foundation was originally set up as a grant-making organization with a library, the foundation's board, all of whom had served on the LA Organizing Committee Executive Board, were very receptive to ideas. Early on, I convinced them that the foundation should create its own programs, rather than just invest money in existing programs. This would better serve the youth of Los Angeles, and we could ensure the quality of the dollars spent.

Initially, we developed everything from the ground up. We had a devoted staff of 20. We were completely independent of any government bureaucracy, which meant that we could do many things that other similar institutions could not.

Our first program was a coaching program to teach volunteers how to coach. From my own experience as a rowing coach at Princeton in 1980, I realized that most coaches were not provided with information on how to coach. They are given a clipboard and whistle and told, "You're the coach."

Even though I had been a competitor at the highest level in rowing, I realized that I had never been trained as a coach. At Princeton, rowers would do anything I asked them to do, despite the fact that I didn't have a base of knowledge for directing them. I felt that I had far too much power for someone with no coaching experience.

I wanted the youth of Southern California to have a more fulfilling experience, and a strong enough one, so that they would someday give back, perhaps as coaches themselves. When you have a positive experience, you are much more likely to give back to the next generation what you have received.

We started the coaching program in January 1986. Through 2016, over 75,000 people went through some portion of the program. To this day, it is the foundation's most successful and far-reaching program, and one that has been adopted by several youth sports organizations.

One of the most important programs we worked on was the "Summer Swim" program. At the time, drowning was the second leading cause of death for children under the age of 14. In Southern California, with the

Pacific Ocean and an abundant supply of pools, teaching children to swim felt like a civic duty.

We formed a partnership with 100 public pools and sponsored swimming lessons and water sports opportunities for at least 15,000 children each summer. Learning to swim not only saves lives, it also opens the door to many other sports, including rowing. Through Summer Swim, kids who learned to swim can then learn other aquatic sports, such as water polo, diving, and synchronized swimming, all of which we also offered. Equally as important, swimming can be a pathway to employment in the field of aquatics.

The Summer Swim program has had a multigenerational effect. Today, the children of parents who participated in our program are now participants in the same program. Many current swim coaches who took part in the foundation's program when they were young have found a professional career in aquatics. By the 30th anniversary of the program in 2016, it had served nearly 500,000 youngsters at 109 public pools across 13 municipalities.

We also started the "Run4Fun" program in 1987, which became a highly successful participatory program. Each year, more than 3,000 youngsters from 50 junior high schools participate in the program learning the skills of distance running. Those who qualify participate in a 2,000-meter run. Celebrity athletes, including the Olympian track and field gold medal winner Jackie Joyner-Kersee, would run with the kids and answer their questions. Operating the event were our volunteers, called "Friends of Sport." The coaches were all teachers who gave their time to run the program. I'm not sure who had more fun at those events, the kids, the parents, or my staff.

· · · · ·

The foundation had – and continues to have – a thriving grants program. At times it was called "sports programming," because the program does more than just give grants to existing youth programs. The program offers an incubator program where we can help people who have not done sports programming before. The foundation assists these people and helps them along until they are capable of operating the program on their own. In addition, the foundation has a small grants program for organizations that

The 1976 U.S. Olympic women's rowing team on our way to the bronze medal.

My mother and me at the 1976 Olympic Games in Montreal, Quebec.

The DeFrantz family at my nephew David's graduation from Indiana University in 1972. *From left to right:* me, my brothers James, Thomas, and David, and Mom and Dad. Very much a picture of its time.

My amazing grandmother, Myrtle May DeFrantz, at the 1976 Olympic Games.

Anne Warner and me, who rowed together on the eight-oared team that won bronze in Montreal, rowed in the pair at the 1977 World Championships in Amsterdam.

Rowing at the 1978 World Championships in New Zealand. *From left to right:* Carol Brown, me, Nancy Storrs, Coz Crawford, and coxswain Holly Hatton.

With my Mom and Dad at the White House during the 1980 Olympic Games boycott.

Touring the 1984 Olympic Village with LA Olympic Organizing Committee President Peter Ueberroth and IOC President Juan Antonio Samaranch.

Talking with President Fidel Castro at the 1991 Pan American Games in Cuba.

With President George H.W. Bush in the Oval Office.

President George W. Bush, IOC member Toni Khoury, and me prior to the 2002 Salt Lake City Olympic Winter Games Opening Ceremonies.

To Anita DeFrantz Best Wishes, *Bill Clinton*

With President Clinton as he welcomes the 1992 U.S. Olympic team. Note the slight photo bomb from USOC President LeRoy Walker.

With Hillary Clinton at the 1994 Winter Olympic Games in Lillehammer, Norway.

Meeting Queen Elizabeth at Buckingham Palace.

With German Chancellor Angela Merkel during
the IOC Session in Guatemala in 2007.

Meeting Vice President Al Gore.

My grandparents and parents would've loved this picture
of me with President Barack Obama.

Nine-time Olympic gold medalist Carl Lewis, whom I am honored to have as a friend, as he continues to serve his sport and the Olympic Movement.

With Juan Antonio Samaranch, IOC President from 1980-2001.

The great soccer star Cobi N'Gai Jones and me at an LA84 Foundation conference.

Rowing with intensity with Anne Warner.

At the 2012 London Olympic Games with proud rowing medal winners.

Working at my dream job at the LA84 Foundation.

The 1976 U.S. Olympic women's rowing team being awarded our bronze medals.

With U.S. IOC member and fellow Olympian Angela Ruggiero, a member of the Hockey Hall of Fame, at the athletes' voting center in Rio.

Olympian and long-distance swimmer Diana Nyad has been a tireless ally in advocating for women in sport.

Working on LA's bid for the 2024 Olympic Games with Mayor Eric Garcetti and the entertainment executive and sports agent Casey Wasserman, chairman of the bid committee.

On the LA 2024 float at the 2017 Tournament of Roses Parade.

"Sam the Olympic Eagle" at the athletes' village of the 2016 Rio Olympic Games.

have done good work and leagues that need just a little bit of help.

In addition to the grants, the foundation does its own programming in areas that would otherwise be ignored. I created the idea of "sports clubs" based on the system used so successfully in Canada and throughout Europe. My goal was to create sports centers where adults would coach kids and, after the kids grew up, they would return as adults and coach the next generation. I also saw this as an excellent means to organize a community. No matter how financially challenged, parents want the best for their children, and with the program's support, they could volunteer their time.

That was the genesis of our sports clubs at the foundation. We went into parts of the cities where there seemed to be a great need, but lacked someone to request the grants to provide programming for youth. That, in turn, led to the development of the sports club concept.

We taught community members how to develop clubs and how to coach. We funded the referees and bought the uniforms so that these kids can be just as proud of wearing their uniforms to sporting events as more affluent families.

In 1994, celebrating the 10th anniversary of the Games, we made a gift to the city. The program was spun off into an independent entity called "Kids in Sports," with its own board and own fundraising. I stayed on as president to help guide the program and make sure that it lived up to the standards we had set, to provide kids with the maximum benefit.

The foundation also inherited a high school sports awards program from the Helm's Hall of Fame. The AAF-CIF (Amateur Athletic Foundation-California Interscholastic Federation) Sports Awards program continues to be the longest-standing high school sports awards program in the nation. For a time, baseball and softball awards were presented at Dodgers Stadium. The look of pride on the faces of parents and recipients was immensely satisfying for my colleagues and me.

The foundation has the best digital sports library in the nation. The original library was inherited from the Helms Athletic Foundation. It contains a collection of books and artifacts, including everything from signed baseballs to Olympic medals. Under the direction of Wayne Wilson, who is married to my former rowing teammate Jan Palchikoff, the library has grown into some 100,000 digital documents, including articles, research papers, and books. We were the first to digitize an official report on each of the modern Olympic Games and more than 60 Olympic athletes' oral histories.

The library, which began to be digitized in the 1990s, allows the foundation to disseminate accurate information about sports and the Olympic Movement, which is especially important in our current era of so much "fake news." In my opinion, it is the best sports library in the world, with the best Olympic library being in Lausanne, Switzerland.

The building that houses the library was constructed during my presidency. The board adopted and approved the library and research center in 1986, but the previous president, Stan Wheeler, had the research center named after the chairman at the time, lawyer and political powerbroker Paul Ziffren. The building was then built and finished on time and under budget, and opened to the public on August 12, 1988, four years after the closing Ceremony of the 1984 Olympic Games.

But the foundation's buildings are about more than bricks and mortar. For years, twice a week we would bring kids to the library to explore the history of sports. For many kids in the Los Angeles Unified School District, this was their only field trip, due to funding restrictions. These interactions were the kind of learning engagement that the foundation was built to support and encourage.

The library has an extensive collection of Olympic footage. It also has footage of the tragic massacre during the 1972 Olympic Games in Munich and its news coverage. David Wolper, a board member and chairman *emeritus*, who made the 1972 Olympic film *Visions of Eight*, donated the footage. The outtakes and additional footage from David's film were used in Kevin Macdonald's Oscar-winning documentary *One Day in September*. This is yet another example of how the foundation serves as a proponent for the Olympic Movement as a whole.

* * * * *

The personal interactions with children are some of my fondest memories at the foundation. At one of the Summer Swim program meets, I noticed a very worried-looking girl getting ready to swim her race. She looked a lot like I did when I was that age, a little pudgy and a little shy.

I said to her, "You look very worried, are you okay?"

"No, I'm afraid I'm going to run out of steam," she replied.

We were using the re-done 1932 Olympic Games pool, which was 50 meters long rather than 25 meters. Thinking I could help ease her anxiety, I tried out my sports psychology skills. I asked, "What's your very favorite thing in the world to do?"

"Swim!" she said.

"Well, that's great because that's just what you're about to do."

"I know, but I'm just so worried I won't make it."

"Tell you what," I said. "I will be at the other end of the pool waiting for you. Okay?"

She nodded.

I took my place at the finish. Her race started. She had a beautiful stroke, but, as she feared, she starting running out of steam in the last 15 meters. But she pressed on and made it to the wall in the middle of the pack.

She pulled herself out of the pool and asked me how she did.

"I'm not sure," I said, prevaricating a white lie. "I was looking at you, I wasn't looking at the other kids."

She sensed that she had finished last. "Oh, no, I really wanted to qualify for the next race," she said.

"That's alright, the best I ever did was a bronze medal," I said.

She looked up at me, and hugged me. "That's alright, you did your best."

* * * * *

The LA84 Foundation also undertook sports research and hosted educational conferences. I felt it was important to study issues relating to sport and to be a leader in presenting solutions to the sports world on important issues.

The first conference we hosted was in 1988, entitled "Doping in Elite Sports." It focused on steroids and PEDs (Performance-Enhancing Drugs). We invited scientists and doctors who were studying steroids in the U.S. to discuss their impact.

The issue went beyond athletes bulking up. The grossly unfair advantage was recovery time during training: High doses of steroids allowed athletes to train longer and recover faster, meaning that they could train that much harder. This was not fully understood at the time by American doctors. What was understood were the side effects of steroid usage, and we wanted to get that message across.

One of the more startling revelations that emerged was how far behind U.S. doctors were in their knowledge of PEDs. Our physicians said that they could not conclude that steroids made a marked difference in athletic performance, because, ethically, they could not give the same high dosages over the same period of time that athletes in Eastern Europe took. Further, they recognized that U.S. athletes who were taking PEDs were self-administering. As a result, it was not possible to undertake a scientifically sound study.

To reach high school athletes, we created a pamphlet called "Sport's Devastated," a play on *Sports Illustrated*. (I cleared the title with the magazine.) We promoted the initiative on television shows, and distributed over 60,000 copies to high school coaches across the region. We also supported national legislation to make the possession of steroids illegal for other than medical purposes, and we supported the Los Angeles Board of Education's efforts to mandate educational efforts about steroids throughout the school system.

A year later, after focusing on doping, we partnered with the National Organization for Women Legal Defense and Education Fund to host a conference on how media portrayed images of race and gender in televised media. "Getting Over the Hurdle: Race and Gender in Sports Media" directed attention to the nature and impact of the portrayal of women and people of color in the sports media. In attendance were distinguished athletes and media professionals from across the nation. It was yet another significant opportunity for the foundation to take the lead on important issues of sport by providing a common meeting place for the diverse elements of the sports industry.

The foundation commissioned a study, and I later presented the resulting report to the head of every network's sports department — except ESPN, which wasn't interested. At that time, the only women's sport ESPN carried was beach volleyball, so I guess it's not surprising that they had no interest. To the credit of ABC, NBC and CBS, they each asked for 100 copies to provide to their producers, directors, and commentators.

The report talked about how language affects how viewers regard athletes. Our researchers compared the NCAA men's and women's basketball finals, and the U.S. Open tennis tournament's men's and women's finals. The results were incredibly sexist.

The NCAA men's basketball games started with trumpets blaring. When the players were introduced, they were photographed from the bottom up so that they looked like giants. To open the women's games, the network showed little girls on a playground using swings and slides to soporific music. A voiceover came on that said, "These little girls grew up to be something their parents never expected."

The production values were also far different. There were seven cameras used for men's games to just three for women's, causing the women's game to look slower, duller, and less dynamic. Every replay captured a different angle for the men, making the plays look all the more dazzling. The women's replays were static shots that looked like old news footage.

The U.S. Open tennis coverage had a different bias. The women were infantilized and called by their first names. They were "Chrissie" and "Steffi." By contrast, the men were "Agassi" and "Sampras." The problem is last names engender respect.

We also found women's sports were underreported and underrepresented in the Los Angeles market. For a six-week period, the study examined the 11:00 p.m. sports newscast on the three network affiliates. Men's sports received 94 percent of the air time, women's sports 5 percent, and gender neutral topics 1 percent. Regrettably, much of the women's coverage made fun of women. In one story, the "kissing bandit" was featured. She was a woman who would run out onto the field and kiss a male athlete.

We repeated the 1989 study in 1993 and again in 1999, and compared the years. Our study initially helped make a difference in the language, although we found that the old bias would creep back in at times. The presentation of some women's sports showed slow, but steady, improvement.

But it was distressing to find that sports news shows failed to adequately cover women's sports. In 1999, the percentage of stories and airtime devoted to women's sports on local news programs remained almost as low as it was in 1989. Much of the coverage still too often treated women not as athletes, but as sex objects. The study also reported that the national sports news program ESPN's "SportsCenter" covered women's sports proportionally less than the LA newscasts.

In the introduction of our report, "Gender Bias in Televised Sports: 1989, 1993, and 1999," I wrote, "The pattern of behavior that ignores and belittles women's accomplishments is sexism, plain and simple." I encouraged advocates of women's sports to work for change until sports media fulfills its professional obligation to properly report on women in sport.

The most encouraging aspect of the studies is their worldwide reach. They were replicated by educational and advocacy organizations around the world. Slow as it might come, perhaps change will come.

Our youth studies focusing on field-of-play safety in particular, which were very progressive and proactive for their time, resulted in corrective actions much more quickly. We conducted a study on the high incidence in girls of ACL injuries, which happen when the ligaments in the knee become overstretched. With a grant we provided, the Santa Monica Orthopaedic and Sports Medicine Research Foundation, led by Dr. Bert Mandelbaum, studied why this was happening and what measures of prevention could be adopted.

As a result of the findings, we developed and implanted the PEP (Prevent Injury, Enhance Performance) Program, a soccer-oriented exercise program designed by doctors, physical therapists, and athletic trainers to reduce the incidence of ACL injuries in soccer players. The PEP Program can be done on a field and requires no special equipment. Best of all, it has greatly reduced the injuries we were seeing.

* * * * *

I remain very proud of the work my team of 20 full-time staffers did at the foundation during my tenure. Interestingly enough, though not by design, the staff reflected the population diversity of Los Angeles. We also had hundreds of volunteers for the sports clubs and other foundation programs. One of the encouraging benefits the foundation's work proved is that lower-income people who work long hours still find time to volunteer. Though giving your time is much more difficult for people who live in economic uncertainty, they care deeply about their children and want to give back to their communities.

Some participants in the foundation's programs went on to become Olympians. Rusty Smith, a short-track speed skater, competed in Nagano. In the Sydney Games, there were at least four medalists, three of them gold medalists, who had taken part in our programs. Lenny Krayzelburg, who won three swimming gold medals, also participated in one of our Summer Swim programs as a coach.

Brenda Villa, who won a silver medal in water polo at Sydney, participated in our program. This was a particular point of pride for me, because the women's event was included in the Olympic program as a result of the support I provided at the international level.

Even more amazing, Venus and Serena Williams, inarguably two of the greatest tennis players ever, both started in our AAF/Junior Tennis League program. This is duly commemorated in a picture published in the *Los Angeles Times* of the Williams sisters at ages 8 and 9 wearing AAF T-shirts, under an AAF banner.

The LA84 Foundation has amassed such a great track record largely because its endowment has done so well. What started as a $93 million endowment grew through investments to over $200 million at its peak. Through 2016, the foundation had helped an estimated three million children and more than 1,000 organizations throughout Southern California — and I am confident it will continue to thrive under the presidency of my successor, Renata Simril.

Chapter Fourteen
Becoming an IOC Member

Olympism is a philosophy of life, exalting and combining in a balanced whole the qualities of body, will and mind. Blending sport with culture and education, Olympism seeks to create a way of life based on the joy found in effort, the educational value of good example and respect for universal fundamental ethical principles.
— From the Olympic Charter

In late 1985, I became aware that an IOC position was open for a member from the United States. Nations seldom have more than three members, and the U.S. was down to one. A journalist, Ken Reich, called to talk with Steve Montiel, vice president for communications at the LA84 Foundation, to tell Steve that Reich was being honored for his work covering the LA Organizing Committee. Reich told Steve that Bob Helmick, president of the USOC and an IOC member who had been elected but not yet sworn in, was asked who he thought the new IOC member would be. Helmick said that one of the names being floated was that of Anita DeFrantz.

Steve came around the partition into my office space and told me that I was being considered for IOC membership. This was news to me. I was aware that Julian Roosevelt, a United States IOC member, had died that fall, but I had heard nothing about his replacement being named.

Given that my name was mentioned, a small possibility was created. In reality, I knew that the chances were slim. At 34, I was on the young side for membership. Also, no American woman had ever been an IOC member, and, to date, only four other women had been elected to the IOC.

* * * * *

The International Olympic Committee was formed in 1894 by Frenchman Pierre de Coubertin. It grew out of a congress in Paris convened by de Coubertin, an educator and historian, to discuss the future of the amateur sports movement. The meeting, which took place at the Sorbonne University, had several agenda items. Interestingly, the possibility of creating a modern-day version of the ancient Greek Olympic Games was the last item discussed, but it was the one that forever changed the face of modern sport.

The IOC's mission is to promote an international movement to support competition in sports among all nations. On this basis, it ensures the celebration of the Olympic Games and the Olympic Winter Games at four-year intervals, supports all affiliated organizations of the Olympic Movement, and strongly encourages "building a peaceful and better world by educating youth through sport practiced in accordance with Olympism and its values."

Based in Lausanne, Switzerland, the IOC is a nonprofit Swiss association with no political ties to any government and is funded by a portion of the sale of broadcast rights, ticketing, licensing, and sponsorships tied to the Olympic Games. Under that legal status, the IOC establishes its own rules and regulations governing all actions of the organization. These rules are laid out in the Olympic Charter, which is amended and updated as needed.

The IOC serves as the governing authority and uniting body of the Olympic family, a web of organizations and athletes that make up the Olympic Movement. Along with the IOC, the main constituents of the Olympic Movement are the international sports federations, which oversee the individual sports and exist with or without the IOC, and the National Olympic Committees, which are in charge of each nation's athletes and teams and exist only because the IOC exists. These interface with the organizing committees of the host cities that stage the Olympic Games and the Olympic Winter Games. Intertwined are many Olympic partners, including broadcasters and sponsors, as well as the Paralympic Games.

Individuals who are members of the IOC come only from nations that have a NOC and are not paid for their work. However, not all nations with NOCs have IOC members. They are elected by the IOC and now serve terms until the age of 70 (if they were elected prior to 2000, their service ends at 80). The IOC is as diverse as the United Nations, with members coming from Kuwait, Guatemala, Israel, Korea, and Monaco, to name just a few of the countries. The Olympic Charter holds the number of IOC members to 115. The IOC is run by an Executive Board consisting of a president, four vice presidents, and 10 other members elected by the full IOC. The IOC is further broken down into commissions dealing with governance issues, including the women in sport commission, the ethics commission, the finance commission, and so forth.

The IOC Executive Board and commissions meet throughout the year. Under the current president, Thomas Bach, most commission meetings are clustered in one week in November. The entire IOC typically meets in full session once a year to discuss and vote on key decisions, such as electing its leaders and selecting venues for forthcoming Olympic Games, although the president may call an extraordinary session if there is a pressing issue that must be addressed. Each member has one vote. A member may not vote for his or her nation to host a Games.

* * * * *

During this time, in 1985, I volunteered on the Anchorage Bid Committee for Anchorage, Alaska working to host the 1992 Olympic Winter Games. I traveled to the IOC's headquarters in Lausanne to attend the session for the vote. Candidates for IOC membership were only present if they were attending on other business.

By then, I had become one of six people named by the USOC as an acceptable candidate for the position. Others included Peter Ueberroth, Olympic gold medalist in swimming and TV broadcaster Donna de Varona, and USOC Vice Presidents Evie Dennis and William Tutt, as well as Harold Henning, a U.S. Swimming officer.

In Lausanne, I was focused on Anchorage's quest to win the 1992 bid, but I was also anxious about the IOC election. The new IOC member would be introduced at the end of the session. Given that my name was under consideration, I knew that it was possible I could be elected a member, but I felt my chances were slim.

Earlier in the day, I was paged to report to the main reception desk.

I assumed it was for news about the vote or my candidacy. Instead, it was message from a journalist that had nothing to do with either one.

Then, I discovered that my accreditation would not permit me into the auditorium to hear the voting results for the bid cities. I went to the president of the Anchorage bid committee and asked about gaining access to the auditorium. He assured me it would be all right to walk in with him.

While we were waiting at the door of the auditorium to enter, an IOC staff member approached me and said that they had been paging me. I told her I had answered the page, but it turned out that she was talking about a different page. She asked me to come with her. I asked if I would be able to see the host city announcement, and she assured I would.

As we walked up the stairs to the second floor, I assumed that IOC President Juan Antonio Samaranch wanted to tell me in person before the formal announcement that I had not been elected. Now I would not only miss the announcement of the host city, but I also had to receive the sad news in person. Alas, he was the IOC President, so I headed upstairs.

I sat down in an open area and waited for what seemed like a very long time. Finally, an IOC staffer appeared and escorted me into a cavernous room.

I was still thinking that I would be told that although I was a very fine candidate, I was not yet ready to become an IOC member. Then Bob Helmick came over to say congratulations. I was still not clear about what was happening, but I was beginning to get butterflies. Could it be possible? I was escorted up to the front of the room, where I was again told to wait.

Another person, Dr. Un Yong Kim, president of the Korean NOC, had been waiting outside the hall with me. He had a very nervous presence and could not sit still. I had met him in 1983. We struck up a conversation and he asked why I was there. I told him that I thought it was about being elected — or not being elected — to the IOC. He told me that he was going to be elected. I congratulated him.

We waited for about 45 minutes. During this time, Dr. Kim left and returned. We chatted on and off about the cities being considered for the 1992 Games. Both Games would be in the same year for the final time. I was fairly calm, especially since I was convinced that I was going to be told to continue my work in the Olympic Movement, but that I would not be elected.

After the long wait, the official who had escorted me to the second floor handed me off to a tall, elegant gentleman, who said with a French accent, "Please, follow me." We entered the main hall.

My first thought was, *This is a big room and they need more light.* I entered, walking behind Dr. Kim. The room was packed. I scanned the crowd and noticed that they were all IOC members. There was a stage at the front of the room. We were stopped at the steps.

Dr. Kim was escorted to the podium. He was told to hold the Olympic flag as he recited the Olympic oath, and then a medal was placed around his neck. Looking back, it seems obvious that he was being sworn in as an IOC member and that I was next, but at the time, I was in a fog.

Then, the IOC *Chef de Protocol*, Louis Girandou-N'Diaye, asked me to come to the podium and hold the Olympic flag. He handed me a card and asked me to read it aloud:

> *Granted the honour of becoming a member of the International Olympic Committee, and declaring myself aware of my responsibilities in such capacity, I pledge to serve the Olympic Movement to the very best of my ability; to respect and ensure the respect of all the principles of the Olympic Charter and the decisions of the International Olympic Committee, which I consider as not subject to appeal on my part; to keep myself free from any political or commercial influence and from any racial or religious consideration.*

When I finished, President Samaranch said, "Congratulations." He put the IOC member's medal around my neck, and shook my hand. The medal is worn by IOC members during the opening celebration of the Games and any time a member presents a medal.

Though I had not previously read the oath, I considered it as solemn an oath as I had ever taken, and I promised myself that I would go above and beyond it and be wholly responsible to the Olympic Movement.

I came down the steps and was immediately surrounded by other IOC members. I remember someone saying, "Welcome to the club."

What a club.

After I was sworn in, IOC members lined up in protocol, the longest-serving member to the newest, which was me. We walked into a small auditorium where all the bid committees had gathered to hear the result. Though I was last, I was somewhat obvious, because I was a tall African-American woman. My friends on the Anchorage bid committee, who had been saving me a seat with them, saw me and stood as they applauded. As all the other bidding cities noticed Anchorage, and as they had done all week, they followed their lead and stood up and applauded.

The results of the vote for the host city for the 1992 Olympic Winter Games were then announced: Albertville, France won. Anchorage, unfortunately, had been eliminated on the second ballot. I took solace, however, not in my election to the IOC, but in how happy the Anchorage committee members were for me.

I was the 98th individual to be elected to the IOC. Protocol holds that IOC members line up for formal events, such as visits with a head of state, according to their election number. As members retire or step down, the other members' protocol number decreases. Interestingly, in some countries this creates a situation where a member with title, such as Sir or Lord, will be placed behind another member from that country when greeting their head of state.

Along with Dr. Kim and me, two other new members who were not present were elected, Jean Claude Ganga from Congo and Lambis Nikolaou of Greece. Under the rules at that time, my term would run through 2027, until I reached the age of 75.

In the early years, IOC members served life terms, but that changed in 1965. The term was first amended to age 72 and then bumped up to 75. The age would eventually be increased to 80.

IOC members are not paid a salary. Until 1980, IOC members paid their own way anywhere they went and housing was only covered at the Olympic Games. That changed when the Los Angeles Olympic Committee sent the IOC a check for $20 million in 1980 from the first payment from ABC, the television rights holder for the U.S. broadcast of the 1984 Los Angeles Games. This was the first time the IOC had ever received money from an organizing committee prior to Games, and the check had the most zeroes ever presented to the IOC. The large payment also led to the realization that the IOC should negotiate the television rights directly with broadcasters in order to potentially receive a larger cut, rather than letting the organizing committees handle negotiations.

As a result, starting in 1980, IOC members were reimbursed for travel and expenses from their homes to an IOC Session, an IOC meeting, or whenever representing the IOC. If the travel is more than 1,000 kilometers, air travel is paid for in first class. If a member has a spouse or significant other and is willing to fly business class, he or she can opt for two business-class tickets. At the time I became an IOC member, the daily stipend was $225. (This has since been raised to $450 for members during the Games, and to $800 for Executive Board members attending an Executive Board meeting.) However, if members are working on a bid committee for a candidate city, they cannot seek reimbursement to those IOC meetings; reimbursement must come from the candidate city's bid committee.

The exception is the IOC president, who works full-time on the Olympic Movement. Rather than having him (or hopefully her someday) request daily reimbursement, the Executive Board in 2014 set the president's reimbursement at $270,000 per year. The president is the only IOC member who draws a salary, because he is the only IOC member acting full-time on behalf of the Olympic Movement. IOC staff members are paid as regular employees, as in any business.

At the time of my election, I was one of only two Americans on the IOC (USOC President Bob Helmick being the other one). At the age of 34, I was also one of the younger members ever elected. At that time, 28-year-old Prince Albert of Monaco was the youngest member serving. More importantly, I was the first African-American member and the first American woman on the IOC.

I called my mother, who was thrilled. It was exactly the kind of path-breaking success that they had hoped for me. I also called the LA84 Foundation office and let my team there know.

The following morning, I left Lausanne and flew home. It didn't really didn't fully hit me until I was halfway over the Atlantic Ocean. I remember sitting on the plane, smiling with pride, wanting to yell, "Yes!"

When I arrived at LAX, two alumni of the Los Angeles Olympic Committee, Valerie Steiner and Steve Montiel, were waiting outside the customs hall. They were holding a huge picture of me with a sign that read: "Welcome Home IOC Member."

Chapter Fifteen
Opening the Games to All Athletes

As a new member of the International Olympic Committee, I was surprised to learn that our duties and responsibilities were not laid out. There was no handbook or written guidelines, and, as it turned out, no orientation for new members. We were just supposed to get busy. The only directive we were given was to "protect the Olympic Movement," a sweeping generality, to say the least. Most boards, and indeed even the United States Congress, have an orientation process.

When I asked a veteran IOC member why there was no orientation, she said she didn't know. She suggested that I work with an IOC staff member and submit a written proposal to create an orientation booklet. Over the course of my first year, as I dove into my new position, I wrote up a report on the information, policies, and procedures that I thought would be helpful to future new members. I submitted it to the IOC, but there was some reluctance to formally adopt it, which I did not understand. Although it took years to work its way through the bureaucracy, a formal orientation program eventually was created for new IOC members.

Without any guidance, I began asking questions and participating. I soon discovered that it was quite unusual for members to speak up during their first session. Of course, I learned that after I had taken part in the debate during my first IOC Session. In the United States, we are taught to speak up; it's part of our culture and our education. I also learned early on that if you didn't speak up on a matter, a decision could be made without your input. I felt that the whole point of being a member was to participate.

The IOC, I quickly learned, was by design an organization that moved very slowly and methodically. At first this frustrated me, but once I became more seasoned, I realized that I would have to be careful and political — as much as I could — and not be just an impatient athlete rights activist. To have any lasting influence, I would have to put in the time and the effort to earn the confidence of the members. That is as it should be with such an august institution.

* * * * *

There were several changes underway at the IOC when I was elected. Prior to 1986, most IOC members only visited bid cities on an *ad hoc* basis, generally when they had other business in that city. And they had to pay their own way.

That year, there were six cities bidding for the 1992 Olympic Games and seven for the Olympic Winter Games. (The Games were then awarded six years in advance to allow the host city enough time to fully prepare. Now the decision is made seven years out.) France and Spain had cities bidding for both the summer and winter Games. For many reasons, it made sense for IOC members to tour the cities and see the venues.

At the 1985 session in East Berlin, a member asked if it was permissible to accept invitations to visit the candidate cities. The response then was, "Why not?" And for the 1992 Games, IOC members began a new effort to visit every bidding city.

One of the biggest issues being addressed in the Olympic Movement at that time was athlete eligibility. The IOC had removed the word "amateur" from the Olympic Charter in 1973 and replaced it with "eligible," which gave the decision to the International Federations for determining who would be eligible to compete at the Olympic Games. Although there was a very fine line between "professionals" and "eligible athletes," so-called professionals were excluded from the Olympic Games.

At my first IOC Session, held May 9-12, 1987, in Istanbul, there was a discussion about which tennis players should be allowed to compete at the Olympic Games, after the sport had been put back on the program. I made an argument for including all tennis athletes in the Olympic Games, whether or not they might be multi-millionaires. Some IOC members felt that athletes who earned millions of dollars should not be allowed to compete, but I disagreed.

My rationale was straightforward. After an athlete has trained so hard for the Olympic Games, he or she wants to be able to say that they competed against the very best in the world, not just the best in the Olympic Games. They don't care how much money someone has in their bank account. They crave the highest level of competition.

I related my own experiences by saying that nobody ever checked my bank account at the starting line. (If they had checked, they would've wondered how I was able to eat three meals a day.) The simple fact was, some people in rowing came from wealthy families and others did not. What did it matter? And why is it an issue that somebody has been able to perfect their skills at a very high level in, say, tennis or basketball and get paid for it? For me, the only relevant question is, are those athletes willing to compete under the same set of rules?

Tennis was the sport on the table for discussion. Tennis had been on the program at the first Olympic Games in 1896, but it was dropped in 1924 due to a dispute between the IOC and the sport's governing body. It returned as a demonstration sport in 1968 and then again in 1984. For the 1988 Games, tennis was coming back onto the program as a medal sport; therefore, the IOC needed to determine who was eligible to compete.

The sticking point for many IOC members was that tennis had many wealthy professional players. The best tennis players earned millions of dollars from prize money and endorsements. My position was that they were the best athletes in their sport, and they had to turn professional to see just how good they could become, as there had been no substantial international competitions for amateurs since the sport's major tournaments like Wimbledon became open to professionals beginning in 1968. To me, it followed that if these athletes were the best in the world in their sport, then they should be allowed to compete in the Olympic Games.

"An athlete wants to see if they can beat the best," I kept harping, "so why shouldn't we let everyone compete?"

In addition, the line was fuzzy. In the U.S., amateurs were defined as those who did not accept prize money and endorsement dollars, such as college players, and professionals were ones who did. But athletes in the rest of the world, particularly in Europe, were technically professional, as they received support from their national federations. No clear line could be drawn even if the IOC wanted to draw one. Hence, we needed an eligibility rule.

The IOC decided that all tennis players would be allowed to compete at the 1988 Seoul Olympic Games. Each nation would select entrants who became eligible based on a system devised by the International Tennis Federation. The result of opening the Games to professional tennis players allowed Steffi Graf to compete and win the gold medal in Barcelona in 1992, the same year she won four Grand Slam tournaments, giving her what was dubbed the first-ever "Golden Slam."

A few years later, I was given a moment of great personal pride from the tennis competition. In the 2000 Sydney Games, Venus Williams, who had participated in the LA84 Foundation's tennis program (then called the AAF/Junior Tennis League program), won her first of four gold medals. I had the honor of presenting Venus with the medal. As I did, I said the words I love to say: "Now and forever you will be known as an Olympic champion."

I'm not sure if my speaking up about allowing professional tennis players to compete, given that I was a rookie IOC member, was any sort of critical factor, but I was delighted that the best tennis players in the world would now be able to be on the Olympic program.

* * * * *

When I was elected to the IOC, I was not a voting member of the USOC. I had stepped down in January 1985 at the end of my eight years on the USOC Athletes Advisory Council when USOC President Bob Helmick asked me if I would chair the USOC Eligibility Committee. I agreed on one condition — that the goal be to end the outdated amateur rules preventing athletes from receiving funding. The work was particularly important to me because it involved advocacy for the rights of individual athletes.

The IOC requires that IOC members have voting rights at the highest level of their NOC. With my election as an IOC member, I went back to being a member of the USOC Executive Board. Because of the way the USOC was then structured, this gave me a vote on the full body, as well as on the Executive Board.

My biggest disappointment with the USOC in 1985 was that USOC rules forbid athletes or even coaches to receive any funding under the longstanding amateur rule. After the experiences I and other Olympians had endured in the 1970s and early 1980s, with many of us training for the Games on shoestring budgets, I was determined to change this rule for the sake of all U.S. athletes.

Although the word "amateur" had been removed from the Olympic Charter in 1973 and changed to "eligible athletes," as determined by each International Federation, it was still the decision of each National Governing Body to enter that eligible athlete.

The word amateur was removed from the Olympic Charter in 1973 because it no longer made sense. Support for athletes varied throughout the world. Athletes in the military can be supported in most countries.

Many of the old guard in the USOC, however, believed that the amateur rule was sacrosanct, notably former president Robert Kane. In conversations I had with these folks, it came out that they actually believed it was right for athletes to have to suffer to make the Olympic team, to claw and scrape together money for training, and somehow against all odds make it to the Games. Worse, it appeared they felt this was an important part of the Olympic spirit.

But my team on the USOC Eligibility Commission persisted and prevailed — to a degree — by finally making it possible for U. S. athletes in all sports to receive funding as they were training, and to allow professionals to compete. As a result of the committee's work, the eligibility rules for U.S. Olympians were changed in 1986. Athletes could now receive financial support from their national organizations, from the USOC, or from sponsors without forsaking their eligibility. Team coaches benefitted from this change.

However, there was a caveat. Due to National Collegiate Athletic Association rules, if the athlete was competing in college, they were not allowed to take the money directly. For example, if an athlete won a medal at the Games and the USOC rewarded them with a stipend of, say, $30,000, that money had to be put into a fund that could not be used while the athlete was in college. On its face, this is ridiculous, but the USOC could not interfere with the NCAA rules.

The most noticeable result of the rule change allowed basketball players who were members of the National Basketball Association to play on the Olympic team. For years, professional basketball players from the European nations had competed in the Olympic Games. Professionals, however, were not allowed to compete for the U.S. because our governing body of the sport, USA Basketball, defined Olympic eligibility as collegiate players.

I found this absurd, especially given the commercial appeal of NCAA basketball. "Amateur" certainly does not describe what happens at the collegiate level. But the NCAA persists in putting forth this notion of amateur athletes who magically and purely spring forth full of wondrous ability with no financial support, and then tear it up on the national stage.

My colleagues on the USOC Eligibility Committee and I pushed hard for the change for two years and were finally successful. In 1986, the U.S. became the very last country to permit professionals on their Olympic basketball team. This rule change allowed for the assembly of the "Dream Team" in 1992.

Composed of future Hall of Famers, including Michael Jordan, Magic Johnson, Larry Bird, Patrick Ewing, and Charles Barkley, the team swept the gold medal, defeating opponents by an average of 44 points. The Naismith Memorial Basketball Hall of Fame called the team "the greatest collection of basketball talent on the planet," and many sportswriters dubbed it the best team ever assembled in any sport.

As the new eligibility rules evolved, they allowed some non-collegiate individual athletes whose primary performance platform was the Olympic Games to become very wealthy and still compete, like swimmer Michael Phelps and runner Usain Bolt. Had these great athletes not been allowed to accept endorsement money and still compete in the Olympic Games, they may very well have moved on for financial reasons after their first Games, thereby depriving the Olympic stage of their talents in multiple Games.

Clearly, changing the eligibility rules was the right thing to do, as it has provided resources to many athletes in unsung sports and also allowed the U.S. to field its best Olympic teams.

* * * * *

During my first two years on the IOC, I learned while IOC members are captains of industry, royalty, and government officials, many do not have an intimate knowledge of sport. They come with different portfolios, but their mission becomes the same: to see that the Games survive and flourish. I felt that my role as an Olympian was to share my experiences in sport to help my fellow IOC members better understand the perspective of the most important element of the Olympic Games: its competitors.

Having worked on the USOC Eligibility Committee and taken up the push at the IOC level for all athletes, regardless of their net worth, to be able to compete in the Olympic Games, I felt that I had put myself on a definitive path as an IOC member who would ensure that the athletes always had a faithful voice. I knew I would to continue to make this the backbone of my work on the IOC.

In 1988, Kenny Moore, who had testified with me in 1977 before the Senate Commerce Committee, wrote an article for *Sports Illustrated* titled, "An Advocate for Athletes: Anita DeFrantz Is an Unlikely Member of the Powerful IOC." Flattered, proud, and humbled by such a declaration, I realized that I had a lot to live up to.

Chapter Sixteen
A Dark Cloud Forms Over the Games

I was attending my first Olympic Games as an IOC member, the 1988 Games in Seoul, South Korea. Early one morning, the phone in my hotel room rang. The caller was Craig Masback, an NBC reporter. I knew Craig from my days at Princeton, when he had been an undergraduate there. He was also a middle-distance runner and a potential member of the 1980 U.S. Olympic team.

Craig told me that late the previous night the sprinter Ben Johnson's drug test had come back positive for a banned steroid. This was going to be one of the biggest stories of the Games.

Three days earlier, on September 24, Johnson had run a race for the ages and won the gold medal in the 100-meter dash, breaking his own world record in the process and becoming the first Canadian to win the 100 since 1928. He had edged out his rival, the American Carl Lewis, by fractions of a second, in one of the Games most anticipated match ups.

After the race, a urine sample had been taken from the three medalists, which was standard procedure. One of the doctors at the Olympic Doping Control Center, Dr. Park Jong-Sei, discovered that Johnson's drug test was positive for stanozolol, a banned anabolic steroid. The IOC Medical Commission confirmed the result and recommended that Johnson be stripped of his gold medal, immediately disqualified from the Games, and removed from the Olympic Village. The IOC Executive Board unanimously voted to affirm the sanctions.

There were other rippled effects. Johnson's disqualification meant that his gold medal would be awarded to the runner-up, Carl Lewis. Additionally, Lewis's second place time of 9.92, a new American record, would also become the new Olympic record.

Lewis had given what was turning out to be a prophetic interview just after losing the race to Johnson. He said that "Ben made a tremendous (time) drop in 24 hours" and "wasn't the same person" in the semifinals as he was in the final. "I don't know how he does it — whether he gets a hypnotist or what to stimulate him," Lewis added.

The world was about to find out what had really stimulated Johnson.

My reaction to the news was immediate and visceral: If he used drugs, he's a coward and a cheat. He doesn't deserve to be in the Olympic Village.

Craig asked me, as an Olympian and an IOC member, to come on NBC to talk about the incident and condemn it. I explained that this was my first Games as an IOC member and I wasn't sure if I should be criticizing an Olympian on the air, even one who had stained the Games. I told Craig I needed to give this some thought.

Craig called me back two more times that morning to lobby me. On one of the calls, he apologized for not being supportive enough of the 1980 boycott protest. He kept stressing how important it was for an IOC member who was an Olympian to speak out on this critical issue.

The more I thought about it, the more I felt I had a responsibility to speak out. Even though it was a sad day for the 1988 Olympic Games, as a premiere event had been tainted, I felt that it was an important day for the Olympic Movement for banning a shameful cheater. The IOC had done the right thing and strengthened itself in the process.

I agreed to go on the air and be interviewed by Craig, because to me the Olympic Games is about mutual respect and fair play. Cheaters had no place at the Games.

It was a difficult and delicate situation. A great deal of hype had surrounded the battle between Ben Johnson and Carl Lewis vying for the title of fastest man in the world, and the race had delivered. But now, the results were being changed. Never before had such a high-profile athlete been stripped of a medal for steroid use.

Canada practically disowned Johnson, who was removed from its Olympic team in the middle of the night. The victory headline in one Canadian newspaper had been "Canadian Wins Gold Medal in 100 Meter." Then after the drug test was revealed, the headline in the same paper was "Jamaican

Shamed by Positive Drug Test." (Johnson was born in Jamaica.) A British tabloid hit ever harder, calling Johnson "The Fastest Junkie in the World."

Predictably, most of the U.S. coverage, which was being anchored by Tom Brokaw, was focused on Ben Johnson and the fallout from his banishment.

By all accounts, Johnson appeared to believe that he would get away with it, despite the fact that all medalists are drug tested. The powerful steroid he had taken had a reputation of being undetectable (at that time), because it spends a very short time in the body. In a race decided by fractions of a second, the drug could have a decisive impact.

Live on NBC, Craig asked me what I thought of the situation. "Ben Johnson is a coward because he wasn't brave enough to stand on his own," I said. "He took drugs. He has cheated, and he needs to leave the Olympic Village." I added that he would "always be an Olympian because he has competed in the Games, even though he has dishonored his competition."

I wasn't quite sure what the response from my fellow IOC members would be. I quickly learned that, at that time, it was unusual for an IOC member other than the president to speak out on controversial issues. However, most members congratulated me. Most importantly, IOC President Juan Antonio Samaranch had seen the interview and told me that he didn't have a problem with it.

As part of a larger investigation conducted after the Games, Johnson admitted to being on steroids when he set the world record in 1987. That record was also erased. He and his coach claimed that Johnson used the steroids in order to have the same advantage as others using them, which to me is a foolish excuse.

As far as how Johnson felt about me calling him a coward on national television, I heard through the grapevine that he did not feel it was appropriate for me as an Olympian to speak out. However, I have never spoken to him directly about it, but would be happy to.

* * * * *

The use of performance-enhancing drugs (PEDs) has a long history in the Olympic Games. Centuries ago when the Games were held in Ancient Greece, athletes ingested all kinds of substances to provide a competitive edge. If an athlete was found to have cheated in Olympia, it is said that a statue in his likeness was erected to embarrass him and his community.

In the twentieth century, this evolved into some athletes taking testosterone to boost their performance. But this was quaint compared to the techniques of doping, and masking doping, that developed in the modern era.

Doping first came into the spotlight as a threat to the Olympic Movement at the 1960 Rome Olympic Games. The death of Danish cyclist Knud Enemark Jensen, the first in an Olympic Games since 1912, was attributed to the use of the blood circulation stimulant Ronical. Jensen's death led to the formation of the IOC Medical Committee in 1961.

In 1964, prior to the Tokyo Games, the IOC voted to condemn doping by athletes and sanction those involved with administering or using PEDs. The IOC Medical Commission published the first list of banned substances, composed of alcohol, pep pills, cocaine, vasodilators, opiates, and hashish. A formal ban on the use of all PEDs at the Olympic Games came in 1967.

To enforce the ban, drug testing began at the 1968 Grenoble Olympic Winter Games and the 1968 Mexico City Games. One athlete was sanctioned at the summer Games, Swedish pentathlete Hans-Gunnar Liljenwall, who tested positive for alcohol use and was stripped of a bronze medal. The 1968 Games also brought the introduction of gender verification tests, as it was widely suspected that some nations were entering men in women's events.

For years, many people suspected that the East Germans were using anabolic steroids. However, the IOC did not test for steroids because a reliable test was not developed until 1972. After the fall of the Berlin Wall, records surfaced that confirmed that the East German coaches and trainers were administering steroid regimens to their athletes. The benefit of taking this type of drug is most effective while athletes are training. Steroids, in particular, allow an athlete to train harder because the recovery time is much shorter. Muscle mass builds up faster, and muscle memory is extended through the increased practice time. Usage was covered up by stopping the drugs far enough ahead of a Games so that the athletes would not test positive. Several East German authorities who ran the doping program were eventually convicted of criminal behavior.

Doping works best when it is done well in advance of competition.

Until the International Rowing Federation (Fédération Internationale des Sociétés d'Aviron, or FISA) started testing in 1984, the only organization that tested for doping was the IOC during the Olympic Games. Scientists in East Germany and elsewhere needed only to avoid the dope testing at the Games.

In 1972, there was a controversial and highly-publicized case in the U.S. involving 16-year-old U.S. swimmer Rick DeMont. After winning the gold medal in the men's 400-meter freestyle, DeMont was disqualified for testing positive for the banned substance ephedrine, which was contained in his prescription asthma medication. The controversy arose because DeMont had originally been using a permitted medication, but switched to one with a banned substance without recognizing the difference prior to the Games. He was barred from competing in the rest of the Games, including racing in the 1,500-meter freestyle, in which he was the standing world record holder. While I had no proof, it seemed to me at the 1976 Montreal Olympic Games the East German women were doping and getting away with it. The "Easties" seemed overall bigger and stronger than other female athletes at those Games. In rowing, they won five of the six gold medals, which seemed statistically impossible in a nation of just 17 million people.

At the 1976 Montreal Games, U.S. swimmer Shirley Babashoff publically accused the "Easties" of doping. Babashoff was the reigning world record holder in six events, but she ended up surprisingly placing second in all four of her individual events to the "Easties." The U.S. media dubbed her "Surly Shirley" and called her an ungracious loser. But after the fall of the Berlin Wall when the records of the doped "Easties" were found, she was vindicated. The IOC recognized her dedication to clean sport and awarded her an Olympic Order, the highest honor given by the IOC.

Part of the problem at that time was that American doctors did not fully understand PEDs and the unfair advantage they gave users.

In 1984 at the LA Olympic Games, a handful of tests — believed to be positive — of track athletes suddenly disappeared before they could be analyzed. We don't know whose tests they were because the file matching the numbers on the samples to the athletes was stolen from the hotel room of the chairman of the medical commission. The file was in a desk drawer.

Someone who clearly did not want those samples tested removed the entire desk.

But the case of Ben Johnson at the 1988 Olympic Games, a high-profile gold medalist who got caught, shined the brightest light yet on doping.

* * * * *

At the IOC Session in 1989, the first meeting following the 1988 Seoul Olympic Games, I asked the IOC to have serious drug cheats and their doctors and entourages banned or heavily sanctioned. To me, it was obvious that if a coach or doctor helped dope one athlete, then they would continue that practice with other athletes.

I cited the disturbing trend among U.S. collegiate athletes, where an athlete found to have cheated would be sanctioned and usually unable to compete for a year. The coaches, however, could transfer to another school and begin coaching immediately. I didn't think it was fair that the coaches would just find another athlete and involve them in doping. To have any chance at stopping the chain, the coaches needed to be sanctioned.

I was later told that I was the first Olympic member in a high-level position to propose such a sweeping ban to the IOC for doping.

There was a very long discussion and debate on the issue, the longest debate to date on any issue. I did not know at the time when you make a proposal to the IOC there was a discussion and you need to respond to each IOC member. (This went back to the lack of orientation for new members.) The problem was, I had not written down the names of the members and what they had said, so when IOC President Samaranch turned to me and asked for my response, I was not prepared to respond to each person.

My basic proposal called for implementing a ban on the entourage involved in doping the athletes. Several members said such a punishment was already available in the Olympic Charter; therefore, no changes needed to be made. The problem was, that was not spelled out: the Olympic Charter merely stated that if there was a doping offense, then the IOC Executive Board would set the sanction.

It wasn't until the year 2000, however, when I was a member of the Executive Board, that the Olympic Charter was used to punish the doctor of an athlete who was found to be doped. That year, a Romanian physician who was found to have doped a gymnast was sanctioned by the IOC. He was told that he had to leave the village and was not eligible to return to the next Olympic Games. It was a long time coming.

* * * * *

As for Rick DeMont's story, it swept me up again 24 years later. DeMont and his team, led by attorney David Ulich and sports psychologist Steven Ungerleider, worked for years to try to have his gold medal reinstated. DeMont had appealed to the IOC and been rejected. As Ulich was preparing a second appeal, his colleague called me in 1996 and asked as an American member of the IOC if I could somehow help. I remembered hearing the story of a 16-year-old asthmatic being stripped of his gold medal for taking his asthma medication when I was at Connecticut College, and felt a kinship with DeMont because I suffered from asthma as a child.

I looked into DeMont's situation and found a few problems.

For over a year prior to the 1972 Games, DeMont had been taking an asthma medicine. At some point, his coach had apparently learned about a more effective medicine called Marax, and he encouraged DeMont to switch. The problem arose when DeMont did not meet with the USOC team doctor in Munich to discuss the new medication. Because this was the first Olympic Games with comprehensive drug testing, all athletes were told several times to meet with the team doctor and discuss medications they were taking so that the doctor could interface with the IOC on drug testing.

DeMont and his coach listed the new medication on his entry form, but they never met with the team doctor. Therefore, the team doctor did not submit to the IOC the paperwork declaring DeMont's use of Marax.

Another problem with DeMont's case came after he tested positive. The IOC Medical Commission doctors who performed the drug test asked how much medication DeMont had taken. He (or his coach) told them that DeMont took one dose before bed the night before the race. However, it turned out that he was nervous and had actually taken two additional doses, which prevented him from sleeping and also created an unusually high amount of ephedrine in his drug test.

Because the medication only stays in the body for a certain period of time, had DeMont told them that he ingested more than the usual dosage, he would have at least been allowed to compete in the next race, rather than being disqualified from all events.

In the ensuing years, the IOC rejected DeMont's appeal to reinstate his gold medal because he was doped during the race. As for the events he did not race, clearly nothing could be done about that after the fact.

Three months after his first appeal, DeMont appealed again. His attorney was pushing on two tracks. The first was he had disclosed the medication to the USOC. The second was that the year following the 1972 Olympic Games, DeMont, who went off Marax, had broken the world record in the 400-meter freestyle, and thus, his attorney argued, the asthma medication did not enhance his performance.

At the IOC Session in March 1996, the IOC again rejected DeMont's petition for reinstatement of the gold medal. When I was asked in the press about the situation, I explained what I had been told about the case. The records indicated that DeMont did not meet with the U.S. team doctor, and he took more of the medication than he had initially told the IOC officials.

In June of 1996, DeMont sued the USOC for not properly supporting him at the 1972 Games, which he claimed led to irreparable damage of his reputation and earning power. DeMont also named me as a defendant, claiming that I had libeled him.

I was floored. Not only had I tried to help him, I had not even been involved in the Olympic Movement in 1972. And now I was being sued over an event that I had had no part of.

USOC spokesman Mike Moran issued a terse statement. "We feel this suit is without merit," Moran said. "The USOC simply will not respond to this kind of threat any more. The IOC officially rejected this appeal, and you're talking about an event that took place 24 years ago at a time when no member of this Olympic committee or its leadership was involved with that delegation."

Be that as it may, I had to defend myself. The USOC refused to pay any part of my legal bills. I was not happy that the USOC abandoned me, to say the least. I hired a lawyer and he asked the judge to release me as a defendant on the grounds that I had nothing to do with the action and could not have libeled DeMont because I did not print the story. The judge refused.

The lawsuit against me was finally dismissed in 1998. My legal costs came to $40,000, which was eventually reimbursed by the IOC. A year after it was all over, I called the lawyer who represented me to thank him. He was surprised to hear from me, as he said that nobody ever calls and thanks him.

Several months later, the lawyer called me back. It turned out that the judge on the case had since become his law partner. Curious, my lawyer asked his new partner, the judge, why I was kept on as a defendant. The judge said that I was kept on because I was an IOC member and therefore must have had deep pockets.

In 2001, the USOC issued a statement saying that it had erred in handling Rick DeMont's medical records at the 1972 Olympic Games. The statement, which did not acknowledge wrongdoing or contain an apology, brought an end to the litigation. The USOC also petitioned the IOC to reinstate his gold medal. Again, the appeal was turned down.

DeMont went on to work as an assistant coach for the South African men's Olympic swimming team at the 2004 and 2008 Games. In 2014, he was named head swim and dive coach at the University of Arizona.

I certainly have nothing against Rick DeMont, and before this episode had respected him and his desire to escape from an unfortunate situation. But looking back, his story has now become one of the more innocent doping scandals at the Olympic Games — in addition to being one of the most avoidable.

Chapter Seventeen
Running as Hard as I Can

My relationship with the United States Olympic Committee was a rollercoaster ride long before the organization refused to defend me in the Rick DeMont case. It was uncomfortable from the moment the USOC ran out of uniforms for the 1976 Olympic rowing team, and I, as team captain, spent months chasing down our clothing. In 1980, I sued the USOC to withdraw its boycott of the Moscow Olympic Games, despite the fact that I served on its Executive Board and board of directors at the time.

I was elected to the USOC board of directors in 1976 and then to the executive committee in January 1977. I served on the Executive Board until April 2003, when the USOC reorganized itself to be governed by a much smaller board of directors, on which I continue to serve. My tenure on both was voluntarily interrupted from February 1985 through October 1986 when my term of office on the USOC Athletes Advisory Council concluded. I was then asked to chair the eligibility committee.

The USOC is often thought be an entity supported by federal funding, though it has never been. Founded in 1894 and renamed the USOC in 1961, the USOC was reorganized in 1978 under the Ted Stevens Olympic and Amateur Sports Act and given the responsibility of coordinating all national governing bodies for individual sports involved in the Olympic Games. It is responsible for entering the U.S. team in the Olympic Games, and later also the Paralympic Games and Youth Olympic Games. A nonprofit corporation that does not receive federal financial support, the USOC is funded by revenue from television rights, corporate sponsorships, and private donations. It is governed by a board of directors, a president, and managed by a CEO appointed by the board.

Over the years, I have had many differences of opinion with other USOC actions and with officials whom I believe have either tarnished or held back the Olympic Movement in the United States. No organization is perfect, and neither am I, but some issues were avoidable and correctable.

* * * * *

One of my more frustrating tussles with the USOC came in 1984 when it set up a foundation — and waded straight into a political and moral swamp.

The U.S. Olympic Foundation was chaired by Bill Simon, a USOC past president. I was named one of the foundation's trustees. The U.S. Treasury Secretary under President Ford, Simon was a pioneer of leveraged buyouts, and insisted that the foundation invest in the highest-return investments he could find. Simon did not want his investment playbook constrained in any way. He believed that large-cap stocks, meaning stocks held in companies with a market capitalization of more than $10 billion, were the strongest investment opportunities. Some of those funds, however, had holdings in corporations doing business in South Africa and supporting apartheid. I believed that such investments were morally wrong and fought to withhold and divest them.

My position was clear: Apartheid was so horrible a blight on the world, such a crime against humanity, that each one of us was forced to choose between being either part of the problem or part of the solution. We either accepted and cooperated with a government that had an evil contempt for its own citizens and fostered racial hatred, or we did the right thing and isolated them until they changed.

I also believed that the USOC should follow the lead of the IOC when it came to South Africa. After the passage of a 1962 United Nations' resolution condemning apartheid as a threat to international peace and security, the Olympic Movement excluded South Africa from the Olympic Games, and eventually expelled the South African NOC from the Olympic Movement.

Of course, this wasn't the first time I had butted heads with Bill Simon. He had been central to convincing the USOC to vote in favor of the boycott of the 1980 Olympic Games.

Not only were these investments morally wrong, I felt they were financially short-sighted. My allies and I pointed out that the Wells Fargo Non-South

Africa Fund, a small- and mid-cap fund, was producing generous returns. The chairman of the finance committee of the LA84 Foundation, the influential film mogul Lew Wasserman, had been instrumental in getting Wells Fargo to set up the non-South Africa index fund. Once the fund was established, the LA84 Foundation diversified its portfolio and invested in the Wells Fargo fund.

I repeatedly pressed the U.S. Olympic Foundation to rid itself of investments in companies doing business in South Africa. Given my own heritage and the sacrifices that my parents, grandparents, and great-grandparents had made fighting segregation, I felt it was my responsibility to do so. But Simon wouldn't budge.

The issue continued into 1988. That July, the USOC foundation trustees voted on a compromise measure to restrict future investments in companies with ties to South Africa, but allow the foundation to maintain its current investments. At the time, the foundation had roughly $12 million of its $155 million portfolio invested in such companies. Simon's position was that restricting investment in South Africa was hurting the people we were trying to help by not allowing money to flow into their country. To me, that was absurd. At all levels, the issue was a moral one — not a financial one.

The measure was defeated by a vote of 4-3, leaving the USOC's values at odds with those of the IOC.

Nine days before the foundation vote took place, the IOC had convened a meeting at its headquarters in Lausanne of leaders from the African nations and reinforced its exclusion of South Africa from the Olympic Movement. President Samaranch further urged leaders of all international sports organizations to increase efforts to isolate South Africa.

The IOC showed that it was willing to welcome South Africa back when apartheid ended. In 1988, the IOC established the Apartheid and Olympism Commission to open discussions about reintegrating a free South Africa into the Olympic family. An interim South Africa NOC, dubbed the South Africa Non-Racial Olympic Commission and led by Sam Ramsamy, a South African living in exile in Britain, had been formed in 1962 in hope of returning a free South Africa to the Olympic Movement.

The movement picked up steam in 1990 when Nelson Mandela was released from prison. Finally, in 1991, apartheid legislation was repealed by the South African government, opening the door for the country's return to the Olympic Family. The IOC reinstated South Africa to compete at the 1992 Olympic Games under an interim flag, as the official flag remained part of the apartheid era.

Ultimately, poetic justice was served on the USOC's investment portfolio. Over time, the Wells Fargo Non-South Africa Fund outperformed Simon's large-cap choices that maintained investments in apartheid South Africa.

* * * * *

My most frustrating and embarrassing time at the USOC came in 1991 when USOC President Bob Helmick disgraced the organization. *USA Today* broke a story that rocked the USOC: Helmick, who had become president after 1985, when Jack Kelly passed away suddenly from a heart attack, and was a member of the IOC, was working as a consultant to six clients who either had or sought business relationships with the USOC and/or the IOC. His clients, including two groups attempting to earn recognition for golf and bowling as Olympic sports, had reportedly paid some $275,000 to Helmick and his Des Moines, Iowa-based law firm.

The only reason Bob was found out, the rumor went, was because he had changed law firms in a year when his junior partners lost out on their bonuses. While his files were being transferred to the new law firm, they mysteriously fell off the back of the moving truck — and into the hands of a *USA Today* reporter.

At the time, Bob and I were the only two Americans serving on the IOC, which made the situation all that much worse for me. With all the allegations flung at the IOC over conflicts and corruption, to have an American be at the center of something so blatantly wrong was embarrassing and demoralizing. I was furious that he had harmed the Olympic Movement both at home and abroad by abusing his position. I had worked with him for years and was both astonished and disappointed that he would cross the line and seek to develop an income stream from what should have been transparent, voluntary work.

I urged him to immediately resign from the USOC and then from the IOC, but he declined. He maintained that his firm had accepted the business in the normal course of events because it was profitable, and denied any conflict of interest and untoward favoritism.

Days after the scandal became public, Helmick traveled to an IOC Executive Board meeting. Before the first day of the two-day meeting, he changed his mind. In the middle of the night, he slipped a resignation letter under IOC President Samaranch's hotel room door at the Lausanne Palace Hotel, and abruptly left town. Bob initially refused to resign from the USOC. On the verge of being removed, he finally relented. Still, as a past USOC president, he was technically welcome to attend meetings. Much to our shock, he did show up from time to time. It was always awkward at best.

It was a sad ending to his service in the Olympic Movement, because he was on track to possibly become the next IOC president. He tarnished his own legacy by his actions, and also the integrity of the USOC. Sadly, when he died in 2003, the scandal was in the first paragraph of his obituary in *The New York Times*.

Helmick's unceremonious resignation opened a spot on the IOC Executive Board for me, if I were brave enough to run. I thought long and hard about it. I was unsure if I had enough years of service or support within the IOC to be elected. Personally, at that time, I was also dealing with a debilitating medical diagnosis that threatened to redirect my priorities.

* * * * *

In 1991, I was formally diagnosed with multiple sclerosis, the degeneration of the nerve covers in the spinal cord and brain. Though I had been made aware in 1989 that I likely had the disease, I refused to fully accept it, in part because I was afraid that I would lose my medical insurance.

The trigger point came when my left eye became foggy. After a day or so, I noticed that if I covered my right eye and relied on my left eye, I could barely see. I went to my ophthalmologist, who diagnosed the eye problem as neuritis, or inflammation of the nerve in my eye.

I also had other symptoms. I constantly felt tired. My adventurousness had dropped a level. As an athlete who was conditioned to be in tune with my body, I knew that something wasn't right. Though I regularly went to the marina to row, I was less and less interested in doing other outdoor activities, such as bike riding, which I had done for years with great joy and abandon.

I ticked through my past history of inexplicably losing my hearing in one ear in the spring of 1980 while at the Olympic camp, and of my legs going numb. Other strange things had happened to me physically, such as tripping and falling on occasion, but I had always pushed through.

My physician, Dr. Laleh Bakhtiar, informed me that my constant fatigue coupled with the other symptoms meant that I more than likely had multiple sclerosis. She was reluctant to give me a formal diagnosis and referred me to a specialist, Dr. Harriet Coakley. Sadly, six years later, Dr. Bakhtiar herself succumbed to progressive MS.

I immediately thought back to the MS collection jar in the corner store in Indianapolis. As a kid, I had been terrified of getting MS, because the sign on the jar said it crippled young adults and had no cure. I held on to that fear for years, but when I turned 30, I distinctly remember thinking that I was out of the danger zone because I had passed through young adulthood.

I saw Dr. Coakley, who had diagnosed me with relapsing MS, meaning that symptoms occurred in isolated attacks rather than continuously deteriorating over time. Between attacks, she said, symptoms might disappear completely, which they generally did.

My approach was not to talk with anyone. My family knew, but I told only a very few friends. I was worried that once people found out, they would treat me differently, and I did not want that.

One friend I told became deeply worried about my health. Once we were in a store together picking up different items and agreed to meet at the cashier in 15 minutes. I became distracted and showed up 10 minutes late. "Oh my God," she said, "I thought you had fallen down in the bathroom and hit your head."

Though I contributed (and continue to contribute) to the National Multiple Sclerosis Society every year, I did not become an advocate.

I knew of one Olympian, American alpine skier Jimmie Heuga, with progressive MS. The disease had ended his skiing career and launched another as an advocate for exercise and activity to keep MS at bay. But while he was dedicating his life to talking about his battle with MS, I dedicated mine to keeping it a secret.

I felt I had enough of a handicap getting through life as an African-American woman, and I did not want to add another challenge. I vowed, however, that if I reached the point where I could not hide it, then I would join the public fight against MS.

At first, I was reluctant to take medication, which is extraordinarily expensive. Although it was affordable to me and insurance covered much of the cost, initially I wasn't willing to give myself that advantage over people who could not afford the medication. It took me a while, along with the prodding of my physician, to be convinced that I should go on medication. The more I read, the more I realized that the only way I could function normally over the long term was to do that.

To me, it didn't seem fair that I could afford to take this outrageously expensive medicine — which has risen in cost from $1,500 a month when I began taking it to $5,000 — while others were forced to seek less expensive, alternative treatments. I attempted to equate my situation with everybody else's, to democratize the situation, which doesn't work for illnesses.

MS is a disease which seems to affect people very differently. In my case, the numbness in my limbs, and a sense of immense fatigue and general pain was a constant problem. The first decade after the diagnosis was challenging. I developed a fear of physical activity, given that heat-inducing activities were thought to exacerbate the condition. And I gained a great deal of weight, which made life more difficult.

It took a long time to learn how to manage the fatigue. Eventually, I found a level of exercise that began to work again. Olympic form and fitness was an idea that I had once embraced; it became a pleasant memory.

To this day I continue to take the medication. Over the years, I have had a couple of attacks that have clouded my vision, dimmed my hearing, and completely numbed my legs. It became very painful to row in my single for more than three or four miles. My legs would go numb and painful. I still love to row, but I have trouble knowing how long I can contribute to the power in the boat. Knowing an attack might be just around the corner makes me appreciate days when I feel completely healthy. Like more than 400,000 people here in the United States, and 2.5 million others worldwide afflicted with an incurable disease, I live with it and get on with life.

Acquisition of insurance became a major issue. This is clearly a pre-existing condition. I was fortunate to have excellent coverage at the LA84 Foundation, but I knew that finding coverage to replace it when I left the Foundation would be nearly impossible. The Affordable Care Act lifted that huge burden, as I no longer could be denied coverage, and made a huge difference in my life outlook. (Sadly, for me and millions of Americans in a similar situation, in 2017 forces in Washington went to work to attempt to strip this right from all of us.)

A friend of mine from high school who became a doctor gave me a piece of advice. He said, "Run as hard as you can for as long as you can." He knew of the punishing schedule I kept. He basically advised me to live my life for as long as I could. So, to keep MS from taking me down mentally, I keep myself on the run.

* * * * *

Not being slowed down by MS was critical to me. I decided that there was no reason not to run for the IOC Executive Board. The election for the position on the Executive Board was held at the IOC session in Barcelona in 1992. Several positions were open. I stood for the position to complete the one-year term of office that Bob Helmick had vacated and succeeded in being elected. (When I completed that term, I then ran for a full four-year term and was re-elected.)

At that time, and until the changes in the year 2000, there were 11 members on the Executive Board: six regular members, four vice presidents, and the IOC president. Reforms were voted in place in 2000, increasing the Executive Board to 15 members. One athlete, one person representing the summer sport International Federations, one person representing the winter sport International Federations and one person representing the NOCs may be elected to the Executive Board, though the election of all is left to the discretion of a particular IOC Session.

Being elected to the IOC Executive Board provided me with a larger platform within the IOC to advocate for issues that mattered the most to me, beginning with bringing equality to the Olympic Games.

Chapter Eighteen
The Push for Olympic Equality

I have long believed that sport is an exclusively human endeavor, and that participation in sport is a birthright. It was one I had been denied until I reached Connecticut College, so it was natural for me to work on behalf of women in the Olympic Movement. After our 1994 Centennial Congress in Paris, President Juan Antonio Samaranch asked me to work on ways to move the Olympic Movement toward equality. As the first president to have women elected to IOC membership, he was certainly the right man to be promoting women.

It was not until 1996, however, that the IOC charter included rules mandating that members of the Olympic Movement "encourage and support the promotion of women in sport at all levels and in all structures with a view to implementing the principle of equality of men and women." Even as the IOC moved to promote gender equality, it was clear that it would need leadership to make that a reality. For me, this was a priority.

Joining the IOC Executive Board provided me with the opportunity to focus on bringing the Olympic Movement into the twentieth century by ensuring an equal number of events for female as well as male athletes. Given that I was only the fifth woman ever elected to the IOC, and the second to the Executive Board, I had no illusions that this was going to be easy. At the same time, looking back, I had no idea how hard it would be.

* * * * *

The physical strength of women has long been known. In ancient carvings and pictures, women are depicted playing sports. If you look back into the far reaches of history, it is not radical at all to think of women as athletes. The dilemma over the millennia and into modern day is allowing us to have the same opportunities as men to compete. Sport is a human endeavor and thus applies to all of us.

At the first modern Olympic Games, held in Athens in 1896, no women were permitted to compete, but a woman named Kalipetria came to Athens with the intention of running the marathon. Officials told her that the entry had closed. Nevertheless, she ran the course the following day, and her time stood up well against some of the men.

Women's competitions were included at the 1900 Paris Games, limited to the sports of tennis and golf. After the French woman, Alice Milliat, hosted track and field competitions that drew crowds numbering 20,000, the International Association of Athletics Federations decided to include a few track events for women at the 1928 Amsterdam Olympic Games.

Then, as now, the International Olympic Committee looks to the International Federations to request the events they want to have contested at the Olympic Games. The problem was, 99.9 percent of the sports administration was male — and it seemed they preferred to keep it that way.

The IOC did not openly promote steps toward equality until its Centennial Congress in 1994, but as women moved into every arena of human endeavor, visible opportunity in sport could not be denied.

It is well known that Pierre de Coubertin, the first IOC president and founder of the modern Olympic movement, was quoted as saying that including women would be "impractical, uninteresting, unaesthetic, and incorrect." He also said, "Woman's glory rightfully came through the number and quality of children she produced, and that where sports were concerned, her greatest accomplishment was to encourage her sons to excel rather than to seek records for herself."

Surprisingly, while he maintained his position against women in competition, he did not ask the IOC to prohibit women from competing in the Olympic Games. Before the 1912 Stockholm Olympic Games, de Coubertin received a letter from the International Federation for Equestrian Sports stating that a woman wanted to compete. His response was, "Well, women are doing everything else in the world, so why should we be surprised at this?"

* * * * *

As was the case since becoming an IOC member, I spoke up at executive board meetings, starting with my very first one in 1992. IOC President Samaranch appreciated my participation and my ideas, which led to him giving me increasingly challenging tasks to accomplish, opportunities I welcomed.

Samaranch was a master at getting done what he felt needed to be done, and I learned a great deal from him in that regard. Before he was even an IOC member, in 1965 he had written an article that appeared in the *Olympic Review* magazine. He stressed the importance of having the International Federations involved with the IOC, and the IOC, in turn, constantly interacting with the National Olympic Committees. Not surprisingly, he was elected to the IOC the following year.

Samaranch rose to the presidency in 1980 just as the U.S. was boycotting the Moscow Olympic Games, a tricky time, to say the least. Part of Samaranch's campaign for president was his promise to elect women to the IOC as a path to putting more women's sports on the program and engaging more women in executive roles. His predecessor, Lord Killanin, had tried to elect Dr. Tenley Albright, an American gold medalist in figure skating, to the IOC, but she preferred to dedicate her time to her practice as a neurosurgeon.

President Samaranch was committed to the election of women to serve on the IOC and increasing the number of women's Olympic sports. After the 1981 Olympic Congress in Baden-Baden, Germany, during the session that followed, he nominated the first two women who became IOC members, Pirgo Hagmen, an Olympian from Finland, and Flor Isava Fonseca from Venezuela, who was deeply involved with equestrian sport.

IOC members are usually nominated by their National Olympic Committee and supported by a current IOC member, typically from their home country. But Samaranch gave me the authority to nominate women from anywhere in the world, thereby bypassing traditional, slow-moving protocol that mandated the NOC from that country make the nomination.

I began nominating women in 1992, and in the coming years several were elected. But because many countries are not as free and progressive as the U.S., women faced extreme pressures at home merely for serving on the IOC. Take the case of Nawal El Moutawakel of Morocco. The year she was elected, the man who had expected to become an IOC member was the General of the Moroccan Army, someone you would want to be your friend in 1998 in a country where women's equality was in its nascent form. But she took on the risk and accepted the IOC position. She has been a very successful IOC member and was eventually elected to her national parliament.

* * * * *

One of the first things I had noticed in the Olympic Village at the 1976 Games was how men overwhelmingly outnumbered women. Baby steps to remedy the gender gap were taking place. That year saw the addition of women's rowing — otherwise I couldn't have competed. For the first time that year, women's basketball was also on the program. Nevertheless, in the 1976 Montreal Games and the Olympic Winter Games, women comprised only 21 percent of the athletes.

More troubling was the slow rate of increase over time. At the 1928 Amsterdam Games and the St. Moritz Winter Games, 10 percent of the athletes were women. By the 1960 Games, only 20 percent were women — meaning that it had taken almost 50 years to double women's participation. From that point forward, we would have expected better progress, but that was not the case. In the 16 years from 1960 to 1976, there was a pitiful 1-percent increase.

There was also a lack of women being elected to the IOC. In 1976, there weren't any. When I was elected to the IOC in 1986, I became just the fifth woman to serve. The first two IOC female members had come on board in 1981. The first woman, Flor Isara Fonseca of Venezuela, was elected to the IOC Executive Board in 1990; I was the second in 1992.

A move to increase the number of women's events to reach parity with the men's was also in motion. In 2000, the IOC took a positive step in that direction by mandating that any new sport seeking to be added on the Olympic program had to include events for both men and women.

After the 1992 Barcelona Olympic Games, which ended up with more athletes than planned for, the IOC implemented a rule capping the number of athletes who could compete in each sport. The International Federations for each sport then had to decide how those spots were filled. The rule, which applied to men and women, was the beginning of pushing federations to enter more women — even if it meant taking away a men's spot.

I was constantly pushing the IOC to add new sports for women. My first step was to become a member of the program commission, which was responsible for reviewing the sports, disciplines and events on the program.

At the first meeting I attended, I brought up softball. Before I was an IOC member, softball was supposed to come on board at the same time that baseball was added to the program. I didn't know what the discussions had been, or the rationale for not putting softball on for the women at the time baseball came on for the men.

So I spoke up, saying regardless of how the slight had happened, we needed to correct the situation. "If we have baseball for men, we must have softball for women," I said. "It's a similar game, not exactly the same, but similar. Let's make this right."

I repeated this rationale at every meeting. It reached that point that when I started to speak, the committee chairman, Vitali Smirnov, would say, "Okay Anita, we know you want softball…anything else?"

In fact, there was. I also wanted women's soccer.

A collaborative effort, including the Atlanta organizing committee, succeeded in bringing both women's softball and soccer on the program for the 1996 Atlanta Olympic Games. As a token of their appreciation for my effort, the International Softball Federation awarded me their medal of honor in June of 1995. I was honored and happy to have helped, but the truth was, no significant change ever happens because of one person's work.

* * * * *

One of the critical aspects to reaching equality was bringing together the entire women's sports movement to support change from the ground up so that the IOC could support it from the top down. Before the 1990s, efforts of promoting women in sport in the U.S. and across the world were only loosely unified.

Ironically, in the U.S., throughout the century of struggle for women's rights, sport was not fully championed. I never understood why. There were discussions about women in all areas of society — except on the importance of us taking part in sport. For whatever reason, leaders of the women's movement did not seem to understand the significance of taking part in team sports and did not consider it something worthy of putting on their agenda of barriers that needed to be removed. I was (and remain) friends with many of these leaders, but I failed to convince them to advocate for women in sport, except sporadically, such as when Title IX was implemented.

Interestingly, Title IX (introduced in 1972 by women's rights crusader Senator Birch Bayh, one of the few reasonable politicians to come out of Indiana in my lifetime) was passed as an Educational Amendment Act designed to promote women in academia. During its entire legislative history, sport was only mentioned once as an educational opportunity, but it did force colleges to provide equal opportunities in sports for women.

I like to say this was an evolutionary, but not revolutionary, idea. As people began to recognize sports as an educational opportunity, it made a noticeable difference in our culture. Today boys and girls think it is quite normal for both sexes to be active in sports, but that was certainly not the case in my youth.

Women's participation numbers have climbed exponentially. From 1966-2001, the number of women taking part in intercollegiate college athletics jumped from 16,000 to more than 150,000 — almost 10 times. This pushed up the high school numbers as well. From 1971-2001, the number of girls playing varsity sports in high school jumped from less than 295,000, or roughly 7 percent, to 2.8 million, or 41 percent.

During this time, we also began to learn that women involved in sport are far more likely to land a job right out of college because of it. I have always believed that sport is an essential part of the fabric of our nation in teaching people about competition, about working together, and about having common goals even though we may not have common approaches to life.

Sport is the crucible in which men have always been expected to take part to learn those lessons of life, but for a long time, women were largely excluded. As a child, I never understood why I could not do what my brothers did in the world of sport. It just seemed plain wrong to little Anita.

Much of the task for promoting women's sports in the U.S. was taken up by the creation of the Women's Sports Foundation. Tennis pioneer Billie Jean King founded the organization in 1974, two years after the passage of Title IX, declaring, "We have to do something to support girls and women in sport."

The idea she launched grew into a formidable presence with a $1 million endowment under Executive Director Eva Auchincloss (1976-1986). Auchincloss enlisted passionate women athletes, including Olympians Donna de Varona and Suzy Chaffee, to fulfill and expand the initial mission of getting women to participate in sports. Donna was significant in leading the charge, especially in the U.S. Congress. The foundation, with the passage of Title IX of the Education Opportunity Act, has certainly been a driving force in supporting organized women's and girls' sports activities.

Over the years, I have worked with the Women's Sports Foundation on various initiatives. The National Women's Law Center was integral in handling legal challenges on behalf of girls and women denied opportunities to take part in sport. I also felt that it was critical to reach out and include all the organizations supporting women in sports, and bring them together with the National Olympic Committees and International Sports Federations. We needed their input about how to increase Olympic participation, thus allowing the IOC to advocate around the world for women in sport.

To help achieve these goals and open an international dialogue, President Samaranch gave me the responsibility of leading the IOC Women and Sport Working Group, a group that would both study the issues and advocate for equality.

At the 1994 "Centennial Olympic Congress: Congress of Unity," we discussed many topics in the area of women and sport. Afterwards, I was appointed to the study group that was asked to make recommendations regarding women and sport. While the field of play in sports was slowly inching toward equality, for sustainable change, women would need to be in policy-making roles as well.

In December 1995, the IOC Women and Sport Working Group was established, and I was named chair. The group would advise and make recommendations to the IOC President and the IOC Executive Board to work across the policy-making spectrum and ensure the equality of women in sport. My goal for the working group was to put itself out of existence by achieving full equality. Only later did I realize that was a mistake: The group needed to be a formal commission with the authority to change policy.

* * * * *

The first major act of business for the IOC Women and Sport Working Group was to schedule and administer a quadrennial World Conference on Women and Sport, which would make recommendations to the IOC Executive Board in all areas of equality in the Olympic Movement. The stated objectives of the conference were "to create awareness about women's role in sport; assess the progress made in the area of gender equality in sport; and define future priority actions to promote women in sport."

To some, these seemed like bureaucratic moves, but I felt that engaging a large sector of those concerned with women in sport directly with the IOC was the only way to begin to address all the issues and long-standing biases. I chaired the first conference, which was held in 1996 in Lausanne at the recently-opened Olympic Museum.

I developed a long-term strategy. At the time, many people were saying, What do women know about high-level sport? My idea was to start working with the International Federations to increase the number of women Olympians and use them to grow the number of women executives. Once a woman had competed in the Olympic Games, the strategy was, no one could say that she did not understand the world of sports. After all, that had been my admission to the Olympic world.

Conference participants included members of the IOC, representatives of the NOCs, representatives of the IFs and athletic advocates, both men and women. The only way the long-term plan could be realized would be to have men and women working together.

One issue we took up at the first conference was gender verification. Gender verification was initially implemented at the 1968 Mexico City Olympic Games. The men in charge of the IOC felt that it was essential. In that era, the Olympic Games were often the first international competition for many of the athletes, as most sports did not have international competitions. This meant that the first time these athletes were seen on an international stage was at the Olympic Games. At that time, the East Germans and potentially other nations were entering men, cleverly disguised as women, in the women's events. Later, we noticed that women athletes from certain countries seemed abnormally capable, and learned that that was the result of steroid use and other performance-enhancing drugs. At the 1976 Montreal Olympic Games, chromosome screening was implemented for all women. I went through the humiliating testing and was rewarded with a card confirming that I am a woman.

The IOC acted on the conference's recommendation to end gender verification. Starting with the 2000 Olympic Games, there was no longer sweeping gender verification at the Games. A new set of rules was drawn up so that not just anybody could point a finger at an athlete and say, "I don't think she is a woman, test her."

The new rules allowed for a NOC to request a test before an individual competed so that a medal would be not later withdrawn. This testing procedure assisted mostly small nations where people were not born in hospitals and a child's parents could designate their sex. These rules were also put in place to ensure that no woman would be maligned by accusations that she is not the sex she intended to compete as. And in the event that an anomaly arose in the testing, the IOC would never disclose the individual's name.

The first conference also brought about significant steps and tangible reforms on women's involvement in the Olympic Movement. By 2001, the International Federations and National Olympic Committees recommended that their Executive Boards would be comprised of at least 10 percent women by 2001 and 20 percent by 2005, and would create a women's sport committee "to design and implement a plan of action to promote women in sport." This move was intended to begin bringing more women into the executive ranks of these organizations. The Olympic Charter was amended to include a specific reference to improving women's participation.

At the conclusion of the 1996 conference, we issued a set of goals to be completed over the next four years which we would use to evaluate progress when we reconvened. Some resolutions, such as hiring more women at the NOC level, were initiatives that were beyond the scope of the IOC's ability to enact them by fiat. Participants needed to take these back to their NOCs to consider and implement. Even so, the IOC could state its goals and use its influence to push the members of the Olympic Family to take action.

For me, the 1996 conference was a high point in my first 10 years as an IOC member. The following year, I was elected the first woman IOC vice president. I planned on using this platform to push even harder for equality in sport, and to put more women on the IOC. A higher profile for me meant that a voice for women in the Olympic Movement would be heard more clearly.

Chapter Nineteen
The Olympic Movement is Compromised

As much as I love the Olympic Movement and respect the IOC members, for better or worse we are human. So while I felt helpless — and even somewhat hapless at times — I knew that my job was to ensure that the Olympic Movement endured and flourished. In good times and bad, that has always kept me moving forward.

The first time many people in the U.S. paid attention to the International Olympic Committee came in 1999. Despite the IOC's 100-plus year history and all the good it had done for sport worldwide — keeping the Olympic flame burning through two World Wars, the Cold War, and countless geopolitical upheavals around the globe — the organization hit the radar of many people as a group of corrupt, insular, self-serving cheats. As is often the case, this was the result of the poor choices and unethical behavior made by a few individuals.

The IOC was thrust into the U.S. media headlines when the Salt Lake City television station KTVX broke the news on November 24, 1998 that the Salt Lake Olympic Organizing Committee had paid the college tuition of Sonia Essomba, the daughter of an IOC member. The TV station obtained a letter addressed to Ms. Essomba from Dave Johnson, a former state economic development professional and the SLOC's senior vice president, stating that they could not continue the "scholarship program" and that the last payment for her tuition was enclosed. The reason given was that the Salt Lake City bid committee was shifting to an organizing committee, but the question was, Why was the Salt Lake City bid committee sending a tuition check to an IOC member's relative to begin with?

This nugget, it turned out, was only the beginning of what became a great many gifts given by the Salt Lake City bid committee to IOC members in what appeared to be an attempt to encourage their votes. The giving of gifts had started before the IOC had awarded the Salt Lake City bid committee the 2002 Olympic Winter Games in 1995, and it appeared to continue after the bid committee became an organizing committee.

As an IOC member, I was automatically placed on the organizing committee of Games taking place in my home country. In a complicated twist, I later learned through a change in the bylaws that I was also a member of the bid committee, though no one told me. Stranger still, there was no requirement to notify me of meetings.

When I first heard about the letter through news reports, I immediately phoned Dave Johnson. He reassured me that there was nothing to worry about, because this was a scholarship that had been awarded to the young woman.

As a trustee at my *alma mater*, Connecticut College, I was very familiar with scholarships. Students and their parents applied for them and after consideration of financial status were accepted. I assumed that this was the case and that the bid committee had helped facilitate the granting of the scholarship. As bad as the news looked, it didn't appear that the Salt Lake City bid committee had attempted to "buy" the vote of an IOC member — but it never crossed my mind the bid committee was directly paying the tuition.

Shortly after the first story broke, it was reported that Salt Lake City bid committee had awarded additional "scholarships" to relatives of IOC members totaling some $400,000. The IOC daughter who had received the letter had, in fact, been given more than $100,000 in college tuition, first by the bid committee and then by the SLOC.

But the scholarships were just the tip of the iceberg. Within weeks, reports surfaced that IOC members had taken numerous financial gifts, in the form of travel, medical care, jobs, and even sweetheart investment deals from the Salt Lake City bid committee in an apparent effort to secure their votes for the 2002 Games.

For the next year, the scandal engulfed the IOC. It spawned investigations by the SLOC, the United States Olympic Committee, the IOC, and the U.S. Department of Justice, as well as two congressional hearings. As the story unfolded, it threatened to undermine the entire process of awarding the Olympic Games, as well as the future of the IOC's authority over the Olympic Movement. As one of the two Americans on the IOC, and as a member of the SLOC and the USOC, I was right in the middle.

* * * * *

The issue with Salt Lake City began in 1985 when Salt Lake City attempted to become the American candidate city for the 1994 Olympic Winter Games, but the USOC gave Anchorage, which had been the U.S. city for the 1992 Olympic Winter Games, a second chance to bid. (For the first time in Olympic history, the Olympic Winter Games were held two years apart, because the IOC had decided to alternate the summer and winter Games at two-year intervals. In the past, both the summer and winter Games were held in the same year.)

Salt Lake City had been on a quest to land the Olympic Winter Games from 1985 through 1995. This effort was led by Tom Welch, an attorney, and Dave Johnson. Over those years, the two traveled to Europe, Africa, Asia, and Latin America to meet with members of International Federations and IOC members.

Despite the fact that Salt Lake City had lost out to Anchorage in the USOC vote, Johnson and Welch would turn up at IOC meetings in Lausanne, presumably to lobby IOC members for some future Games. They were being introduced to IOC members by Alfredo LaMont, the director of international relations for the USOC, who was a friend of mine.

This behavior was totally inappropriate. It meant that the USOC had bid committees at an IOC meeting from two American cities, one of which was not even in the running for the 1994 Games. At best, it was confusing to IOC members, and at worst, it was unfair to Anchorage. I pulled Alfredo aside and told him that Johnson and Welch had to leave.

Anchorage ended up losing the 1994 Games to Lillehammer, Norway. Both Salt Lake City and Anchorage tried again to be the American candidate city for the 1998 Olympic Winter Games. This time, the USOC selected Salt Lake City over Anchorage, which wanted to bid for a third time. The circumstances of that USOC voting process were somewhat odd.

The first ballot ended with Salt Lake City and Anchorage tied. After the second vote, USOC President Bob Helmick, who was also an IOC member, announced that Salt Lake City had won, but the results were never shown to the Anchorage members. Given Helmick's soon-to-be-discovered unethical behavior that led him to eventually to resign the presidency, it seems, in retrospect, that there was something fishy about the result.

But America likes winners and discards losers, so Salt Lake City took the American mantle and moved on to bid against Nagano, Japan; Ostersund, Sweden; Jaca, Spain; and Aosta, Italy for the right to host 1998 Olympic Winter Games. The vote was taken seven years in advance of the Games at the 1991 IOC Session in Birmingham, England.

The IOC vote went five rounds and came down to Salt Lake City and Nagano. Looking at the two bids side by side, Salt Lake City's was the stronger bid. The village of Nagano was hard to reach in the mountains, whereas Salt Lake City was a major city with an international airport. This meant that athletes from around the world would be able to train there. Because of the dominance of the Mormon faith, Salt Lake City also had an international flair. In their efforts to bring more people into the faith, the Mormons went on missions around the world, resulting in people from many different cultures coming to Salt Lake City.

But there were some hijinks at the 1991 IOC Session that should have raised red flags. The four bidding cities were inviting IOC members to dinners. I was invited to a dinner hosted by the Nagano bid committee, which started with a presentation about the bid and ended with a formal tea service. One by one, I noticed that many IOC members were invited out of the room for a period of 15 to 20 minutes. Although I wondered what those sidebar meetings were all about, I never found out because I was not invited out of the room.

Nagano also had a confidante of IOC President Juan Antonio Samaranch lobbying IOC members. This member was telling IOC members that Samaranch favored Nagano over Salt Lake City, which was totally improper. When Tom Welch told me, I insisted that we take the issue to Samaranch. We did, at which point Samaranch insisted that the man write a letter saying that he did not have the authority to represent the president's wishes, and told the man he needed to apologize.

The vote came down to the fifth and final ballot, with only Salt Lake City and Nagano remaining. In a bitter defeat, Salt Lake City lost the 1998 Olympic Winter Games to Nagano by a vote of 46-42. Rightly, the Salt Lake City contingent was upset. They were convinced that Nagano had undermined their efforts by providing perks to IOC members and by pressuring IOC members to vote for them. This turned out to be true. The Japanese media later reported that the Nagano bid committee had spent an average of $22,000 per IOC member on travel and gifts for 62 IOC members.

After losing to Nagano, the leaders of the Salt Lake City bid committee decided take a page out of Nagano's playbook in their quest for the 2002 Games and began what turned out to be a corrupt effort to influence the votes of IOC members. In the end, the Salt Lake City bid committee ended up spending a total of $16 million on the bid, including paying for 70 of the 100 IOC members to visit Salt Lake City. The decision was made by a few members of the committee who executed the plan and did not share it with the entire committee.

One issue that must be understood is that many IOC members wanted — and even expected — to be treated like royalty. The IOC had members whose parents had been leaders of their countries and had been showered with gifts all of their lives. Unfortunately, that sense of entitlement had stayed with them.

Early on, I decided to accept nothing from bid cities, rather than try to decide what was reasonable and what was not. I made my decision after I visited a bid city in Europe. The visit came on a stopover en route to another destination. The bid city offered to pay for any increase in my airfare. I told them that I didn't think there would be any, but I would let them know. I made the trip, but forgot about the conversation. When I left the bid city, I was handed a wrapped present that I didn't open until I got home. It turned out to be a box with cash inside. I had my assistant count the money, and I mailed a check for the full amount, telling them politely that there had been no cost to my stopover.

Gifts were always destined to be an issue with some IOC members. In different cultures, it is important to give gifts to visitors, frequently in the poorest nations. So for Americans to decry this was a misunderstanding of these international cultures. That said, college tuition was outside the boundaries of most people's ethics — though clearly not everyone's.

But with the Salt Lake City revelations, the issue of bid cities providing gifts and trips to IOC members had to be dealt with head on, or the IOC would be in danger of losing all of its credibility.

* * * * *

Weeks after the story broke, at a previously scheduled Executive Board meeting on December 12, we set up an *ad hoc* commission to conduct our own investigation into the allegations. Because I was from the U.S. and on the SLOC, I, of course, could not be on the commission; in fact, I was investigated by the *ad hoc* commission, and asked to present my knowledge, such that it was, of the situation. I told them the truth, that I was astonished by the charges, and could never imagine a bid committee offering scholarships. It turned out that I had no idea of the depth of the problems at that time.

At that Executive Board meeting, a bizarre and ultimately damaging situation also unfolded involving Marc Hodler, an Executive Board member who led the IOC's coordination committee overseeing the organization of the 2002 Games. Hodler was taking pain killers for a recent surgery on the day of the meeting. This was rare for him, as he was the consummate Swiss outdoorsman.

As a result, he was a little bit off his game and gave an interview to the news media that fanned the scandal's flames. He began talking about corruption in his federation and the bribes that had been offered during the bidding process for the 1990 and 1996 Skiing World Championships and then he went on to describe the bidding for the Olympic Winter Games. The media believed that he was talking about the IOC and the recent scandal.

While Hodler was meeting with the press, the IOC Executive Board was meeting to figure out how to progress and what the next steps should be, while the media was detailing stories of widespread corruption. Our mission is always to save and protect the Olympic movement. We formed a commission led by Dick Pound, a Canadian who was an IOC vice president, to investigate the Salt Lake City allegations and any other corruption in the bidding process. His work resulted in the Pound Report made to the IOC.

By January 1999, some six weeks after the first story broke, four separate investigations into Salt Lake City's bid for the 2002 Olympic Winter Games had been launched — by the U.S. Department of Justice, the IOC, the USOC (led by former Senator George Mitchell), and the SLOC Board of Ethics.

Before any of the investigations could even get underway, both Tom Welch and Dave Johnson resigned their posts. Their resignations were followed shortly by Frank Joklik, the chair of the SLOC board, and Craig Petersen, the SLOC chief executive officer.

The IOC Executive Board met again from January 23-25. Pound had found that at least a dozen IOC members or their relatives had received cash, gifts, or other enticements from boosters or organizers of the Salt Lake City Games. Two IOC members had already resigned. Six members were suspended pending a final vote on their possible expulsion at an extraordinary IOC Session scheduled for March, as every IOC member has the right to defend themselves against allegations.

The IOC standard for members to remain in good standing is that members cannot embarrass the IOC with their actions. It is not a question of criminality, because the IOC has no powers of investigation under the law and cannot pursue criminal or civil penalties, but rather a question of responsibly discharging one's duties ethically and upholding the Olympic Charter. Undoubtedly, if these members had accepted the gifts being reported from the Salt Lake City bid committee, they had embarrassed the IOC.

The SLOC Board of Ethics report was issued on February 8. It detailed widespread payments to IOC members, including $108,350 in educational expenses for Sonia Essomba, the revelation that began the scandal. The most egregious, however, was the largest extended to Jean Claude Ganga from the Republic of Congo.

Ganga had accepted numerous trips to Salt Lake City for him and his family. During his visits, the Salt Lake City bid committee had paid for him to be treated for hepatitis, for his mother-in-law to undergo knee replacement surgery, and for his wife to have cosmetic surgery. In all, he accepted travel expenses worth more than $115,000. Ganga was also involved in business ventures with bid committee members, and had made a $60,000 profit on a land deal. Other payments to him totaled more than $70,000.

This was entirely unacceptable behavior for an IOC member, and was certainly an embarrassment to the Olympic Movement.

The next shoe to drop, although a much smaller one, nearly landed on me. On March 1, Senator Mitchell's report commissioned by the USOC, dubbed the Mitchell Report, was released. A member of the investigative team had interviewed me and asked me about gifts I had received from bid committees. I told them that I had not received any gifts. In the report, they referenced a "fur coat" I had been given while volunteering for the Anchorage bid committee. This pushed the bounds of the absurd.

The jacket I had received, along with the other bid committee members and volunteers, was a cloth coat that had a hood trimmed in coyote fur. Estimated value by the president of the Anchorage bid committee: $45. Had they bothered in their investigation to call the bid committee and talk with the CEO, he would have given them that number. Yet they wrote in their report that I had received a "fur" coat, an altogether different implication. I was irritated that they were conducting an investigation of me without following up, particularly in such an accusatory climate. Further, the USOC never sent me a copy of the Mitchell Report commissioned by the USOC, despite the fact that I requested it several times.

* * * * *

The IOC took its first action in March 1999. An extraordinary session was called to review the Pound Report commissioned by the IOC and adjudicate the cases of those accused of sullying our reputation. By this time, the negative media coverage of the IOC was piling up.

The IOC Executive Board met first. After reviewing the Pound Report, we recommended expelling six IOC members, including Ganga. One had already resigned, and three others under investigation would eventually resign. Nine others were investigated and given warnings. Three members who had been investigated were eventually cleared. We also recommended the IOC implement sweeping reforms so that this would not happen again.

It turned out that these six expelled IOC members had accepted thousands of dollars in travel and other incentives from the Toronto bid committee in 1990 when the city was bidding for the 1996 Games, which ultimately were awarded to Atlanta. The fact that they were recidivists made the decision to remove them a bit easier.

During Toronto's bid, the committee's chairman, Paul Henderson, who was also president of the International Sailing Federation, had revealed that there were IOC members who had misbehaved by either demanding or accepting support, but he refused to name names. He claimed that the volunteers supporting the bid were afraid they could be sued. I thought that was highly unlikely.

Just before the misdeeds of Bob Helmick became public, I wrote a note to the IOC president suggesting that he set up an ethics committee so that he didn't personally have to do a review of the members. That suggestion went nowhere until the Salt Lake City scandal broke.

Another irony was that Dick Pound, the person investigating the Salt Lake City bid scandal, knew the names of those who had taken the graft from the Toronto bid committee. He had access to information about behavior embarrassing to the IOC at that time. Had he reported those members, we may never have ended up in the Salt Lake City mess.

Alas, there we were.

It appeared that the nexus of the trouble were all those visits by IOC members to the host cities. Most countries have a national air carrier. The U.S. does not have one. This led to the Salt Lake City bid committee to spend hundreds of thousands of dollars bringing IOC members to the city. Host cities had been selected from 1896 to 1985 without visits from IOC members and without gifts exchanging hands. A change to this policy had been innocently made at the 1985 IOC Session in Berlin. A member asked if it would be alright to make a visit to a candidate city, and the response was, "Why not?" The first time IOC members visited a bid city was in 1985 and 1986 for the 1992 Games.

On paper, it made sense for members to visit the cities and evaluate them before voting. But some IOC members spent more time touring a city, rather than visiting and evaluating potential Olympic venues.

I understood how you put the Games together, as I had worked on the LA Olympic Organizing Committee and been part of Anchorage's bid committee. When I visited a city, I wanted to know about the technical issues. For me, it was important to know how the athletes would be treated, and there were a lot of questions to be answered in that area. I also wanted to know how the Olympic Movement would be treated as a whole. And then I wanted to know how the Games would affect the city.

Under each of those headlines, I had a number of questions. Often committee members wanted to take me to dinner or other events. I would typically be in a city for a day or maybe a day and a half, so I wasn't interested in being entertained. I wanted to be polite, but I had very precise things I was looking for. I preferred to be able to do things on my own to get a feel for the city.

The only way to stop those IOC members who were now abusing the privilege and accepting free trips from bid committees was to implement a rule that IOC members cannot visit a candidate city at the invitation of the bid committee. If a member travels to that city in the normal course of events, they would no longer be allowed to contact the bid committee while they were there or to accept any gifts or travel perks for the trip.

To implement further reforms, two new commissions were formed at the extraordinary session, the IOC Ethics Commission and the IOC 2000 Commission. The ethics commission would be composed of senior members of nations from around the world, including former Senator Howard Baker, and charged with enforcing the new ethics rules. The IOC 2000 Commission was given the task of reforming the structure of the Olympic Movement. This commission would be composed of 82 members, 13 of whom were IOC members.

Though the perception issues would take years to fix — if they ever could be — I was encouraged that we were taking the necessary steps to reset the IOC back to its original mission, of protecting and advancing the Olympic Movement.

* * * * *

The IOC's reputation in the U.S. was tainted by negative publicity from the Salt Lake City scandal. After the release of the Mitchell Report, the Senate Commerce Committee held a hearing on the scandal on April 14, 1999. I was among those asked to testify by Senator John McCain, the committee chairman, along with Jim Easton, the other American member of the IOC.

Easton had been elected to the IOC in 1994 and walked into a buzzsaw. Prior to that, he had been (and remained) president of the World Archery Federation. He ran a family-owned aluminum manufacturing company that specialized in camping equipment, some sports equipment, and famously, arrows for archery. I had known him since 1981. He was a longtime friend of Peter Ueberroth. Both of them had their business headquarters on the same street.

Easton's company had a manufacturing hub in Utah, where he also maintained a ski condo. He had been asked by the Salt Lake City bid committee to help them by offering his condo for IOC member visits, which he had done until he became an IOC member. So while he had technically done nothing wrong, there may have been an appearance of impropriety.

Senator McCain also invited a journalist named Andrew Jennings, a detractor of the IOC and critic of Samaranch. Former Senator Mitchell testified at the hearing, as did USOC President Bill Hybl. The Senate committee asked Samaranch to appear, but he declined.

Senator McCain took direct aim at Easton and me, as the two U.S. IOC members. Easton struggled to answer questions, as he had never been in such a hot seat before. While I had lots of practice, things weren't all that much easier for me.

When the Senate hearing was called to order, the senators made their presentations about the scandal and lambasted the IOC. Senator Fritz Hollings called for Samaranch to be fired. "What are y'all waiting for?" Hollings asked. "Why not get rid of Samaranch?"

McCain was annoyed that Samaranch didn't appear. When McCain asked me about his absence, I replied, "English is his fourth language," which predictably did not go over well.

Much of the focus was on the Mitchell Commission's recommendations to the IOC. These included term limits and periodic re-election for IOC members, disallowing any country that does not sign an international treaty against bribery from being the host of an Olympic Games, allowing access to all financial records, and requiring IOC members to pay for their own trips to candidate cities. A version of all of these recommendations were already under consideration by the IOC.

Senator McCain was annoyed that the IOC hadn't already acted on these recommendations. I explained that the IOC was in the process of reviewing them, but that it would take time because we were an international organization that met once a year, not every week like congressional committees. I assured him that the IOC would take up the suggestions at the next session in June.

Though not entirely satisfied with my answer, Senator McCain moved on and pressed me on several other issues. At one point, he asked me how I was sure that funds from the IOC earmarked for the various federations actually reached the athletes. I told him we didn't know for certain if they did, which further irked him.

What I should have said was that I would get back to him with specifics. The day before, I had been in one of the offices of the IOC's attorneys and seen copies of the biannual report, which had been released for the first time. I thought, I should take one of those with me, but I didn't. The report was hard to decipher because it was done with international principles of accounting, but it might have mollified McCain.

He also harped on why the minutes of IOC sessions were embargoed from release for 10 years and Executive Board minutes for 30 years. I explained that the policy allowed people who reside in more treacherous countries to voice opinions without the fear of repercussions from their governments. What I could have added was that the Red Cross embargoes its minutes for 50 years.

Oddly, after Jennings, the journalist, had testified, the only senator left in the room was Senator McCain. Thus, for anyone watching from outside of the room, it looked that Senator McCain was truly grilling the U.S. IOC members. But had he not continued to ask questions, the hearing would have been over.

The hearing was well-covered in the press. Most of the stories were decidedly negative toward the IOC, following the general pattern after such hearings. Referring to the treatment of the panel's aggression toward Easton and me, *The New York Times* wrote in part, "...members of a Senate committee harshly reprimanded two United States members of the International Olympic Committee today for a 'culture of corruption.'"

The U.S. Congress seemed intent on taking full control of the situation and trying to punish the IOC with legislation. Senator Ted Stevens proposed to limit the IOC's tax-exempt status in the U.S. and to shift control of all TV payments in the U.S. from the IOC to the USOC. On the House side, Rep. Henry Waxman, who was my congressman, had introduced a bill to prohibit U.S. corporations and individuals from providing financial support to the IOC until it fully adopted the Mitchell Commission recommendations.

Much of this was grandstanding, because the U.S. Congress does not have jurisdiction over the IOC. While the USOC was chartered by Congress, the IOC is a Swiss association. But the IOC was obviously on the defensive, and Congress seemed intent on using the circumstances to pressure the IOC.

Weeks after the hearing, I was called back to Washington. My attorney told me that they wanted to interview me further because they felt that I had not expounded on my answers to their questions. So I returned to Washington.

The committee had done its homework. During the meeting, one of the attorneys said that they had examined all of my USOC records from the Salt Lake City and Atlanta bid committees and discovered only two times when I had accepted anything that could be construed as a gift. Once was in Atlanta when I neglected to pay a $2.15 phone bill. The other time was in Salt Lake City, when I accepted a milkshake without paying for it.

When I heard this, I laughed. "If the milkshake was chocolate, I plead guilty," I said.

The U.S. House Commerce Subcommittee on Oversight and Investigation held its hearing on October, 14, 1999. It had requested an investigation into Atlanta's bid for the 1996 Olympic Games. Headed by former Attorney General Griffin Bell, the investigation found instances of gifts given to IOC members, including 38 that exceeded the IOC limit of

$200. It was also revealed the Atlanta bid committee kept a dossier on every IOC member to track how they might be pressured. The report concluded, "This is not a corrupt system, but it is subject to abuse."

President Samaranch testified before the House Committee. Former Senator Howard Baker, who had been named to the newly-formed IOC Ethics Commission, also testified. I attended the hearing, as did Dick Pound, who headed up the IOC commission investigating the Salt Lake City scandal.

The House committee expressed skepticism over the proposed IOC reforms that were to be presented to the full IOC in December. One member asked Samaranch to resign on the spot, an increasingly popular move among congressmen. Many of the committee's questions were ridiculous. Another member wondered if they trusted Samaranch to initiate the reforms, and what would happen when he stepped down as president. Samaranch replied, "You know, congressman, cemeteries are filled with irreplaceable people."

Baker, an old Washington hand at dealing with congressional committees, eased the tension by vouching for the proposed reforms. "While I was initially skeptical about whether the IOC would undertake serious ethical and structural reforms in a fairly short period of time, it is now my distinct impression that the IOC — its leader and its members — fully recognize the need to restore the Movement's credibility," the former Senator said. That was about as positive an endorsement as the IOC could hope for at that point.

* * * * *

The IOC met again in an extraordinary session on December 11-12, 1999 to vote on the IOC 2000 Commission recommendations, all of which I fully supported. The IOC approved all 50 recommendations, resulting in several amendments to the IOC Charter.

For starters, we implemented a policy that stopped IOC members from accepting trips paid for by candidate cities.

We also set a policy that no member could vote on an issue concerning their own country.

The last time IOC members visited bid cities was in 1997 for the 2004

Games. For the 2006 Olympic Winter Games, which were awarded at that December session, there were no paid visits by IOC members.

IOC membership was also restricted to a maximum of 115 members. The breakdown would be: 15 athletes who had taken part in the Games within four years of membership; 15 International Federations presidents; 15 NOC presidents; and 70 members elected on an individual basis. The IOC Executive Board was increased to 15, staying with four vice presidents.

Further, stricter limits on service were also imposed. The president's term of office was limited to eight years, renewable with one re-election of four years. Consecutive Executive Board terms were limited to two terms of four years each. After serving a term on the Executive Board, there would be a four-year period before the possibility of re-election. The age term limit was lowered from 80 to 70, although members already on the IOC were grandfathered in until age 80.

An important change that I had pushed hard for was to have athletes serve on the IOC. This began in 1996 when athletes were first elected to serve on the IOC Athletes' Commission. This was repeated in 1998 for the Olympic Winter Games athletes. Now, as part of the IOC 2000 Commission reforms, athletes elected from that point forward were also elected to the IOC for an eight-year term. The athlete had to be no more than four years, or one Olympic Games, removed from competition.

My executive assistant at the LA84 Foundation, Wanda Dowding, assisted me in this from 1996-2014. Her work was nothing short of extraordinary. In a couple of the elections, we had to sort and count paper ballots from the Olympic athletes because the electronic counting system broke down. Wanda stuck with this quest through thick and thin. By 2014, in a tribute to our efforts, 75 percent of the athletes voted, which was extraordinary. I was satisfied enough to hand off the elections to others.

This effort also helped boost the number of women on the IOC. In 2010, Angela Ruggiero, an American ice hockey player, was elected to the IOC, making her the second American woman IOC member. In 2016, she was elected to the Executive Board.

Another woman elected to the IOC was Manuela Di Centa, an Italian cross-country skier. In an interesting twist, she was re-elected to a second term and served from 1998-2010. Because she crossed the 10-year threshold, she became, at age 47, an honorary member for life, meaning that for the rest of her life, she can attend the IOC Sessions, as well as the Games.

As far as the reforms went, critics of the IOC, mainly those in the media, questioned how the IOC could police itself. My response was that I had lived in a community at Connecticut College that did just that. The students were responsible for upholding our honor code, just as the IOC was for upholding its code. I believed the IOC had shown that we held our best interests at heart by removing and sanctioning members. But in the years to come, the Salt Lake City scandal, and its reaches into the Toronto and Nagano bids, would leave a stain on the IOC that remains to this day.

* * * * *

The entire ordeal left me confused and disappointed. As the events unfolded over the course of 1999, it appeared to people who did not know me and what I stood for that I was in the center of this mess. I was one of only two Americans on the IOC, a member of the IOC and USOC Executive Boards, IOC Executive Board and the Salt Lake City Olympic Organizing Committee, in addition to my full-time job running the LA84 Foundation. Unbeknownst to me, I was also officially a member of the Salt Lake City bid committee.

This somewhat shocking revelation came from a journalist, who had long insisted on that fact. I had consistently maintained in the media that I was not, but when I was in Salt Lake City for a meeting while we were finalizing bringing Mitt Romney on to run the Games, the journalist took me to his office and showed me a copy of documents I had never seen.

According to the SLOC documents presented to me, articles had been amended to say that IOC members are automatically bid committee members, but they didn't have to be notified about meetings, and didn't count as quorum unless they were attending the meeting. What!? This was outrageous. I had been placed on the bid committee board after the fact, without my knowledge.

I felt that the Mormon members of the SLOC were unlikely to fully confide in me as an African-American woman. The Mormon Church did not renounce its discrimination against people of color until 1978, but I didn't expect to be lied to outright. I actually had some experience with the Mormon church. When I was in the fourth grade, my family had moved from Indianapolis to Bloomington so that my mother could pursue her master's degree at Indiana University. My mother's mother had been a Seventh-Day Adventist, so she thought it would be fine for me to go to Saturday school. It turned out that the school was at the Mormon Church. Except for my skin color, I would have made it all the way through the catechism.

The fallout from the Salt Lake City scandal continued for a couple years. In July 2000, both Tom Welch and Dave Johnson were indicted by a federal grand jury for paying $1 million to improperly influence votes of more than a dozen IOC members. They rejected plea deals, and the judge dismissed their case in December 2003.

In the end, two individuals pled guilty to crimes. One was David Simmons, a Salt Lake City businessman, who pled guilty to tax offenses related to an alleged sham job he set up for Jung Hoon Kim, the son of Un Yong Kim of Korea. (Jung Hoon Kim was indicted but fled the U.S. to avoid facing the charges.) The other was my friend Alfredo LaMont, who I had known since we worked together at the 1984 Los Angeles Games.

LaMont, who was the Justice Department's primary witness against Welch and Johnson, pled guilty to tax evasion charges related to payments of more than $400,000 that he secretly received over a five-year period from the Salt Lake City bid committee for his effort as a "consultant" to help secure the 2002 Games.

It was devastating enough to be lied to and deceived by the Salt Lake City officials, who did things they knew I would have blown the whistle on, but the fact that my friend had lied to me and acted so unethically was even more troubling. In addition to concealing the payments, he had also abused his USOC position. I never fully understood how he could so irreparably compromise his integrity. He has since apologized to me, and our friendship has been restored.

When Samaranch finally stepped down as IOC president in 2001, he called the Salt Lake City scandal the worst part of his presidency and expressed deep regret for what had happened.

Dick Pound, who conducted the IOC ethics report, ended up as more than a footnote in the story. During Samaranch's tenure, Pound had done a great deal of work negotiating the deals on IOC sponsorship platforms (that had been created by Peter Ueberroth to finance the 1984 LA Olympic Games). I understood that the IOC was paying something, but I thought it would be for support staff to assist him with scheduling around his travels. I assumed the amount was in the $50,000 range annually.

After Samaranch left the presidency, his successor was Jacques Rogge. It was discovered that Pound's firm had been reimbursed in the neighborhood of $3 million. The head of the investigation commission had his own story of profit from the Olympic Movement. The funds were for his firm, he said; he made no income personally. Further, President Samaranch had agreed to make the payments, so it was known at the highest level of the IOC.

Ten IOC members ended up losing their positions, all of whom deserved to be removed. An upsetting part of the scandal was that the reputations of some IOC members who had done nothing wrong were damaged. Though they were investigated and cleared, the names remain associated with the allegations.

I never felt like I was personally on the defensive, as I knew that I had done nothing wrong. But I knew that to rebuild its reputation and show itself worthy of being responsible for leading the Olympic Movement, IOC members had to step up on ethical behavior. This was the only way that we could restore international public trust in the IOC and maintain the integrity of the Olympic Movement.

Chapter Twenty
Honoring My Ancestors

On February 4, 2001, I announced my candidacy to become the eighth president of the International Olympic Committee, making me the first woman in the 107-year history of the IOC to run for its highest office.

I decided to make my announcement in Dakar, Senegal at the Executive Board meeting. It was one of the few times the board had met in an African nation. As a descendant of Africans, I wanted to honor my ancestors, notably my mother's ancestors who had come from the Cameroon area, and also to honor the people of Africa for all the work they had done over the years on behalf of the Olympic Movement. I felt that they had not received the recognition they deserved. I wanted my announcement to be a tribute to them as well.

I had put a lot of thought into my decision. I asked myself how I could move the Olympic Movement forward. President Juan Antonio Samaranch had built the Olympic Museum in Lausanne, which now stood as a symbol for the unity he had built. He believed that the Olympic Movement had to be unified: that the National Olympic Committees, the International Federations, the IOC, and the athletes all had to work together. I call these four constituencies the four sides of the Olympic Pyramid.

Now that we had unity, my platform was to foster inclusion. As Olympians, all athletes are members of the Olympic Movement, but I felt that more athletes should be IOC members. I sent a series of proposals to my IOC colleagues for review, and promised to contact each one of them. I wanted to hear their thoughts, how they felt about the direction of the Olympic Movement, and what their vision was for the future of the IOC.

The vacancy was created when the current president announced he would step down at the 2001 IOC session in Moscow. The fact that the election for the new president, the first in 21 years, would be held in Moscow was also alluring to me. Moscow had been an important city in my life. It was the site of the boycotted 1980 Olympic Games that I had qualified for —the Games that had tested my devotion to the Olympic Movement.

* * * * *

I declared my candidacy for the presidency the day before the meeting started. I felt it would be inappropriate to have the news coming out of the Executive Board meeting. President Samaranch, who was suffering from the flu, was in Barcelona, Spain and restricted from traveling, meaning that he would not arrive before the third day of the meetings. As first vice president, I became president *pro tem* and took on Samaranch's duties on the same day I announced my candidacy.

First, I gave the awards at the Judge Mbaye Golf Tournament, the first ever held in honor of Judge Keba Mbaye, an IOC vice president and member of the International Court of Justice. I had a great deal of respect for Judge Mbaye, a very intelligent and savvy jurist, as well as an excellent judge of character. He had been instrumental in reincorporating a free South Africa into the Olympic Family.

That afternoon, there was a trip scheduled to the Île de Gorée. For me, it would be an emotional journey. A UNESCO World Heritage site, the Île de Gorée was where much of the trade of enslaved human beings occurred from the 1500s through the early 1800s. So while I had fully intended to go there, I had never expected to be traveling in an official capacity.

I not only had to deal with the very personal emotional experience of the Île de Goree, but also the unplanned experience of acting as president *pro tem*, which added another dimension to the trip, as I was representing the Olympic Movement.

Our boat traveled the same route to the island that the people enslaved in Senegal were forced to take. We were told that these unfortunate people had already traveled many miles across Africa as captives of war, or been sold at the whim of their leader. The people were disoriented and exhausted, and had suffered unspeakable atrocities. Then, they were put on a boat to take a short, horrific journey to a human trading ground.

On our diesel-fueled boat ride to Île de Gorée, I tried to politely chat with my colleagues — as I needed to round up votes — while going through all my personal set of emotions. I felt a profound sadness for the enslaved people of the past, the men, women, and children forced to make this journey that I was able to make voluntarily.

The conversations weren't helping much. People would say, "Didn't they know what was happening? Couldn't they see what was going to happen?" Of course they couldn't. This was in the 1500s to 1900s, and people were going about their daily lives. These war captives were not their family or friends; they were complete strangers to them. Our guide also explained that, during that time, using captives of war in such a manner was also normal in Europe as well as in other parts of the world.

As we got closer, it became clear that the port was another part of the island, completely distant and not visible from the shore of Dakar. After the boat made its way around the tip of the island and came into port, it was clear that the mainland was not visible. The island is structured in such a way that it completely blocks any view of the city of Dakar, probably one of the reasons it was chosen for the slave trade.

We put in to shore, climbed down from the boat, and began our visit of Île de Gorée. My emotions were on the surface, as I thought about my own family history, and others who might not have been as fortunate as I was. I also empathized with the people and the history of the great and longstanding nation of Senegal, and the harrowing struggle that came with the recognition that they were complicit in sending off millions of enslaved people from all nations of Africa.

The guide informed us that the continent of Africa probably lost about 13 million people: six million gone missing at sea and seven million being taken to the Americas. The guide talked about how the American Indians, after receiving many diseases from the Europeans, could not do the enormous work demanded by the Europeans who were developing tobacco, sugar cane, and cotton farms in the New World. This led to them looking for people who could be enslaved to help fulfill the enormous amount of labor needed.

The descendants of enslaved people are primarily African Americans, obviously meaning those of us who are now in the United States. Others were taken to the Caribbean islands and many more throughout South America, with a large number in Brazil.

We walked through the community and saw the larger houses built for the wealthy people who had engaged in the slave trade. Eventually, we reached the actual place where the enslaved people were traded.

I managed to hold it together when the guide showed us the very tiny space where the captured men were kept, and told us about the huge number of men who were crammed in there, the length of time they were confined, and what was done to keep them subdued.

When he got to where they kept the children, I lost it. Fortunately, I had on my shades. I didn't have enough Kleenex for that experience, and unfortunately, I'd left my handkerchief back at the hotel. I just sort of melted to the back of the group.

Being at the actual site was overwhelming. To look out at the sea and think of how lost these people must have felt. There was absolutely no respect for human life — zero.

Standing in the room where the transactions were finalized was a difficult struggle for me. As much as I felt I had sorted out the baggage of my past, an experience like this assured me that I could never fully reconcile it.

Then, as president *pro tem*, I was asked to sign the visitor's book. While this was a great honor, when I first grasped the pen, I had a flash that I was signing one of those contracts involving human transactions. I snapped back to the present and realized that my signing the book could only be occurring because the descendants of the enslaved African people, like me, were now free.

The people who worked at the site were so proud, seeing that I was an African American and knowing that we were all connected through our common past. Of all the places I have been in my life, this was one place that would never leave me. As difficult as the experience was personally, it helped me focus on another aspect of my candidacy: to bring respect to the people who had devoted their lives to the Olympic Movement.

* * * * *

Four others candidates declared they were standing for election: Dick Pound of Canada, Pál Schmitt of Hungary, Un Yong Kim of South Korea, and Jacques Rogge of Belgium. Despite the Salt Lake City rebukes and the actions of Kim's son, Kim himself had managed to escape censure. All served on the executive committee, and three had seniority over me. The response to my declaration for president was positive both within the IOC and in the press.

In *Sports Business Daily*, Richard Lapchick, director of Northeastern University's Center for the Study of Sport in Society, wrote a flattering endorsement of my candidacy, titling his article, "What the IOC Needs, Anita DeFrantz Offers." Calling my candidacy the best news he had heard coming out the IOC, he wrote: "She would be the only choice for anyone wanting a clean slate from which to operate the organization along with a promise to return the Olympic Movement to its founding ideals."

As solid a footing as the IOC was on, the IOC needed a president who would make it a priority to weed out perceived corruption and to make the IOC's reputation a priority. There were still plenty of lingering public clouds at the time, not the least of which was that Kim was still a vice president and a candidate for the presidency.

The 2000 Sydney Olympics had been hit by allegations of vote buying to win the Games, and the 1999 Salt Lake City scandal still stuck in many people's minds. In Dakar, the executive committee also referred two of our members to the IOC Ethics Committee: Mohamad Hasan, who had been sentenced to a two-year jail term for corruption in his native Indonesia; and Lassana Palenfo, a top general in the Ivory Coast's military junta, who had recently been charged with crimes, including arms trafficking. Because he was convicted, Hasan was expelled from the IOC. Palenfo, however, was jailed without trial as part of a military coup.

The rules on running for the presidency were ill-defined and ever changing, due in part to the fact that the IOC had not elected a new president in 21 years. I struggled to figure out how to campaign without breaking the rules, which prohibited campaigning during IOC meetings.

Distance was the first obstacle. I lived in Los Angeles and the bulk of my IOC colleagues lived in Europe. At one point, I let it be known that I was trying to raise funds to finance my travel to meet with several key colleagues, only to be warned that this was not allowed. So I did my best to talk to them by phone. At every turn, I felt that I was facing an uphill battle.

* * * * *

The vote for president was taken on the final day of the IOC Session in Moscow, and held from July 13-16, 2001. At that time, there were 100 IOC members. The candidate receiving the majority of votes would win. Each round of voting would eliminate the lowest vote-getter until a winner was declared.

Prior to the vote for president, the host city for the 2008 Olympic Games was selected. Beijing won on the second ballot, beating out Toronto, Paris, Istanbul, and Osaka.

By the time the IOC members were ready to cast their ballots for president, I felt like I was in a hole. One candidate, Un Yong Kim, had promised IOC members $50,000 per year for their service, a clear violation of election rules. He initially denied making the promise, but unfortunately for him, one member had recorded him.

Kim seemed to have nine lives. His son had been indicted in the Salt Lake City scandal for accepting a job, and then fled the U.S. to avoid prosecution. Not only had Kim survived the scandal, he was an IOC vice president, because Kim himself had maintained plausible denial and not done anything himself to embarrass the IOC. It seemed like splitting hairs, but that was what I was facing.

Kim had previously brought corruption into the bidding process. When Seoul was competing against Nagoya for the 1998 Olympic Winter Games, Kim had convinced his government to provide two roundtrip, first-class airline tickets for each IOC member to visit Seoul. The fact that Kim was offering tickets at the Baden-Baden Session where the vote was being held meant that they could not be realistically used — that turned out to be exactly the point. He set up an office where members could turn in their tickets for the cash value.

In May 2005, Kim's actions caught up with him. He resigned from the IOC during his expulsion proceedings resulting from his conviction in

Korea of embezzling corporate donations given to the World Taekwondo Federation.

In the run up to the election, Samaranch made it clear that he preferred for his successor to be European and in any event not Un Yong Kim. He was meeting with people individually and lobbying them; in fact, he told me as much. My reply: "I have ancestors from Europe. Does that count?"

Due to Samaranch's behind-the-scenes maneuvering, 11 members who had indicated that they would vote for me came to me the day before the election and told me that they could no longer vote for me. I was devastated. Their reasoning was that there was a concern that the wrong person — Kim, who had violated ethics rules — would be elected on the first round of votes. I countered with the fact that it was mathematically impossible that anyone would receive a majority of votes on first ballot, because there were five candidates.

I felt if I could make it through the first round, I would have a chance of drawing more votes in second and third rounds, but that didn't happen. Losing those 11 votes turned the numbers against me. I was eliminated on the first ballot. Jacques Rogge was elected IOC president on the third ballot. I was crushed. In retrospect, I wish I would have handled the defeat better. I started to cry, and I couldn't stop.

Part of it was the added pressure that I was under leading up to and during the meeting. In addition to running for president, being the first vice president meant that I was the point person on the issues concerning the outgoing president. I chaired the meeting on his departure package and made it work for him — knowing full well that he had wanted a European president. I didn't take his wishes as a personal slight, but it was not easy.

I was, however, proud that President Samaranch went out with the dignity and respect he deserved for all that he had given to the Olympic Movement. It was decided that he would be elected honorary life president and maintain an office in his home city, as well as have his travel on official trips paid for.

The fact was, I made many mistakes during my bid for presidency, and I needed to accept responsibility. I had talked to Samaranch frequently about what I was doing. But each time I did, those tactics suddenly became illegal.

I should have worked more quietly behind the scenes to build a coalition. I needed more members working on my behalf rounding up votes, especially in light of the IOC being such a diverse group. I planned to take what I had learned to build coalitions going forward for my goals for the Olympic Movement.

Chapter Twenty-One
Women and Sport Should Be a Non-Issue

Although I was not elected president of the International Olympic Committee, and my term on the Executive Board had ended, I dedicated myself to focusing on women's issues across the Olympic Movement. Jacques Rogge, who succeeded Juan Antonio Samaranch and beat me for the IOC presidency, ultimately supported my efforts, dubbing my strategy "Name and Shame" at IOC meetings.

He was right. I felt that the only way to make progress was to call out those who weren't doing enough. I would report on the number of International Federations who still did not have women on their executive boards. I took to task any IOC member who did not support bringing equality for women. My goal was simple: *to make the issue of women and sport a non-issue*. Was it easy? No, it was an uphill battle at times, but one I felt that I owed to myself, to all other women athletes, and to my family constitution of working for equality.

* * * * *

Prior to my bid for the IOC presidency, the second World Conference on Women and Sport had been held in March 2000 in Paris to celebrate 100 years of women competing in the Olympic Games. The event was a huge success. At least 200 more participants registered in the week leading up to the conference, and altogether, nearly 500 leaders in women's sports from around the world attended the conference. Because the original room was not large enough, we had to divide the participants into two rooms and run a video feed into the second room.

We assembled a distinguished list of speakers, and laid out what we wanted to accomplish at the conference and beyond. People had known about our first conference, which had been well received. The second one built on the first as a world conference with multi-national participation. In fact, it had the largest participation level of any IOC issue-oriented conference.

We reviewed the progress that was being made, which was steady, if a little slow, for my taste. The Olympic Games and Olympic Winter Games had added women's sport events. From 1996-2000, eight additional sports were voted onto the women's program, including ice hockey, taekwondo, bobsleigh and weightlifting. There had been a 4 percent increase in the number of total female athletes competing.

In Paris, we put forth the goal of at least 20 percent that the IOC had established for increasing female members on their board. This challenged the International Sports Federations, the National Olympic Committees, and the National Federations to establish their own targets of 20 percent of decision-making positions across the Olympic Movement by 2005.

We felt that if the IOC took the lead, then these goals could be realized. The IOC needed to encourage the NOCs to send at least one woman to the regional and world assemblies; historically, there had been only men attending those meetings. Our hope was that if NOCs engaged women in their countries, then those women could work their way up and become leaders in the IFs.

The conference also issued a resolution on sexual harassment. We sought to establish a policy against sexual harassment that governed coaches' conduct toward athletes and work throughout sport at all levels. This was a sensitive area that many NOCs did not talk about. We hoped that by including the issue in conferences and workshops, and showing the NOCs how to address sexual harassment, that progress could be made much faster.

Our group also called on the Olympic Solidarity Commission to provide more scholarships and training specifically for women. The Olympic Solidarity program was started in 1960 to provide funds to emerging nations for athlete development, training of coaches and administrators, and promotion of Olympic values.

The IOC Women and Sport Trophy, another important tool to spotlight the involvement of women at all levels of sport, was established. At every Olympic Games, six trophies — one for each of the five continents and one at the world level to a woman, a man, or an institution — were presented during the Opening Ceremonies to individuals, groups of persons, and teams or institutions that had done the most to advance women's causes in or through sport. This represented a real opportunity to leverage the recognition of women in the field of sport around the world.

Though the 20 percent target goal to put women in leadership positions by 2005 in the NOCs and IFs was beyond the IOC's control, we could at least use our bully pulpit to push these groups. The NOCs exist only because the IOC exists, and the IOC can also exert pressure on the IFs because the IOC ultimately decides whether their sports stay on the Olympic program. By having their sports on the program, the IFs benefit financially, as well as from the added publicity their sports receive.

For these reasons and to engage the media, it was critical that the IOC President, and not just our working group or the Executive Board, make a statement backing these goals. President Samaranch had done that at the Solemn Opening — the IOC's formal opening of the Games — of the 2000 Sydney Olympic Games. His speech made the proposals the official policy of the IOC going forward, and we needed to assure that continued level of support.

* * * * *

With the backing of the new IOC President Jacques Rogge, the IOC Women and Sport Working Group became a full-fledged IOC commission in 2004, 10 years after it was formed. Despite our advances, over the years I realized I had made a mistake by not insisting the working group be a commission from the onset. At the time, I had not pushed for a commission because I did not want the issue of gaining equality to be ongoing; I wanted it to be solved, thereby eliminating the need for an open-ended commission. I also did not want the group to be a dumping ground for women's issues that needed to be addressed by the full IOC.

Over time I learned that the status of a working group in the Olympic house did not come close to the status of a commission. It was also harder for the IOC staff to work on our behalf because of their other responsibilities.

It became clear that the momentum of measurable progress had slowed because a working group does not have the same leverage as a commission to push recommendations through the IOC. As we were planning the 2004 conference, we reviewed the statistics indicating how far women had come in the Olympic Movement. Some were encouraging, while others had lagged.

Based on information provided by 187 NOCs in 2003, 160 NOCs had at least one woman on their executive committees and 117 had met the minimum of at least 10 percent, but less than 25 percent (48) had more than 20 percent on their executive committees. Of 35 International Federations reporting, 31 had at least one woman serving on their board, 11 had met the minimum target of 10 percent but, again, less than 25 percent (eight) had more than 20 percent women on their Executive Boards.

Sadly, the IOC was out of compliance with its own goal. The IOC had met the 2001 goal of at least 10 percent, as Samaranch was determined to make that goal before he left office. Specifically, to meet the 20 percent goal, we would have to double the number of women. With a total membership of 115, the IOC would need to have 23 women members; in 2003, we had only 12. There were many qualified women eligible for election, and at the 2004 conference, I asked all the conference attendees for their help in identifying the best candidates so that they could be nominated for election to the IOC.

And, yes, at the IOC Session meeting I "named and shamed" the IOC for not meeting our goal. In my best IOC diplomatic speak, I said: "As you know, we committed to having at least 20 percent of our membership be comprised of women by 2005. We are well short of that number, and I hope that we correct this right away."

At the 2004 Women and Sport conference in Marrakesh, we focused on reaffirming all of our goals. Part of the advantage of meeting every four years was the ability to regroup and redouble our efforts. As a commission, we also adopted a broader mandate. We wanted to become involved in developing and implementing programs that used sport as a tool to empower girls and women to contribute to the overall development of women worldwide.

One of my central beliefs is that sport is a mirror of society, as well as an extraordinary tool for social change. Sport provides access to all parts of society. More than ever, sport is a tremendous medium of communication and emancipation that can help build girls' and women's physical and psychological well-being. With that enhanced personal awareness, women can take on new roles in society, particularly in countries where they have been left out.

Going into the 2008 conference, we expanded our horizons to reach into this area. Held in Jordan, the conference's theme was "Sport as a Vehicle for Social Change."

At the conference, as chair of the IOC Women in Sport Commission, I offered a call to action for delegates to put forth the idea that sport is a powerful tool for addressing women's issues around the world and is also a common language that strengthens diversity. I encouraged the removal of all barriers that discourage participation. I asked for those in positions of power to develop protégées. And I also asked the NOCs to put forward women candidates for the IOC and support their election.

In the tailwind of the conference, a major step forward came in 2009 at the XIII Olympic Congress, the gathering of representatives from all constituencies of the Olympic Movement. Held in Copenhagen, it was the first congress since 1994. We convinced the congress to issue a recommendation aimed at strengthening the women and sport policy of the Olympic Movement.

The recommendation stated:

> *"High priority should be given to the advancement of women both in sport and through sport. The Olympic Movement should at all times seek to promote equal opportunities for women, both in their participation in sports competition and in administration and coaching. Wherever necessary, the Olympic Movement should identify and implement changes to achieve gender equality, and should also provide incentives and appropriate educational and training programs for athletes, sports leaders, and administrators in support of this goal."*

Previous work had been done under President Samaranch, but we needed a reaffirmation under the current president, Jacques Rogge. In an earlier speech, Rogge told a European group that the Olympic Games needed to move toward 50-50. Now we had an official declaration of that intent.

The conferences had a thematic accretion to them. They started by pushing for more women to participate in the Games and advanced into putting women in positions of power in sport. To keep moving forward, the 2012 conference focused on having men and women work together. Titled "Together Stronger: The Future of Sport," the conference was held in Los Angeles and had by far the largest participation, with 700 people attending from 121 countries.

Two main recommendations came out of the LA conference:

The first: "The IOC should revisit and review the minimum number of women to be included in leadership roles which it set for its constituents, and set up a mechanism to monitor and ensure that this minimum number is being respected."

The second: "The IOC should establish closer working partnerships with the UN and its agencies, especially UN Women, and share in the work of the UN Committee on the Status of Women in order to foster its own gender equality agenda."

Unfortunately, the 2012 women's conference was the last. The problem was that every other commission had conferences every two years, which made no sense because change took longer than two years to register. It was also a huge expense, and except for ours on women and sport, where you could see progress, there was no practical way of measuring results. To correct this, Thomas Bach, who took over as president in 2013 after Rogge served the new two-term limit, mandated discontinuing separate conferences on individual issues and discussing all issues within an overall IOC conference, to be held next in Lima, Peru in September 2017.

I strongly felt that women's sports conferences should have continued on a quadrennial basis. Having the women's discussion as part of a larger conference relegates it to being just one item on a long agenda. Attendance from the women's sport movement would also be significantly diminished, as outside groups could not attend IOC conferences. But I committed myself to push forward through all available channels.

* * * * *

The quadrennial conferences helped build a wider movement in women's sports across all continents and create a better understanding of what the IOC was doing to help. In the U.S., we often think that we are the center of the universe. The Olympic Movement has been the greatest source of opportunity in sport for women worldwide. If it hadn't been for the Olympic Movement, and the efforts it has directed toward providing opportunity in sport for women throughout the world, we would not see the level of performance and participation that we see today. Over time, the Olympic Movement has been one of the greatest sources of opportunity for women worldwide.

From 1994, the year we formed the Women and Sport Working Group, through 2017, substantial progress was made around the world.

The resolution to have at least 10 percent of women in decision-making positions of legislative bodies by the end of 2000 was achieved. At the 1996 Games, women competed in 26 events. From then through the 2016 Games, 13 events for women were added, and more are coming. Karate, sport climbing, surfing, and skateboarding for women will be on the program in 2020. The participation of women athletes in the Games increased from 30 percent to 47 percent in 2016. By the year 2024, I anticipate the Games will be 50-50.

Further, the number of women competing at the Games has increased significantly. From 1900-1984, slightly more than 12,000 women Olympians competed. From 1988-2016, the numbers increased two and a half times, to 30,000 women Olympians. To me, that means there is a pool of 30,000 Olympians ready to take on volunteer and professional roles in world sport.

As much as any single entity in the Olympic Movement, Olympic Solidarity has contributed to the empowerment of women, setting aside substantial budgets for training and collaborating with the commission to ensure funding for national initiatives has a better chance of reaching women. All high-level training programs are open to women. The popular sports administration programs have seen an upsurge in women's participation.

From 2009-2011, 542 female athletes were awarded training scholarships in preparation for the 2010 Olympic Winter Games in Vancouver and the 2012 Olympic Games in London; 47 NOCs received grants to train their women's team sports; 68 female coaches received a scholarship; and 86 initiatives in the women and sport program were awarded financial grants in 62 countries.

The 2012 London Olympic Games had several firsts on the women's front. It was the first-ever Games in which women competed in all sports on the program. That summer, also for the first time, the U.S. team had more women athletes (269) than men (261). This was the case for 31 NOCs. And, in a development that was nothing short of amazing, every participating country in the Games had at least one woman competing, a vast improvement over the 1996 Games when 26 countries did not enter a single woman.

At the 2012 Olympic Games, the rising popularity of women's sports was also evident. NBC actually devoted more air time to women's events than men's, with women's coverage receiving 55 percent of the total air time.

Leading up to the 2012 Olympic Games, I had lobbied the NOCs of Saudi Arabia, Qatar, and Brunei, the only countries that had never sent women to the Games. In another milestone, all three entered women athletes. This, of course, came with difficulties, due to the cultural mores and religious customs of these nations. Nevertheless, the women are now Olympians.

In 2012, two Saudi Arabian women athletes sought to compete in the London Olympic Games. They had to compete in hijabs, the head covering for Muslim women. Some sports still maintain that a head covering will somehow endanger women competitors, although there are no studies to support that conclusion.

The IOC will not make rules based on religion and we do not interfere with the International Federations on athlete safety, but we ask that rules be based on evidence, not supposition. At present, there is only one International Federation, basketball, which prohibits head coverings. Now, in 2017, I am happy to report that no federations ban the use of head coverings by women.

Those two athletes, along with a Saudi women's official, marched in the

Opening Ceremony. But following custom in their homeland, they walked behind all of the men. Other countries from this region had women as their flag bearers. At the 2016 Rio Games, the four Saudi women who competed walked behind some of their male teammates, but in front of others.

The IOC is closing in on equality of athletes at the Games. For the 2020 Tokyo Games, women will be 48.8 percent of the athletes. The 2020 Lausanne Youth Winter Olympic Games will be 50-50. So, we are getting our goal met.

* * * * *

All of these numbers matter. To me, they are not merely statistics. They represent movement toward equality: Women actively competing in the Games and becoming involved in sport leadership positions. With more female athletes participating in the Olympic Games, we anticipate that these Olympians will in time fill more of these leadership roles. Most of the men in sports positions within the Olympic Movement have come up through sports, so we anticipate that the same will occur with women over time.

Of course, additional challenges lie ahead. There are still inequalities for women, in training opportunities, prize money, sponsorships, and marketing. In many areas of the world, access to sport by girls and women is often restricted due to cultural or religious barriers. Physical education, often the entry point to sports at the school level, is not a priority in many societies. This affects both girls and boys.

I remain optimistic because the IOC continues to make women's participation in sport as athletes and leaders one of its major goals. The practice of sport — whether in Olympic competition or community-based sport — and the values it brings are important tools for communication, education, and emancipation that favor the social integration of all human beings, men and women alike.

Chapter Twenty-Two
Keeping Politics a Spectator Sport

The list of controversial cities awarded the Olympic Games has grown in recent years, and critics have had a field day prosecuting the International Olympic Committee for many of their host city selections for the Games. This process has varied over the century of the modern Olympic Games, but some history provides context for the selection of more recent host cities.

The first three host cities of the modern Olympic Games, Athens, in 1896, Paris, in 1900, and St. Louis, in 1904, were simply asked to host the Olympic Games. The 1904 Olympic Games had originally been awarded to Chicago, but the IOC gave the Games to St. Louis. While the specific reasons for the change to St. Louis are somewhat murky, the fact that the 1904 World's Fair would be in St. Louis had a great deal to do with the decision; there would be a guaranteed audience that could visit the World's Fair and the Olympic Games at the same time.

By the late 1920s, having a large audience in attendance became a deciding factor, although IOC President Pierre de Coubertin did not want the Games to be part of the World's Fair. In order for the U.S. to host the Olympic Games the second time, civic leader William May Garland, representing a group of civic leaders from Los Angeles, attended a meeting of the IOC and asked if Los Angeles could host the 1928 Olympic Games. He was informed that Amsterdam had been selected. He was asked if LA had a main stadium to host the Opening Ceremonies and the track and field events. He said that such a stadium was under construction and should be finished in time for the Games — then he got to work on expanding the stadium. When the Los Angeles Memorial Coliseum was finished, Garland went back to the IOC headquarters, declared that the stadium was ready, and the IOC offered the

1932 Olympic Games to Los Angeles.

Looking back, no host city was more controversial in the early years of the modern Olympic Games than Berlin, which won the bid for the 1936 Olympic Games.

* * * * *

The vote to award those Games occurred in 1931 during the Weimar Republic, two years before Adolf Hitler's Nazi party rose to power in 1933. In fact, Hitler initially had no interest in the Olympic Games, but his adviser, Carl Diem, leader of the German Organizing Committee, who was instrumental in discovering the site of the ancient Olympic Games, helped convince Hitler that the Games were an opportunity to show off the strength of the new Germany under Nazi control. With Diem at the helm, the Germans built several new facilities, including a 100,000-seat track and field stadium, in an attempt to show up the 1932 Los Angeles Olympic Games. Diem also instituted the Olympic torch relay to put Germany on display. Hitler then used filmmaker Leni Riefenstahl to chronicle the Games.

After Hitler's rise to power, many people in the U.S. and in other countries called for a boycott of the Berlin Games. United States Olympic Committee President Avery Brundage was adamantly opposed to a boycott. He had struck up a friendship with Diem when the German visited the 1932 Games. The USOC met to discuss and vote on the matter.

Ironically, the meeting was held at the New York Athletic Club, which did not allow Jewish or African-American members. The USOC voted to send the U.S. team to the Games. In announcing the decision, Brundage declared that "politics have no place in sport."

Brundage served as president of both the USOC (1928-1953) and the IOC (1952-1972). As much as I appreciate Brundage standing up for the athlete's right to compete, I am not an apologist for Avery Brundage by a long shot. He never spoke with kindness of people outside of the Christian faith. He presided over an Olympic team in 1932 that barred two African-American women who were eligible from competing in the Games. In 1936, he denied two Jewish men and one African-American woman the opportunity to compete, despite the fact that they were in Berlin to compete at the Games.

As for the 1936 Games, the goal of the Nazis to show the dominance of the Aryan people over the rest of the world failed as the great Jesse Owens, an African American, lit up the new track stadium with several performances for the ages. Owens won four gold medals and became the most decorated athlete at those Games. Other African Americans also became victors in their sports and events. Sadly, Owens returned home to a nation whose leader, President Franklin D. Roosevelt, did not congratulate him.

* * * * *

IOC members are put in the position of predicting the future when we select host cities for the Olympic Games and Olympic Winter Games, and sometimes that comes with costs, and often with criticism. Our mission in selecting a host city is to take the long view to make sure the Games endure and flourish. With a few exceptions, Olympic Games are awarded to a host city seven years, or at least six years in advance, to give the city time to prepare. In many countries, six or seven years can turn out to be an eternity in terms of what happens politically and economically.

This was clearly on the minds of IOC members at the IOC session in 1970 when selecting the host city for the 1976 Olympic Games. The IOC members were aware of the political unrest that had taken place just two weeks before 1968 Opening Ceremonies in Mexico City, during which 200 students who were taking part in a large rally were murdered. The mystery of who shot the first bullets was publicly reported recently. It was confirmed that the Mexican Secret Service started the shooting, and it was long felt that the government had been responsible.

After Mexico City, the IOC members were looking for a safe place for the Games to be hosted. (Munich had already been selected for the 1972 Games.) At the 1970 Session in Amsterdam, the city of Montreal was selected over the candidates Los Angeles and Moscow. At the 1974 session in Vienna, Lake Placid was selected to host the 1980 Olympic Winter Games, and Moscow was selected for the 1980 Olympic Games over Los Angeles, which bid for the second consecutive time. Finally, after its third consecutive bid, Los Angeles was the only city bidding for the 1984 Games, and so it was selected.

The IOC had avoided political issues by selecting Montreal first, so it was logical to go to Europe for the Moscow Games next. Finally, it was logical to return to the American hemisphere for the 1984 LA Games. Los Angeles faced the outrage of the public from the Montreal Games going well over budget in construction of the village and sports venues. However, the success of the LA Games, which was funded by sponsorships, television rights, and ticketing and careful contracting with the venues and the three villages, left a very large financial surplus.

Although only two cities had bid for the 1988 Games at the 1981 session in Baden-Baden, Germany, six cities entered the contest for the 1992 Olympic Games and seven for the Olympic Winter Games at the 1986 session in Lausanne. For the subsequent six Olympic and Olympic Winter Games selections, there were more than three candidates. It was only after reports of how much Russia spent on the Sochi 2014 Olympic Winter Games that the interest in hosting the Games dried up.

* * * * *

I am often asked, Why did the International Olympic Committee award the Games to Sochi and give Russia's president, Vladimir Putin, a world stage for his regime? How did a polluted Beijing, with its deplorable human rights record, get the Games — twice? How did Rio, with its crumbling economy, political unrest, and dirty waterways, land the Games over Chicago, whose bid was backed by President Barack Obama and Oprah Winfrey?

Having reviewed 74 bid proposals during my time on the IOC and served on eight bid committees, I can explain some of the ideas that were present among those who made the decisions, but the only accurate way to get an answer to that question would be to ask each IOC member what motivated their decision.

Some people suggest that the choice of Beijing began the process of placing the cost of the Games out of reach for most cities. The cost of the 2008 Beijing Games is not known with specificity. It is assumed that the Chinese government would spare nothing to put on a Games that would thrill the athletes and astonish the world. Every host city seeks to put its city in the best possible light as the world comes to visit. When one has the will and fortune of over one billion people, a great deal can be accomplished.

So, how did Beijing get selected to host the 2008 Olympic Games?

Beijing certainly has been one of the more politically controversial cities to secure the Olympic Games. In 1993, Beijing bid for the 2000 Games. In the months leading up to the vote for those Games, due to China's human rights record, several members of the U.S. Congress opposed Beijing's bid. The House of Representatives passed a resolution urging the American IOC member — me — to vote against Beijing's bid, as I was the sole American on the IOC from 1991-1994.

The U.S. Senate introduced two resolutions opposing Beijing's bid on the grounds of China's record on human rights. The Senate Commerce Committee held hearings in July of 1993. The hearings focused on whether Senate opposition would represent a political stance against the Chinese government's treatment of its citizens, or become an unintended punishment for Olympic athletes and even provoke a boycott of the 1996 Atlanta Games.

USOC President LeRoy Walker and I testified at the hearing. We both made it clear that as African Americans we fully, and very personally, understood issues of human rights. I told the Senate panel that the substance of the resolution did not speak to the issues involved: Passing the resolutions might negatively impact our IOC members' voting freedom on future Games. In the end, the resolutions were not sent to the Senate floor.

The Senate Committee may not have understood my role as an IOC member. I had taken an oath to represent the IOC in the United States, which is different from being the U.S. representative to the IOC. I could not be more American than I am, given my family's activist history and my years of competing for the U.S., but I was not on the IOC to push the U.S. agenda. As much as people did not like hearing this, the distinction is clearly there.

The vote for the 2000 Olympic Games host city was held in August 1993 at the IOC Session in Monte Carlo. Beijing led through the first three rounds of bidding. (The number of votes each city receives during the rounds of voting is not announced until after the host city is revealed.) As three other cities were eliminated, support for Sydney increased. In the fourth round,

Sydney was preferred over Beijing by a vote of 45-43. (In keeping with the vote by secret ballot, I do not reveal which city received my vote.) The leader of the Chinese delegation felt so slighted by the defeat that he threatened that China would not compete in future Olympic Games.

In 2001, however, Beijing bid for the 2008 Olympic Games. There was talk that the delegation leader's statement after China's last bid might have a negative impact, but the evaluation committee report gave Beijing's bid high marks for government support in curbing pollution and regulating inner city traffic.

In September 2000, however, as the IOC was reviewing candidate city bids for the 2008 Games, the U.S. Congress again pushed back against China hosting the Games. Rep. Tom Lantos, a Democrat of California, introduced a bill to express the sentiment of the House of Representatives, that the Olympic Games not be awarded to Beijing. The bill said:

> *"...because the deplorable human rights record of the People's Republic of China violates international human rights standards which that Government has pledged to uphold and its actions are inconsistent with the Olympic ideals that express the sense that without improvement in human rights, the Olympic Games in the year 2008 should not be held in Beijing in the People's Republic of China."*

Prior to the vote, I was again called to testify before the U.S. Senate Commerce Committee in Washington, D.C. — my home away from home. Again, the U.S. government was concerned about the Games being awarded to China.

I testified that the mission of the IOC was to take a long view and ensure the Games endure and flourish. I used the analogy that one farmer should not open a levy to save his farm if it would flood all the farms below his. This analogy was offered after a major flood of the Mississippi River, which was in the news. I made it to show that IOC members have a responsibility to not look out only for themselves, but more importantly to look to the way that the IOC will be best positioned to reach the largest number of people with the message of the Olympic Movement.

I would never apologize for the Chinese government, but since the United Nations hosted the Fourth World Conference on Women in Beijing in 1995, then what negative international message would the IOC be sending if it voted for Beijing to host the 2008 Olympic Games? I led a delegation from the IOC to the UN conference. The keynote speaker was First Lady Hillary Clinton, who spoke clearly about her concerns on women's rights in China.

It was interesting to me that Congress wanted to punish China by rejecting their opportunity to host the Games, but others believed that some problems could be cured by hosting the Games.

The vote was held in Moscow in 2001, during the same session where I ran unsuccessfully for IOC president. Beijing was chosen over Toronto, Paris, Istanbul, and Osaka in the second round of voting. In addition to Beijing's strong bid, members expressed their belief — and may continue to believe — that when the Olympic Games come to a country, the Games provide the opportunity for positive change and help open closed societies. Another argument expressed for Beijing was the country's large population. China has one-quarter of the world's population that the Olympic Movement could reach with its ideals. IOC members expressed the belief that the Olympic presence and media spotlight that accompanies the Games would help end some of the repression. (Many outside the IOC thought that this was wishful thinking and held that the political regime was terrible and decried the limits put on free speech among journalists.)

In a quiet moment, former IOC President Juan Antonio Samaranch explained that Beijing would be a good choice, because the Games there would reach the most people and be certain of coming off as a success. The city is home to more than 10 million people. One journalist asked me why we selected Beijing, given that the government was installing cameras all over the city to follow people. I asked, "When was the last time you were in London?" Yes, we live at a time when privacy is rare. Of course, the question is always, What purpose is the State using to intervene in its citizens' privacy? Clearly, these matters have a great deal to do with one's perspective, as well as sense of freedom.

Was the IOC successful in bringing positive change to China, or at least to the city of Beijing? It is very difficult to make a fair analysis as an outsider.

After Seoul hosted the 1988 Olympic Games, Korea was able to establish diplomatic relationships with more than 40 new nations, and their economy expanded greatly. In China, it was a bit more challenging to determine the beneficial outcomes. But one should not conclude that nothing positive happened. There are reports that child labor laws came into existence. Factories producing dry goods for export began allowing inspections to ensure these laws were being followed. Is this enough for the privilege of hosting the Olympic Games?

My view is that freedom of speech, freedom of the press, and human rights are the most important measures of quality of life, so I remain disturbed by the policies of the Chinese government and the way it has treated journalists and dissenters. But I met some wonderful people at the Games who wanted a more inclusive nation, and I became convinced that they are taking steps to work toward that end.

In 2015, Beijing bid again, this time for the 2022 Olympic Winter Games. The only other city bidding was Almaty, Kazakhstan. Other cities, including Oslo, Norway, had dropped out of the running because of the drumbeat of media reports that it cost Sochi $51 billion to host the 2014 Olympic Winter Games. Overlooked was the fact that Sochi had to build everything, including all the venues and housing, from scratch.

The original estimate of $12 billion scared other nations away, because it appeared the Sochi Games were one giant cost overrun. (One IOC member famously said that bid documents are the most amazing fiction you'll ever read.) Still, when all factors were considered, the true cost for Sochi to host the Games was significantly less than the $51 billion spent. There was actually a $50 million surplus from the operation of the Games, which is not the same as the capital construction costs. And also, the facilities they built will remain for a very long time and will be available for the future use by Russians and their athletes, leaving the Games as an investment in a resort area that the Russians were willing to make.

The IOC did not do a good job, however, of getting out front with this information in explaining the level of capital investment necessary if you start with nothing.

Interestingly, the reason that Kazakhstan bid for the 2022 Olympic

Winter Games was because it had the facilities. Its mountains had been the site of the winter training center for the former Soviet Union. And the prime reason the Russians wanted the Sochi Games was so it could build a winter training center for future use.

There was some concern about the weather for the Olympic Winter Games in Beijing, which averages in the 40-degree range in the wintertime. Kazakhstan tried to use that to its advantage. Their theme was, "Keeping It Real," because they have tons of snow throughout the winter months. However, Beijing made assurances that they would be able to produce and keep enough snow.

* * * * *

To the American onlooker, Sochi brought its share of baggage to the table while bidding for the 2014 Olympic Winter Games in 2007.

For starters, it had no facilities. The bid committee overcame this as the government pledged to build everything needed in seven years.

But the bigger issue for many, particularly in the U.S., was Russian President Vladimir Putin and his government's policies against homosexuals, crimes against humanity, and overall, Russia's abysmal human rights record. Though this line of thinking may be unacceptable in Western countries, its existence can be a mitigating factor when the IOC chooses a controversial host nation.

From the moment Sochi won the 2014 Games over PyeongChang, South Korea and Salzburg, Austria, there were calls from activists and politicians, mainly in the U.S., for a boycott of the Sochi Olympic Games over various issues. They cited such concerns as safety of lesbian, gay, bisexual and transgender athletes and allegations of state-sponsored doping of Russian athletes (plenty more on that later).

In the summer prior to the Games, the Russian government passed what they called a "child protection law," which was purportedly designed to protect children from sexual molesters who were LGBT. But while they viewed it as a protection law, it basically said that LGBT individuals could not come to Russia nor could they exist in Russia.

This was a major problem for the Games, and also begged the question,

How could the IOC stage a Games in a country with that type of law? There were LGBT athletes, as well as support staff and the staff of Olympic sponsors, who would be coming to Russia.

In the end, the government pledged to the IOC that there would be no problems related to the Games. This, however, did little to stop the criticism of the Russian government and the IOC.

Again, I am not an apologist for any government and certainly not one that discriminates against an individual for any reason, but my position for the right to compete was the same as it had always been: Taking away the opportunity of any athletes to compete would not solve any of these problems.

The question becomes, does the IOC award the Games to a country in an attempt to make it better, or does it punish a country by not awarding it the Games?

This has always created a dilemma. It is not the role of the IOC to punish countries for their political positions, yet at the same time, we cannot ignore human rights abuses. We can only hope that any nation hosting the Games, with the world's eyes upon it, will become better at adopting mutual respect and fair play.

The Olympic Charter prohibits political demonstrations on the medal stands and in Olympic venues. The goal is to have the celebration of the athletes for this quadrennial event be the sole topic at the Olympic Games. This is a challenging concept in today's world and yet it is a central concept for the Olympic Games.

* * * * *

So what happened to Chicago?

In 2009, Chicago was one of four cities bidding for the 2016 Olympic Games. One challenge that the Chicago bid faced was an ongoing dispute between the IOC and the USOC over how certain funding was being dispersed. Some influential IOC members felt that the USOC was receiving an unfair share of sponsorship and television revenue.

The first issue was funding from The Olympic Partner Programme (TOP), a program where sponsors pay big money to have exclusive rights to the Games in their product category for a quadrennial or longer. The overall agreement had been signed in 1986 without any time frame for the contract. When the program was initiated, all of the TOP sponsors were U.S.-based. Even later, when sponsors based in other nations were added, the U.S. market remained a key part of the program. Without the U.S. market, the program would have failed, or at least been far less robust. Be that as it may, the IOC was looking to cut the USOC's share.

The second issue was that revenue was being paid to the USOC for TV rights payments from the rights holder in the U.S. The USOC was the only NOC to receive funding from a portion of their television rights fees. Many IOC members were working to have this changed, and felt that the USOC was not being open to a new formula. After the 1986 contract was signed, the IOC created several programs for the good of the Olympic Movement. It was felt that the USOC was not contributing funds to those efforts, which compounded the bad feelings toward the USOC.

Clearly, as the Chicago bid went forward, it was handicapped by the overall ill will in the Olympic movement ranks against the USOC built up from those issues. The financial payment problems were eventually resolved in 2012, when USOC President Larry Probst and CEO Scott Blackmun brought a proposal to the IOC that met the needs and concerns of the IOC and continued fair support for the USOC. But this was obviously too late to help Chicago's bid.

There were also several cosmetic missteps that contributed to Chicago losing the bid at that time, notably having two of Chicago's most prominent citizens attend the selection meeting in Copenhagen: President Barack Obama and Oprah Winfrey.

Prior to the vote, consultants hired by the Chicago committee were telling them that the vote was in the bag, but I had done a head count and I told them that was far from the case. Things only went downhill from there.

It hurt having Oprah in Copenhagen, because she was not well known to IOC members and therefore held no sway with them. Oprah's staff also did things that annoyed many IOC members, like having an entire section of the only restaurant in the hotel cordoned off for her entourage. This meant that IOC members were inconvenienced, which is not what you want to do the day before the vote. I learned about this many days later, unfortunately.

Another interpretation was that she had welcomed IOC members to dine with her, but somehow that good intention was lost.

I have always been uncomfortable inviting heads of state to host city selection meetings. The Chicago bid team put pressure on President Obama to attend because the leaders of the other bidding countries were attending. Russian President Putin had attended Russia's winning bid, and British Prime Minister Tony Blair had done the same when London successfully bid for the 2012 summer Games in 2005, so there was precedent.

In Chicago's case, the president's presence led to a potentially costly misunderstanding. Several IOC members were irritated that they had to be at the voting session by 8 a.m., because they thought the streets needed to be cleared for President Obama's motorcade. That was not the truth. The local police insisted that the busses depart early so they would not be stuck in morning rush hour traffic. But once the rumor spread, the damage was done.

Chicago was eliminated on the first ballot and finished fourth to ultimate winner Rio de Janeiro.

* * * * *

Rio was awarded the 2016 Olympic Games because it offered two compelling reasons to host the Games that Chicago did clearly not present: The summer Games had never been held in South America and the infrastructure spending would help modernize the city.

Interestingly, Chicago was also handicapped by the IOC's ban on members visiting bid cities, which was put in place in the wake of the Salt Lake City scandal. Few IOC members had been to Chicago, and most had no idea what a beautiful, cosmopolitan city it is.

When Rio was awarded the Games, Brazil was on the upswing. Rio had hosted the Pan American Games in 2007 and done a good job, while many previous Pan Am Games in South America had been severely challenged. Brazil's economy was booming. It had gone off the fossil fuel standard, and alternative fuel for motor vehicles was available at nearly every fuel station. They had discovered a huge oil field off the coast, which they believed would give them income for the foreseeable future and ultimately put Brazil in position to exist without importing oil.

Rio had not seen a major investment in 50 years, since losing the opportunity to become the country's capital city. Having the Games was an opportunity to clean up the bay, build more hotels, and shore up the infrastructure.

Brazil's challenges grew over the seven years leading up to the Games. First, Brazil's economy took a nosedive. Then the oil find proved hard to refine and deliver. The project was beset with corruption; it seemed many politicians had their hands in the pockets of the drilling company. This started a political drama that triggered the virtual collapse of the government. In May 2016, just months before the Games began in August, President Dilma Rousseff was suspended from her duties pending impeachment proceedings (which came just after the Games ended). The massive funding promised from the federal government turned out to be nonexistent.

Rio fell far behind in construction of Olympic venues and housing. Though the city punched through the mountains to build a railway system to serve the public during the Games and the people of Rio for decades thereafter, Brazil was criticized for spending on the Games and for ignoring the basic infrastructure needs of its citizens. The plan to clean up the bay was slow, if barely executed. To make matters worse, there was widespread fear of an outbreak of the Zika virus, something that had not been on the public's radar when Rio was awarded the Games.

As the Games grew closer, a predictable pattern emerged that has become a tradition in the run-up to the Olympic Games, not only for Rio but for all host cities: As usual, the number of athletes qualifying to compete at the Games decreased. At the beginning of 2016, there were approximately 20,000 athletes who woke up each morning and asked, "What can I do today to increase my chances of winning a medal in Rio?" But month by month, the numbers diminished as the teams were selected by the 206 National Olympic Committees around the world. By July, a month out, that number of hopefuls was nearly half. But this winnowing of the young men and women during the Olympic trials is part of finding out who is the best of the very best.

Another less appealing pattern emerged and received just as much — if not more —attention in many forums: persistent criticism that the host nation was not ready. It has happened from the 1984 LA Games, with stories of gridlock and smog that never materialized, to the 2014 Sochi Games, with predictions that the housing would not be ready and security would be insufficient. Much of what was written in the months before Rio made it sound as though Rio de Janeiro was the last place on earth a person would want to go. The fact was, the people of Rio had been working on this project for seven years and, in the end, they pulled it off.

* * * * *

Looking back, the two weeks before the Opening Ceremonies of nearly every Olympic Games is always described in the media as a disaster, a prime example of unpreparedness, an utter disgrace that the host nation was even considered.

I now realize that the denigration of the host nation's preparations has become an Olympic tradition of sorts. Instead of the media tearing down the host city, it would be nice if it would acknowledge the enormity of the task and recognize that they have worked day and night for years on the preparations.

Yes, there will always be lingering issues that need attention up to and through the Games. But once the starter's command is given at the venues, the real Olympic stories are written, which is as it should be. The efforts of the thousands of athletes seeking to stand on the awards podiums are celebrated in the headlines.

So while there is often much handwringing over the selection of the host city and the preparations, it is my role as an IOC member to remind the world that the Olympic Games are a unifying event of many different nations whose people hold different values, but come together to compete in sport.

Chapter Twenty-Three
A Call to Arms on Doping

Doping — and the masking of doping — is the single greatest threat to the Olympic Movement and an affront to the fair competition for which the Olympic Games stand.

Over my 40 years in the Olympic Family, from my days as a competitor to now being the seventh-longest serving member of the International Olympic Committee, the issue of taking and masking performance-enhancing drugs has become the single most volatile issue facing the Olympic Family.

In April 1988, the LA84 Foundation hosted a "Doping in Elite Sports" conference. To me, this was an important topic that needed to be discussed at all levels. In fact, many of the ideas that came out of the conference were later presented to the IOC.

A few months later, at the 1988 Seoul Olympic Games, I was the first member of the IOC to speak out publicly when sprinter Ben Johnson tested positive for steroids after winning the gold medal in the men's 100 meter. An IOC neophyte at the time, I went on NBC the following morning. I called Ben Johnson a coward because he wasn't brave enough to stand on his own and said that he had competed with dishonor, which he had.

At the IOC Session in 1989, the first meeting following the 1988 summer Games, I asked the IOC to have serious drug cheats and their entourages banned from the Olympic Games. I was the first IOC member to propose such a sweeping ban. It was not until 2000, however, when a Romanian doctor was found to have doped a gold medalist, Andrea Raducan, that a member of an entourage was sanctioned by the IOC for his actions.

A few years later, in 2003, I was named as a defendant in a lawsuit filed by Rick DeMont, a swimmer who had tested positive for amphetamine and was stripped of his gold medal back in 1972. The irony was, I had tried to help him explain himself after I reviewed the file. He had tested positive for taking too much asthma medication, which contained a banned substance. Yet I was named as a defendant because the judge assumed that as an IOC member I had deep pockets. That was not the case, and it was costly for me both financially and psychologically to defend myself against a fellow Olympian.

But nothing has come close to the bombshell story that broke in 2016 about state-sponsored Russian officials who clandestinely carried out a doping scheme during the 2014 Sochi Games and then hid it by tampering with test samples. These revelations, which were detailed and confirmed by the director of the program tasked with switching the urine samples to cover up the doping, left a dark cloud over many of the medals won by Russian athletes at the 2014 and 2012 Games, and came with calls for Russia to be banned from many international competitions, including the Olympic Games.

The harsh criticism of the IOC and demands that we take decisive action have shined a spotlight on the systems we have put in place to weed out cheaters. It has also shown that the entire drug testing system needs to evolve to keep Olympic ideals from being subverted. Yet much incomplete information has been published about the IOC's anti-doping procedures.

* * * * *

The IOC has a detailed procedure for drug testing at the Olympic Games, the only place where it has control over the testing of athletes. This came about as a result of the increased usage of PEDs in elite sport throughout the 1970s and 1980s. National and international governing bodies, lacking a unified approach to the problem, seemed to many critics to be unable or unwilling to take steps to stem the tide. The growing crisis came to a head in 1998 as a result of a series of much-publicized doping scandals at the swimming world championships and the Tour de France.

In February 1999, the IOC convened the World Conference on Doping in Sport to deal with elite-level doping. The conference, attended by sport and government leaders, took place in February 1999 in Lausanne, Switzerland, at the home of the IOC.

In preparation for that conference, working groups were created. I chaired the group for the protection of athlete rights. There was lively discussion, which included recommending that elite athletes become card holders that would make them available for drug testing at any time. This card would also verify that a baseline for the athlete had been developed, so that if there were changes over the years in the testing results, the baseline would prove whether or not the athlete had begun using banned drugs.

Participants were not unanimous in their recommendations. There was, however, support for a universal, no-notice, out-of-competition testing system. While some International Federations had already developed testing programs outside of competition, very few were taking the problem seriously. Although the IOC was becoming more committed to finding drug cheats during the Games, the IOC had no jurisdiction over athletes at any other time. This created a problem, because athletes taking PEDs would generally cycle off of the drugs in time for their systems to be clean at the Olympic Games. This then left it up to the International Federations to find the cheats in the intervening four years.

Broad agreement on the concept of out-of-competition testing led to the conference's most important decision: the call for the formation of a world anti-doping agency, along with the development of a worldwide anti-doping code in sport.

In November 1999, the IOC established the World Anti-Doping Agency, which is guided by an independent board. The first order of business was to develop a world anti-doping code to coordinate the approach to anti-doping in all sports and across all nations. The code was eventually adopted in 2003. Every National Olympic Committee and IF was required to sign on by the 2004 Athens Games.

Today, every NOC and IF, as well as every athlete who competes in a world championship or the Olympic Games, must agree to abide by the World Anti-Doping Code before they are allowed to participate. In addition, all parties are subject to the rules of the IOC.

An appellate process for athletes who test positive for banned substances at the Olympic Games was also established. The internal structure required the IOC Medical Commission to test athletes and notify the IOC president of any positive results. The president in turn notifies the athletes and their NOC. A hearing before the medical commission with the athlete, their

NOC and/or personal representative, and a representative of their sport's IF follows. The medical commission then presents its recommendation to the IOC Executive Board, which determines any discipline. Their decision can then be appealed to an *ad hoc* commission of the Court of Arbitration for Sport, the international court governing world sport.

This system of doping adjudication, known as the Olympic Standard, was a major step forward. The IOC also strongly encouraged the NOCs and IFs to implement testing rules along these lines at all international competitions. Some IFs took their responsibility seriously and put these in place. Rowing, for instance, started conducting blood testing so that we could have a base analysis of the individual's body chemistry, a baseline from which to test.

However, some sports, such as weightlifting, are chronic offenders and don't have appropriate measures in place to stop doping. At the 2015 world championships in Houston, a staggering 80 out of 300 athletes tested positive. Even more startling was that not all of the competitors had been tested, only the top four in each event, meaning the overall percentage was likely much higher. But it didn't really matter how many positives were found, because the International Weightlifting Federation allows athletes who test positive to pay a fine and continue competing. This is egregious and must be changed, or weightlifting should be taken off of the program at the Olympic Games.

To ensure full enforcement at international competitions throughout the year, I believe the IFs need to be taken out of the process because many of them cannot be trusted to police themselves. Ten years ago, I believed they could, but I am no longer optimistic.

In a horribly corrupt twist, the president of the International Association of Athletics Federation, the international governing body of track and field, was being paid by the Russian government to allow doped Russians to compete in international track and field events. He was removed. It goes without saying that IF leaders must have the highest ethical standards.

The only effective solution is for the IFs to give over control of testing and adjudication to an independent body that will continuously mete out sanctions. That way, there would be less possibility of a third party intervening and allowing an athlete who is doped to continue competing.

The IOC has some influence over the IFs, because they rely on the IOC to put their sports on the Olympic program. The IOC has direct control over the NOCs, which would not exist otherwise, but it has no direct control over the IFs. They can exist with or without the Olympic Games and stage competitions in their sports on their own timetables. Recognition by the IOC is a prerequisite for inclusion on the Olympic Program. The IOC has authority on the conduct of athletes in a particular sport only during the Olympic Games; at all other times, the IF or the individual NOC holds that responsibility.

Outside of the Olympic Games, the national federations for a particular sport are notified of a positive test and must then report the results to their IF. The NF can also decide to hold a hearing with the athlete and report the outcome to the athlete's IF. If the IF doesn't like the outcome, it (or the athlete) can appeal through the Court of Arbitration for Sport. CAS is the last court of appeal for the athlete.

Some governments, however, fund their NFs, and reporting procedures are not always followed.

The best way to ensure clean athletes will be through an independent testing agency. Currently, athletes are tested by WADA, which adjudicates the tests as well.

But WADA cannot be both prosecutor and judge outside of the Games. We need another yet-to-be-formed organization, or arm of CAS, to adjudicate. We have to show the athletes that we are serious. If the IFs won't adopt a new procedure, then we must provide a portal for the athletes to allow themselves to be tested and receive a certificate that they are clean.

Many countries also have National Anti-Doping Organizations. The U.S. Anti-Doping Agency is one of these. Even though the USOC provides some of its funding, the U.S. NADO remains independent of the USOC. The problem with relying on the NADOs is some of them aren't completely independent of their governments, or are controlled by their governments.

The fairest solution is to have an independent testing authority do the testing, with funding coming from the Olympic Movement. The IOC has tried to get the governments of the member nations, which are supposed to put up half of the cost, to help financially, but it has grown harder to persuade the governments to put up their end of the money. In the end, the IOC must put up the money if necessary.

My priority for athletes is to be able to compete in a safe and fair arena. If the IFs won't ensure this, then we need to call upon the athletes who want a clean playing field to step up and agree to have themselves tested. Therefore, the IOC must show the IFs that we have created a system that will work for them, because clean athletes are losers in a tainted system, and if an IF won't participate, then we must provide an avenue.

Athletes themselves are clearly in favor of this. The most decorated Olympian of all time with 28 medals, Michael Phelps, said at a 2017 congressional hearing: "I can't describe how frustrating it is to see other athletes break through performance barriers in unrealistic time frames knowing what I had to do to go through that. To believe in yourself through sport, you need to be able to believe in a system that safeguards clean sport and fair play."

* * * * *

Although PEDs were clearly not eliminated from the Olympic Games despite testing procedures put in place by the IOC in 2004, there was evidence that rigorous testing worked as a deterrent until the 2014 Olympic Winter Games.

At the 2006 Turin Olympic Winter Games, only one athlete failed a drug test and had a medal revoked. Six Austrian athletes were given a lifetime ban for possession of doping substances and the conspiracy to cover them up, marking the first time the IOC had banned athletes without a positive or missed drug test. This was another step forward. At the 2004 Athens Games, the IOC announced the samples would be held for five years, so that the testing could catch up with the science. (That has since been increased to ten years, because the integrity of the samples can now be maintained over a ten-year period.)

Heading into the 2008 Beijing Games, the slogan "Zero Tolerance for Doping" was adopted. There were 4,500 samples taken from the athletes. Six athletes tested positive and were disqualified. By the 2012 London Games, the drug testing had increased. In addition to all medalists, who are always tested, 6,000 samples were taken, and half of all Olympians were tested. Six athletes were disqualified for failed drug tests before or during the Games.

Over this time, many athletes were sanctioned by their IFs and barred from the Olympics Games for testing positive at other international events.

But just as the IOC established these firmer testing procedures for the Olympic Games and saw them work, the biggest doping scandal in the history of sport occurred at the 2014 Sochi Games.

After the Games, a German television station reported that Russia had engaged in a systematic doping system, which led to an investigation by WADA. In a November 2015 report, WADA concluded that the reports were true, and identified the leader as the director of the Russian Anti-Doping Agency, Dr. Grigory Rodchenkov. Over the course of 2016, evidence continued to mount that Russia had conducted a comprehensive state-sponsored doping program. The final salvo came when Dr. Rodchenkov, who had run the anti-doping lab since 2005, revealed the full scope of the operation to *The New York Times* after he moved to Los Angeles, where he had fled in fear for his life.

The details were staggering. The Russian doping program at the 2014 Sochi Olympic Games involved a massive cover-up apparently endorsed at the highest levels. Long before the Games, Russian officials had athletes give urine samples when they were clean. They then started a protocol of doping that continued through the Games. At the Games, however, after these athletes were tested, Russian doctors and members of the Russian intelligence would switch positive urine samples of doped athletes in the middle of the night. They were able to open the tamper-proof bottles of as many as 100 samples, including those of at least 15 gold medal winners.

Dr. Rodchenkov also told the *Times* how he had developed a "cocktail" of anabolic steroids and a system to speed up absorption and shorten the detection window for athletes for the 2012 Games. All of this, he claimed, was a result of the Russian government pushing him to ensure that Russian athletes won the most medals on their home turf at the 2014 Games, which they did, after finishing sixth at the 2010 Olympic Winter Games.

These revelations led to strong action from the IOC. In July 2016, the IOC established two commissions, one under the chairmanship of IOC

Member Denis Oswald of Switzerland, called the Oswald Commission, and another under the chairmanship of Samuel Schmid, the former president of the Swiss Confederation, called the Schmid Commission. The Oswald Commission is examining the evidence against individual Russian athletes and their entourages who may have committed a doping violation at the 2014 Sochi Olympic Winter Games 2014, and also retesting the samples of all Russian athletes. The Schmid Commission is investigating the sweeping allegations about the potential systematic manipulation of the samples.

Further, the Oswald Commission is investigating all samples from the 2008, 2010, and 2012 Olympic Games. If an athlete is selected for testing at the Games, half of the amount of urine collected is tested, and the other half is stored for ten years. If an athlete is not tested, the full sample is stored for later. This is done because there are ongoing breakthroughs in the science of testing that penetrate the masking agents for certain substances.

Retested samples from the 2008 Beijing Games and the 2012 London Games resulted in 27 Russian athletes being sanctioned. It was not possible to complete the testing prior to the 2016 Rio Games, so the IOC asked each IF to determine whether the Russian athletes were clean and had been tested outside of the Russian system. As a result of the retests, the IOC banned 180 Russian athletes from the 2016 Rio Olympics. As of February 2017, the retesting of the stored samples had so far resulted in sanctions against 18 Russian athletes from the Beijing Games and 20 from the London Games. Several former Soviet states have also been caught doping from 2008-2014 in the retests. In many cases, medals were withdrawn.

Addressing the Russian doping scandal is a complex process. Some of the athletes whose tests were redone have a different status from those who were banned as part of the doping system in Russia. There are two groups of Russians: the first is composed of athletes who were banned from Rio, and the second are those whose original tests were retested with the new technology and found to have been doped in Beijing or London. Some in the second group are in the process of appealing to a special division of CAS that was created to hear those appeals. Looking forward to the 2020 Olympic Games, the IOC is giving Russian athletes the opportunity to show that they are no longer doping by being regularly tested.

As for the switched samples at the Sochi Games, the investigators can tell which samples were tampered with. In order to switch the samples, the Russian officials had to remove the seal and replace it. In the process of doing this, the bottles ended up with tiny scratches visible only under a microscope. The fact that those athletes' bottles were manipulated shows that they were potentially positive, and that is enough circumstantial evidence to disqualify those athletes.

* * * * *

Going forward, the IOC must build a consensus to fight what the Russians have done, and everything, including banning an entire nation, must be on the table. It is outrageous that Russian track and field athletes would give urine samples when they are clean, start a protocol of doping, which they would continue through the Games, and then have the clean urine sample available to be substituted for the positive one — all orchestrated by the Russian government.

Due to the high level of suspicion cast over Russia, the IOC is working with WADA and Russia to re-establish independent anti-doping institutions in Russia. In the period leading up to the 2018 Olympic Winter Games in PyeongChang, the IOC has requested that every eligible Russian athlete undergo anti-doping tests with higher benchmarks than for athletes from other countries.

The ultimate solution requires that the IFs and NOCs turn over control of both the doping testing and the adjudication to an independent group that will mete out sanctions. This eliminates the possibility of a national sports federation intervening and allowing an athlete who is doping to continue competing. The ethical standards of the leaders of the IFs and NOCs must be reinforced, and anyone proven to be complicit in doping must be sanctioned.

The IOC's goal remains the same: to punish the cheaters and make the Games fair for those who compete with integrity.

Chapter Twenty-Four
The Future of the Olympic Movement

Olympism is a philosophy of life, exalting and combining in a balanced whole the qualities of body, will and mind. Blending sport with culture and education, Olympism seeks to create a way of life based on the joy found in effort, the educational value of good example and respect for universal fundamental ethical principles.
— Olympic Charter, Fundamental Principles

Years ago, I was an answer on *Jeopardy!*.

The question was: "Who was the first African-American member of the International Olympic Committee?" As flattering as this was, and as proud as it made me personally, that "first" was just a small step toward inclusion. I see the Olympic Movement, both at home and around the world, as being inclusive of different races, cultures, and religions. The strength of the Olympic Movement relies on its inclusion — not on singling out any one individual's accomplishments — while recognizing excellence and appreciating effort.

* * * * *

The Olympic Movement is growing stronger and more inclusive each year, but keeping it that way will require effort on behalf of all of its supporters. The news media constantly runs negative stories about the Olympic Games, the IOC, and to a lesser extent about the US Olympic Committee.

As a recent example, in 2016, one journalist wrote about deserted Olympic venues and unfulfilled promises left behind in the wake of the Rio Olympic Games. This was unfortunately the product of Brazil's crumbling government that was not able to follow through on its promises, and the fact that during the Games there was much hope of good to come, but its attachment to the Olympic Games makes it headline news. Overlooked were significant milestones from the Games.

At the Rio Olympic Games, 206 national Olympic teams competed, and for the first time, there was a special delegation made up entirely of refugee athletes. They competed under the Olympic flag and anthem and entered the stadium next to last, just before host nation Brazil. These young people sought refuge from war and other life tragedies they faced in Syria, South Sudan, the Democratic Republic of Congo, and Ethiopia. Some had lived in refugee camps for more than a decade.

The Refugee Olympic Team was made up of 10 inspirational athletes, six men and four women, and the Independent Paralympic Team with two men. Despite having their lives upended and being displaced from their homelands, these athletes were able to keep alive their desire to excel on the field of play. Living in a refugee camp with all of the stress of such a life did not extinguish their dreams to compete at the Olympic level. With the bare minimum of opportunity, they each were able to achieve the qualifying standards for eligibility at the Rio Games.

The IOC assembled the team in response to the refugee crisis spurred by Syria's civil war and the geopolitical tension wrought by terrorist groups such as ISIS, or the Islamic State of Iraq and Syria, by establishing a $2 million fund to find the displaced athletes a sponsor NOC and fund their training.

Their stories were as inspiring as they were harrowing. Yusra Mardini, a 17-year-old swimmer from Syria, fled from Turkey to Greece in an inflatable boat. When the motor died, she and her sister swam, pushing the boat, for three and a half hours to reach shore. They saved everyone aboard, including many who could not swim. She made her way to Germany, where she lived and trained for the Games under an IOC Olympic Solidarity scholarship.

These athletes' reach went beyond the Games. As a symbol of the Olympic Movement's unity with refugees, the United Nations Refugee Agency arranged for one of the athletes, Ibrahim Al-Hussein, a Syrian refugee living in Greece who was a member of the Paralympic team, to carry the Olympic torch through the Eleonas refugee camp in Athens, home to some 2,300 refugees.

The team was more than a gesture by the IOC. Assembling and funding it was a responsibility and an example of how sport can lift people and provide an off-the-field moment of excellence that everyone can appreciate.

* * * * *

There are also many positive stories and events on the Olympic Movement that the news media covers. In the fall of 2016, I attended a White House ceremony honoring our Olympians who competed in Rio.

President Barack Obama and First Lady Michelle Obama recognized the athletes' achievements, as presidents typically do. President Obama and the First Family also made two extraordinary gestures of inclusion: They invited the family members of the 17 African-American Olympians from the 1936 Games whom President Franklin D. Roosevelt did not invite to the White House, along with the 1968 Olympians Tommie Smith and John Carlos.

The story of Smith and Carlos, whom I am pleased to call my friends, resonates to this day. Smith and Carlos won gold and bronze medals, respectively, in the 200-meter sprint. When they accepted their medals, they took the podium wearing black socks with no shoes. Smith had a black glove on his right hand; Carlos had one on his left hand. When they turned to face the American flag for "The Star-Spangled Banner," they both raised a gloved fist and kept it raised until the national anthem ended. In a show of solidarity, the Australian silver medalist Peter Norman wore the same Olympic Project for Human Rights badge on his warm-up suit as Smith and Carlos, and stood on the podium without shoes.

The salute, which Smith and Carlos made as a human rights gesture, was interpreted to be the Black Power salute, which was used to reflect the struggles our country was going through at that time. Things were already on edge. To bring attention to the Black Freedom Movement, U.S. basketball players Lew Alcindor, Wes Unseld, and Elvin Hayes had refused to compete in Mexico City. The all-white Harvard University men's crew team also issued a statement of support for Smith and Carlos. IOC President Avery Brundage, whose removal was a goal of the Olympic Project for Human Rights for his sympathetic views toward the Nazis, deemed their gesture a domestic political statement and ordered that they be suspended from the U.S. team and banned from the Olympic Village. When the USOC refused, Brundage threatened to disqualify the entire U.S. Track & Field team. Rather than risk having their teammates barred from competition, Smith and Carlos left the Olympic Village, but they stayed in Mexico City until the Games ended.

"We're proud of them," President Obama said of Smith, now 72, and Carlos, now 71. "Their powerful silent protest in the 1968 Games was controversial, but it woke folks up and created greater opportunity for those that followed."

I thought it was fitting that President Obama honored Smith and Carlos on the same day as the descendants of the 1936 African-American Olympians. Just blocks from the White House, the National Museum of African-American History and Culture features a larger-than-life size statue of Smith and Carlos on the medal podium just a few feet from the cleats worn by Jessie Owens in 1936.

President Obama also highlighted the diversity of the U.S. team, which has reached the point where every single boy or girl competing at a sports venue can now imagine themselves becoming an Olympian based solely on their performance.

"We've become something more than just the sum of our parts," our 44th President said. "We've become Americans together. And there's something special about that. All races, all faiths, all traditions, all orientations, all marching together under that same proud flag, not bound by a creed or a color but by our devotion to an enduring set of ideals that we're all created equal, that we can think and worship and love as we please and that we can pursue our own version of happiness."

I was so pleased that he said those words in the context of the Olympic Movement. Those are the moments that illuminate the Olympic ideals that so many of us have fought so hard to preserve.

The IOC has worked consistently to spread those very ideals. While the IOC cannot solve many of the world's problems, we do have a strong voice. We are showing that sports can be a unifying factor in world affairs.

* * * * *

Closer to home, I serve on LA 2024, the Los Angeles bid committee for the 2024 Olympic Games. Los Angeles is bidding against Paris. Our committee includes Mayor Eric Garcetti, Earvin "Magic" Johnson, Olympic swimmer Janet Evans, and sports entrepreneur Casey Wasserman, Lew's grandson. Our bid was one of the strongest in history from every standpoint and will celebrate the city's cultural diversity at the first wholly-sustainable Olympic Games.

Because both the Los Angeles and Paris bids were so strong, the IOC took the unprecedented step of awarding each city an Olympic Games. An agreement was reached for Paris to host the 2024 Olympic Games and Los Angeles to host the 2028 Olympic Games. Because of the 11-year waiting period from 2017 to 2028, the IOC agreed to advance LA2024 a legacy payment of $160 million, which is normally made after the Games, to be used to support youth sports programs in the Greater Los Angeles Area.

For me personally, it will be a great pleasure to see the Olympic Games return to Los Angeles. In 1981, I moved to Los Angeles to join the organizing committee of the 1984 Games. It took me all of 10 minutes to figure out that the City of Angels would be my home. After the Games, I spent more than three decades working on behalf of the LA84 Foundation and watching it improve the lives of millions of children in the Greater Los Angeles Area. I want to continue to give back to this city, my own.

I believe that people were put on this earth to experience and to create their own history. I have a sense that I was put on this earth to help other people have the opportunities they need to develop their own history. To that end, I feel that my work is an extension of those who came before me in my family.

In my small place in the Olympic Movement, I hope I am seen as someone who has helped provide opportunity to those who might not have otherwise had it. I have done my utmost to give more than I receive; in many ways, however, I feel that the Olympic Movement has given me far more in return: It has inured in me purpose and faith and shown me how an ideal, if turned into action, can positively affect the lives of people in all reaches of the globe.

Addendum
The Olympic Movement's Alphabet of Organizations

International Olympic Committee (IOC)
Formed in 1894 by Frenchman Pierre de Coubertin, the IOC is the supreme authority and uniting body of the Olympic Movement, a web of the organizations and the athletes that make up the Olympic Movement. Based in Lausanne, Switzerland, the IOC is a nonprofit Swiss association with no political ties to any government and is funded by a portion of the sale of broadcast rights, ticketing, licensing, and sponsorships tied to the Olympic Games. Under that legal status, the IOC establishes its own rules and regulations governing all actions of the organization. These rules are laid out in the Olympic Charter, which can be amended and updated as needed. The IOC is governed by the IOC Executive Board. As of March 2017, there were 95 members. For more information, www.olympic.org.

National Olympic Committee (NOC)
A NOC is the organization in charge of developing, promoting, and protecting its nation's athletes and teams. It is also responsible for promoting the Olympic ideals in its nation. As of 2016, there are 206 NOCs. To be a NOC, a nation must be recognized by the United Nations.

United States Olympic Committee (USOC)
The USOC is the NOC in the United States. Based in Colorado Springs, Colorado, the USOC is governed by a board of directors and run by a CEO who is appointed by the board.

International Federation (IF)
The IFs are the governing bodies of individual sport recognized by the IOC. They stage and manage international competitions throughout the year

and exist with or without the Olympic Games. Each Olympic sport is represented by an IF. The IOC has no direct control over the IFs, though the IOC must recognize an IF for its sport to be on the Olympic program.

WORLD ANTI-DOPING AGENCY (WADA)
WADA is a foundation established in 1999 by the IOC to develop a World Anti-Doping Code to coordinate and monitor the approach to anti-doping, in all sports and across nations. WADA is guided by an independent board.

UNITED STATES ANTI-DOPING AGENCY (USADA)
USADA is the independent national anti-doping organization in the U.S. It is a nonprofit corporation, and a non-governmental agency. USADA has control over drug testing both in and out of competition for the U.S. Olympic programs held in the U.S.

LOS ANGELES OLYMPIC ORGANIZING COMMITTEE (LAOOC)
The LAOOC was responsible for staging the 1984 Los Angeles Olympic Games. (In this book, it is referred to as the LA Organizing Committee.)

ATHLETES ADVISORY COUNCIL IN THE USOC (AAC)
Instituted by the USOC, the AAC was established in 1973 to represent athletes from all the Olympic sports and ensure their rights.

AMATEUR ATHLETIC UNION (AAU)
Established in 1888, the AAU was created to promote and develop amateur sports. For years, the AAU ran the trials in many sports to determine the Olympic team. Due to complaints from athletes and conflicts with the influential NCAA, in 1978, as part of the Amateur Sports Act passed by Congress, the AAU was removed from controlling multiple sports. Legislation required that each sport be vertically managed.

NATIONAL GOVERNING BODY (NGB)
NGBs are U.S. organizations responsible for governing individual sports, such the United States Tennis Association (USTA).

National Collegiate Athletic Association (NCAA)
The NCCA oversees all collegiate sports.

President's Commission on Olympic Sport (PCOS)
The PCOS was created in 1972 by President Gerald Ford in response to problems at the 1972 Munich Olympic Games.

Amateur Athletic Foundation of Los Angeles (AAF)
The AAF was the initial name of the organization created in 1984 with 40 percent of the surplus from the LA Olympic Games to fund sports programs in Southern California, where the Games had been held. In 2006, the name was changed to the LA84 Foundation.

Court of Arbitration for Sport (CAS)
CAS is the international body that settles disputes in sport. Established in 1984, CAS deals with disputes arising during the Olympic Games, such as an athlete's appealing of a ban for doping.

Association of National Olympic Committees (ANOC)
ANOC looks after the interest of National Olympic Committees, and ensures that they do what the Olympic Charter asks of them, dispersing Olympic ideals within their countries. Each continent has an association:

ANOCA — Association of National Olympic Committees of Africa
OCA — Olympic Council of Asia
PASO — Pan-American Sports Organization
ONOC — Oceania National Olympic Committees
EOC — The European Olympic Committees

Fédération Internationale des Sociétés d'Aviron, or International Rowing Federation (FISA)
FISA is the international governing body of rowing, which is, of course, the most noble of all Olympic sports.

Acknowledgments

Throughout my life, I have been surrounded by people who have helped me find my way.

No doubt my parents had the greatest effect on who I am. My mother gave me her name, and I have worked to live up to the standards of that brilliant woman. And my father gave me experiences with community organizations, so I learned to listen and be compassionate about people at every station in life.

My brothers, David, James, and Thomas, are my support group. I was never afraid when they were around. David, the firstborn in our family, saved my life at least two times before I reached the age of five. Equally important, our mother taught us that there was one race, the human race. Skin color may vary, but we were all human. Thus, the Golden Rule, learned in Sunday school at Witherspoon Presbyterian Church, "Do unto others as you would have done unto you," became a central concept for action throughout my life.

Those who have guided me stretch all the back to nursery school when I was prevented from entering school through the front door by giant lawnmowers. That teacher let me climb over a fence to safety. Later, my first grade teacher, Mrs. Grimes, began our public school education with a focus on how we should treat each other. I returned to her classroom when I was in 5th grade and was shocked at how mean she seemed. Then I realized her sternness was well received to a beginner at the social norms needed for the classroom. And it was not easy to get those across to six year olds. It had worked well for me!

During the time we went to school in Bloomington, Indiana, I was filled with fear about the other kids not liking the color of my skin or of having an asthma attack, because there was a lot of mold on campus. But we survived all that with the help, again, of my big brother, David.

I can still remember the boy at PS 43 a few years later. After the seventh and eighth graders were presented awards for their outstanding achievement in each subject, he told me that he thought I would win all of the awards next year. I don't recall even thinking that I could accomplish that until he said that – and I did!

After we moved and changed schools, I remember the new friends I made at PS 86 in eighth grade who would be with me through high school and, to a certain extent, for the rest of my life. Recently, I received a note from two counselors who worked at the Girl Scout camp I attended the summer after my senior year in high school. I guess I impressed them, because they have followed my career ever since.

I thoroughly enjoyed Shortridge High School, where we were given so much opportunity to explore. We were privileged to have a remarkable teacher named Thomas Prebble, who ran the music department. He taught us so much about music and music theory that I was able to take college-level courses with little trouble.

We performed the Sacred Service by Bloch at the Clowes Hall, the top symphonic performance hall in Indianapolis, with professional musicians and a professional soloist. And our Madrigal Group was the best around. We sang *a cappella* with no leader in front of us. One member used the pitch pipe to give us the note. Then Vickie Lewis set the pace with a nod of her head, and off we would go. Vickie and I are still in contact.

We had great fun in Junior Vaudeville, a group of performances created and performed by junior class members. I still remember the words to the song we performed "We're going to stamp out hate!" Richard Borman was our senior class president, and I was the treasurer. Ricky has been an elementary school teacher in New York over his career. We are in contact from time to time.

Connecticut College introduced me to Dr. Jewel Plummer Cobb, an eminent scientist and college administrator. We communicated at every change in my life. She insisted that I go to law school. After I finished law school and began practicing law, I then moved to Princeton to train so that I could to win a gold medal in Moscow. I learned that she had become provost at Douglass College, the women's college associated with Rutgers University. I called to tell her I would be moving to Los Angeles, and she told me she had just been offered the job as president of California State University, Fullerton. We were able to spend time together until she retired from the university and then moved back to the East Coast.

My two favorite professors at Connecticut College were the Woodys — Mrs. Woody and Mr. Woody were both professors in the philosophy department. Their courses were challenging and helped me learn about my own philosophy of life.

Law school at the University of Pennsylvania was quite challenging. The 13 of us who were minority students were not made to feel very welcome. But within that class, I have three friends who will remain with me for the rest of my life. Gerald Early, who left before the end of his third year and instead pursued his doctorate at Cornell, and has been teaching at the University of Washington in St. Louis; James Johnson, who achieved his goal of becoming the in-house counsel for a major corporation at Boeing, and my housemate, Gurujodha Singh Khalsa, once known as Reece Couch, a saxophone player who became a student of martial arts and now works in Bakersfield, California as a Deputy County Counsel. Those three kept me sane through law school and supported my rowing exploits. I am grateful they were there.

The Juvenile Law Center of Philadelphia was a perfect choice for me to start my career as an attorney. The principals, Marsha Levick and Robert Schwartz, were great at demanding the best and sharing their knowledge. And, they understood my rowing career.

Speaking of rowing, my life at Vesper Boat Club was deeply enriched by the women and men who trained there with the ultimate goal of winning Olympic and World Championship medals. Many of the men were able to sleep at the boathouse and did part-time labor jobs. That kept their cost of living down. The women all had to find full-time jobs or jobs that could keep us afloat financially. I am not certain that I wanted to wake up at the boathouse. We women supported one another. At one time I had what was called "Anita's home for wayward women rowers."

I was fortunate to have a great friend from Connecticut College join Vesper when I did, Cathy Menges, who had been in the varsity boat our senior year. She was attending the school of nursing at the time I was in the school of law. It was great to have a friend from our shared past. I was a member of her wedding party after the 1976 Games. I am proud that her daughter became the first U.S. gold medalist in fencing during the 2004 Athens Olympic Games.

From the time I appeared in the boathouse telling them that I was also attending Penn Law School, I felt welcomed by the women. What a great group of women. The personnel changed from year to year, but during the time I rowed at Vesper, Pam Behrens, Ann and Marie Jonick, Cathy Menges, Nancy Storrs, and several others were fixtures at the club. The coaching staff that worked with us included Woody Fischer, the great Dietrich Rose, who had come from East Germany to coach and row at Vesper, and John Hooten, who started with us in 1975 and stayed with the women until after the 1980 Games.

I came to know John Kelly, Jr. (aka Jack), who was an Olympic rower and won the Diamond Sculls at the Henley Royal Regatta. (His nephew, Prince Albert of Monaco, is also an IOC member.) He went on to become the president of the United States Olympic Committee, but passed away one month into his term of office. While not all of the men were supportive of the women or of my presence, overall Vesper stood for excellence in rowing. Over time, I met and became friends with many of the women's and men's team. Jan Palchikoff became a lasting friend, even though she was a sculler (i.e., one who had a blade handle in each hand) and did not train in Philadelphia. It was at the international regattas that I was introduced to rowers from every country. At the 1976 Olympic Games, the Cubans presented a team that was strong, although they seldom raced internationally. They were the first team I saw that had people with my skin color.

Returning home after the Games, I went to Washington, D.C. for the first term of my third year in law school. I interned at the Center for Law and Social Policy. It was a great job working at a public interest firm. There I met three people who became lifetime friends: Christine Hickman, who was working on the third floor with the Women's Law project; Robert (Bob) Friedman, who sat across the hall from me, in the room where the interns had desks, and his soon-to-be, long-time wife, Kristina Khiel. And, because the Democrats had just won the presidency, several of the staff wound up serving in the Carter Administration; in particular, Joe Onek, who became Deputy White House Counsel.

I salute all of the members of the Athletes Advisory Council, all members of the Olympic team or members of their national teams who worked to make the USOC a better and more responsive organization for the athletes. We worked hard to develop solutions that would serve the Olympic Movement in good stead. There were two members of the original AAC that I met in Montreal looking for our uniforms who became longtime friends, Col. Mickie King (Air Force retired), a diver, and Larry Hough, a businessman and rower.

In 1977, Larry loaned me the boat that had been built for him and his pair partner for the 1972 Olympic Games. He became a close friend.

During my many trips to Washington, D.C. to support the athletes' right to compete in the Moscow Olympic Games, I was welcomed to stay at either Bob Friedman's home or the home of Larry Hough. Without these welcoming homes, it would have been much more difficult to make my presentations to Congress.

My move from Philadelphia to Princeton was eased by being hired at Princeton University as an assistant house master and the pre-law advisor. Dean Joan Girgus made certain that I was safe, especially during the time I was getting hate mail and death threats. The following year, I stayed at Princeton and became coach of the freshman women's rowing team.

Given that I had no income from the coaching, I also worked for The Corporation for Enterprise Development (CFED) for Bob Friedman. That job opportunity kept me going through a challenging year. And as the coach at Princeton, I met a group of talented and optimistic young women who were willing to take a chance on me as their coach. I became friends with Janette Payne, who much later told me that my race speeches (stories that they demanded I tell them to get ready for the race) actually scared them, and few slept well the night before.

Moving to Los Angeles, I called upon my one LA friend, Christine Hickman, to help me figure out how to live there. She introduced me to her book group. The members were all professional women, including attorneys, academics, physicians, journalists, civil rights workers, sports managers, and jurists. Over the years, some members moved away, but we still kept in touch. We continue to meet monthly, or whenever we can get together.

It has been a wonderful group of women and their families to rely on since 1981.

During the 1992 Olympic Games in Barcelona, I was in the athlete's office in the Olympic Village. A gold medalist from the 1984 Games, Benita Fitzgerald Mosley, stopped by. She wanted to discuss staying involved with the Olympic Movement. We developed a plan that we have continued to watch grow over the decades.

The staff at the LA Olympic Organizing Committee was a remarkable group of fairly-young people lead by two remarkable leaders, Peter Ueberroth and Harry Usher. Many of us remain friends to this day. From this period onward, I came to volunteer for many organizations working for the common good and to better our nation.

Over the years, I have met people during the Olympic Games who have become lifelong friends. Anucha Browne-Sanders was working at IBM for a LA Organizing Committee friend, Eli Primrose. Given that we were probably the only two African-American women who were 6 feet tall or taller in Nagano, Japan during the 1998 Olympic Winter Games, we decided to meet. And we continue to do so around the world.

And to my team at the LA84 Foundation, to whom I shall be grateful forever as we helped to bring opportunity to youth and understanding of the role of sport in society to Southern California and to the broader world: I wish all of my colleagues well as the work of the foundation continues. I certainly could not have imagined a better person taking my place at the Foundation than Renata Simril. I am certain she will lead the foundation in new and better methods to fulfil its mission. Meanwhile, I have the pleasure of working with a young woman who started as a volunteer in the LA84 Foundation library. After graduating from high school, she invited me to a luncheon, where she explained that she wanted to have a career in the Olympic Movement. I am proud to say that she now has her undergraduate degree and an MBA. Currently, Corine Taylor is working at the LA24 bid committee. Her brother, Creighton, who is my godson, is doing well in the work of technology.

My work in the Olympic Movement has introduced me to remarkable people. For example, in Salt Lake City, I met Bob Bills and his family.

Bob got me through the black hole in the White Canyon, a remarkable experience. And his firstborn carries my name; since he is a male, it is my last name. And during the 1988 Seoul Olympic Games, I met Jerry Thomas, who is the most knowledgeable person on African and African-American art in the U.S. He started as executive at the Turner Games and now works in another field of artistic endeavors. I am grateful for having met my dear friend Jarogin Gilbert at the Baden-Baden IOC Congress in 1981. This brilliant man has greatly enhanced my life.

I appreciate the many athletes I have met over the years, as well as the many administrators, board members, staff, and volunteers with the USOC. Similarly, the scores of staff and volunteers I have met through the International Olympic Committee, the many colleagues, staff, and volunteers over the 31 years that have been with me through the Games have deeply enriched and continue to enrich my life.

I realize that this acknowledgment is becoming nearly as long as my book, but it is difficult to thank all of the people who have contributed to my life. I'll end with saying again: "Thank You!" You know who you are, and I hope I will have an opportunity to thank you in person sometime along the road.

Finally, to the team at Klipspringer Press who worked so diligently and professionally on the book. They include Gabriel Levinson, designer Will Petty, associate editor Jenna Bernstein, promotional and jacket copy writer Debbie Harmsen, and in particular, Dorianne Perrucci, who spent countless hours editing and honing the manuscript. Thanks also to Ryan Azevedo and his team at MediaBlitzz for deigning my new web site and handling social media. Finally, this book would not have happened without the help of my coauthor, Josh Young. Our mutual friend Cathy Griffin recommended I contact Josh, and I am certainly glad she did!

INDEX

Photo insert images indicated by *"p"*.

Amateur Athletic Union (AAU), 10, 65, 66, 67, 73, 238
Amateur Sports Act of 1978, 67, 68, 78, 85–86, 89, 153
Association of National Olympic Committees, 239
Athletes Advisory Council (AAC), 64–65, 68, 105, 238

Bach, Thomas, 111, 129, 202
Behrens, Pam, 41–42
boycotts, ii, 51–52, 63, 71–82, 85–90, 95, 107–8
Brown, Carol, 49, 97, *p*
Brundage, Avery, 208, 233–34

Carter, Jimmy, 67, 71–73, 75–79, 81–82, 87, 89–90, 100
Cobb, Jewel Plumber, 22, 31
Connecticut College, 21–26, 28–32, 43, 186
Coro Fellowship program, 31, 32
Couch, Reese, 43–44
Court of Arbitration (CAS), 225, 239
Crawford, Connie, 70, 89, 90, 92–93, *p*
Culver, John, 65, 66–67
Cutler, Lloyd, 78, 80–81

de Coubertin, Pierre, ii, 128, 162, 207, 237

DeFrantz, Alonzo David, 2
DeFrantz, Anita, *p. See also specific topics*
DeFrantz, Anita Page, 6, 7–9, 89, *p*
DeFrantz, David, 7, 18, *p*
DeFrantz, Faburn E., Sr., 2, 3–6, 22
DeFrantz, James, 7–8, 43, *p*
DeFrantz, Robert David, 6–8, 13, 22, 87, *p*
DeFrantz, Thomas, 7, *p*
DeFrantz et al. v. U.S. Olympic Committee, 85–86
DeMont, Rick, 147, 149–51, 154, 221–22
de Varona, Donna, 67
Dowding, Wanda, 117, 185

Early, Gerald, 43–44
Easton, Jim, 181, 183
Elizabeth II, 53, 59–60, *p*

Ganga, Jean Claude, 132, 177–78
Greece, 145–46, 161–62
Greig, Marion, 49, 58, 59
Gullong, Bart, 29, 30, 32

Hatton, Holly, 91–92, 97, *p*
Helmick, Bob, 127, 130, 133, 138, 156–57, 160, 174, 179
Helms, Paul, 116
Hitler, Adolf, ii, 76, 208
Hooten, John, 39–40, 46, 48–49, 60–61, 66
Hough, Larry, 103–4

International Federation, 237–38
International Olympic Committee, 127, 129–34, 171–84, 187, 189–90, 193–96
International Rowing Federation, iii, 42, 45, 91, 239

Johnson, Ben, 143–45, 148, 221
Johnson, Dave, 171–72, 173, 177, 187
Johnson, James, 43–44, 111
Johnson, Rafer, 65, 109, 111
Juvenile Law Center of Philadelphia, 43, 64, 66, 68–69

Keller, Thomas, 42, 45, 91
Kim, Un Yong, 130–31, 132, 187, 193–95

LA84 Foundation, iii, 115–26, 221, *p*
Lapchick, Richard, 193
law school, 32–33, 35–36, 44
Lewis, Carl, 97, 111–12, 143–44, *p*
Los Angeles Olympic Games, 68, 105–12, 115
Los Angeles Olympic Organizing Committee (LA Organizing Committee), 68, 101–03, 105, 107–08, 111, 112, 116, 117–18, 127, 180, 238

McCain, John, 181–82
Miller, Don, 50, 72
Mitchell, George, 177, 178, 181, 183

Mondale, Walter, 81–2
Montiel, Steve, 115, 116, 117, 127, 134
Montreal Olympic Games, 45, 48–58, 63, 102, 164, *p*
Moore, Kenny, 66–67, 141
Moscow Olympic Games, 71–82, 85–90, 95
multiple sclerosis, 10, 157–60

Nash, Cora, 12
National Collegiate Athletic Association, 29, 65, 68, 239
National Governing Body, 238
National Olympic Committee, 63, 64, 91, 237

Obama, Barack, 217, 218, 233, 234, *p*
Olympic Charter, 127, 129, 148–49, 231
Onek, Joe, 73, 76, 80
Owens, Jesse, ii, 107, 112, 209, 234

Page, Savelia Ann, 12
Palchikoff, Jan, 92, 120
Paralympic Games, 128, 153
Parker, Harry, 39, 46, 49, 54, 58, 109
PEDs, 63, 122–23, 143–51, 169, 221–30
Phelps, Michael, ii, 140, 226
Pound, Dick, 176–77, 179, 184, 188, 193
Pratt, John H., 88–89
President's Commission on Olympic Sport, 239
Princeton University, 69–71, 87

Putin, Vladimir, 210, 215, 218

racism, 1–9, 13–14, 43, 48, 51, 76, 79, 123, 154–56, 208–9
Refugee Olympic Team, 232
Ricketson, Gail, 49, 56
Rodchenkov, Grigory, 227
Rogge, Jacques, 188, 193, 195, 201–2
Ruggiero, Angela, 185, *p*

Salt Lake City Olympic Winter Games, 172–77
Samaranch, Juan Antonio, 130–31, 145, 148, 155, 157, 161, 163, 167, 174, 181, 184, 187–89, 190, 195, 197, 199, 200, 201, 213, *p*
Senate, U.S., 66, 181–84, 211
Shortridge High School, 13–15, 18, 19
Silliman, Lynn, 49, 55
Simon, Bill, 79, 81–82, 154
slavery, 2, 16–18, 190–92
Smith, Tommie, 233, 234
Sochi Olympic Games, 210, 214, 215, 220, 222, 227–29
Sommers, Myrtle May, 2–3, 4, 58, *p*
Stevens, Ted, 65, 72, 153, 183

Title IX, 28, 166–67
Truth, Sojourner, 17–18
Tubman, Harriet, 1, 16–17, 18

Ueberroth, Peter, 102–7, 109, 112, 116, 129, 181, 188, *p*

University of Pennsylvania, 32–33, 35–38, 43, 44
U.S. Anti-Doping Agency, 238
Usher, Harry, 103, 104, 105, 115
U.S. Olympic Committee, ii, 51, 64, 68, 78–79, 81, 85–86, 153, 154–57, 160, 237
USRowing Association, 40–41, 50, 66, 91

Vesper Boat Club, 31–32, 33, 36, 38–42, 46–48, 60, 66, 68

Walker, Leroy, 211, *p*
Warner, Anne, 49, 69, *p*
Wasserman, Casey, 235, *p*
Wasserman, Lew, 118, 155
Welch, Tom, 173, 174, 177, 187
Williams, Ed, 65–66, 68
Williams, Serena, 126
Williams, Venus, 126, 138
Winfrey, Oprah, 240, 247
Wilson, Wayne, 117, 120
Wolper, David, 105, 117–18, 121
Women's Sports Foundation, 221
World Anti-Doping Agency (WADA), 225, 227, 229, 248

YMCA, on Senate Avenue, 3–6, 9
Youth Olympic Games, 153

Zagoria, Robert, 86